NARRATIVE
OF THE
VISIT TO INDIA

THE KING-EMPEROR AND THE QUEEN-EMPRESS.

Frontispiece.

NARRATIVE OF THE VISIT TO INDIA

OF

THEIR MAJESTIES

KING GEORGE V. AND QUEEN MARY

AND OF

THE CORONATION DURBAR HELD AT DELHI, 12TH DECEMBER, 1911

By

THE HON. JOHN FORTESCUE

GYAN

Published by

Gyan Publishing House
5, Ansari Road
Daryaganj, New Delhi-110002
Phone: 011-47034999, 9811692060
E-mail: books@gyanbooks.com

Distribution Network
gyanbooks.com
India, USA, Canada, UK, Australia, France

ISBN : 978-81-212-9832-2 (HB)
First Published, 1912

2nd Impression 2023

Printed at: Gyan Press, Delhi.

NARRATIVE OF THE VISIT TO INDIA
Author: The Hon. JOHN FORTESCUE

NARRATIVE

OF THE

VISIT TO INDIA

OF

THEIR MAJESTIES

KING GEORGE V. AND QUEEN MARY

AND OF

THE CORONATION DURBAR HELD AT DELHI

12TH DECEMBER 1911

BY

THE HON. JOHN FORTESCUE

1912

DEDICATED

(BY GRACIOUS PERMISSION)

TO

HIS ROYAL HIGHNESS

THE PRINCE OF WALES

ILLUSTRATIONS

ILLUSTRATIONS

PLAN

I

INDIA. What does this name signify to ninety-nine out of a hundred of us beyond a triangle, coloured red, upon the map of Asia? We are told that the said triangle measures nineteen hundred miles in length from north to south, and about the same in breadth, at its widest point, from east to west; and that it contains an area rather larger than that of Europe west of the Vistula. The statement conveys little to us. We accept it as undoubtedly true, and, if we look at a map of India superimposed upon one of Europe on the same scale, we are perhaps a little staggered. But we in our little island are accustomed to reckon by acres, not by thousands of square miles; and, strive as we may against the tendency, we find ourselves always attempting to apply our own puny standards to things Asiatic. We hear of great rivers, and instinctively recall the Thames at London Bridge, forgetting that a great Indian river in flood would fill the space from Westminster Abbey to the Crystal Palace. We are told of mighty mountains, and commit to memory the bald fact that some of them soar to twice the height of Mont Blanc; we are aware, perhaps, that they form a barrier practically impassable by man along the immense northern frontier of India; possibly we may even realise with awe that they make the vast reservoir of water, in the form of snow, which feeds the gigantic rivers already mentioned. So much we may gather, with moderate intelligence, from our maps. But there is one thing more, the most important thing of all, and of all the most impossible to grasp. This red-coloured triangle contains three hundred and twenty million people, six times the population of France, thrice the population of the United States, one-fifth, as it is reckoned, of the men, women and children living upon this planet.

No one man has ever seen, nor will ever see, the hundredth part of them. No one man has ever seen, nor will ever see, in spite of motor cars and aeroplanes and railways, one hundredth of the eighteen hundred thousand square miles over which they are spread. No one man has ever visited, nor will ever visit, all the cities, living and dead, which they have builded. No one man has ever mastered, nor will ever master, all the languages which they speak. More than this, though for centuries men of mighty and commanding genius strove from time to time to bring the whole of India under their sole sway and sovereignty, not one of them succeeded; and it was only in the nineteenth century that the task was at last accomplished by the agents of an alien Queen, the first ruler in Indian history who looked upon all races in India as her children, the great and good Queen Victoria.

We English take this thoughtlessly as a matter of course; yet surely it is one of the strangest circumstances recorded in history. Here is a country which, while we were sunk in barbarism, had worked out a great civilisation and a very remarkable scheme of social organisation for itself; had produced great engineers, great astronomers, great thinkers, great artists, great poets, great soldiers and great administrators; and has always abounded, as it still abounds, in men of signal ability and exceptional valour. Could we teach her anything in the matter of commerce? On the contrary, bills of exchange have been in use in India for countless centuries; and her credit, based on the thrift of the peasantry, is stabler than that of any Western race, even than that of the French. Could we, except by keeping the peace—a very important exception—better the social relations of man with man? We may think so; and yet let us take the most insoluble of the problems that for centuries has confronted ourselves, the question of the relief of the poor. India has solved it. There is not, nor has ever been, a poor law in India, for there is no need of one. The difficulties which demand a complicated, yet always imperfect and unsatisfactory mechanism of State in the West, are not so much vanquished as quietly and imperceptibly suppressed by the organisation of the village and the caste in the East. Could we offer higher ideals of citizenship, or stronger bonds of civil obligation? The native of India fulfils far more readily than ourselves the duty which we have laid down as owing to a neighbour. He is imperfect, as are all other men, yet he loves, honours and succours his father and mother; he honours and obeys the King and those that are set in authority under him; he orders himself lowly and reverently to all his betters; he learns and labours truly to get his own living; and he has mastered, better than the Western races, the crowning lesson—whatsoever his station is, therewith to be content. It is useless to broach to him in his natural state the theory, with the conclusions which follow upon it, that all men are equal. He knows that they are not, and is content to accept the consequences. In time of famine he will lie dying slowly, hard by the bountiful table spread for the British Commissioner, without envy and without complaint. It is not that he knows or cares that the said Commissioner, for all that he eats so well, is killing himself in the effort to save starving men from death. To the Indian it is the order of a higher power that a few shall be full while many shall fast, and he bows himself before it without a murmur. We call such resignation fatalism. It makes us impatient that men should submit tamely to eternal injustice. As a younger nation, we—or at any rate some of us—are still confident that we can set the whole world right ; and we have accepted the phrase *divine discontent* to dignify our aspirations. But the native of India, untainted by European thought, sees nothing divine in dashing himself against the decree of the Most High. He has the courage to face inexorable fact, and sets little store by this transitory life. Not the more, however, on that account, does he hold himself released from his duty towards his neighbour. Every Hindu from the moment of his birth is bound over to good behaviour by his caste, under the terrible penalty of being cut off from communion with it, and thrown upon the world alone, without a friend, without a hearth, without a hope, until he joins the great company of the dead.

Lastly, could we offer India any romance of leadership or sovereignty which she enjoyed not before ? On the contrary, she has for centuries possessed natural leaders and a nobility whose social pre-eminence is recognised throughout the length and breadth of the land, a nobility prouder and with longer and sublimer traditions of chivalry and heroism than any that is to be found between the Atlantic and the Ural Mountains. The pedigree of the Guelphs is one of the grandest among all European families, yet it pales before that of the oldest of the Rajputs. None the less, India has passed under the sway of a nation which is, comparatively speaking, of yesterday, which hails from an insignificant island six thousand miles away in the most distant corner of Europe, and which is as remote from the Asiatic in character, training and environment as can be one race of men from another. The great position which was denied to the Mogul Emperors has been attained by English kings; and, so far as they are conscious of a ruler at all, the three hundred millions of India acknowledge one ruler only, King George, the grandson of Queen Victoria.

How did this come about? It is worth while to look back very briefly over the history of the past, for only thus can we realise the true significance of His Majesty's visit to India. It will give us at least an opportunity to unite with our Indian fellow-subjects in praising famous men and the fathers that begat us.

II

India, as every one knows, is divided into a northern portion named Hindostan, which extends from the Himalayas south-west to the Vindhya Mountains and the Narbada River, and a southern portion, named the Dekhan, which includes the remainder of the Peninsula southward from those boundaries to Cape Comorin. This division at first sight seems arbitrary, until we realise that India is, in fact, nearly cut in two by a belt of rugged, broken and mountainous country, through which for all practical purposes there was, before the days of railways, but one principal passage, famous in military history as the Ajanta Pass. Within this belt have taken refuge the remnants of the aboriginal tribes, which in remote times were driven from the more favoured districts by an invading host of Dravidians. Whence these Dravidians were derived and what they were is unknown. Possibly they came from over the sea, as did the Maoris in New Zealand, for they were a seafaring folk ; but they were at any rate a fighting race which founded kingdoms. In later times —apparently about the seventh century before Christ—they in turn were subdued by a fresh horde of invaders, the Aryans, who entered India from the north-west ; but, though they took from their conquerors some veneer of the Hindu religion, the Dravidians remained distinct and apart from them, preserving their own languages, of which the most important are Telugu, Kanarese, Malayalam and Tamil, the last named a speech of many dialects. Besides these there is one Aryan language, Marathi, spoken by the Aryan invaders who now occupy the north-west of the Dekhan, and several more tongues confined to small tracts. Hindostani is alien to Southern India, and is used only as a kind of *lingua franca* for purposes of convenience.

But though, as shall be seen, the English, owing to peculiar circumstances, were concerned at the outset mainly with the Dekhan, the India alike of history and romance is the vast tract, for the most part alluvial plain, which bears the name of Hindostan. For not only is it the richest, and therefore the most attractive to invaders, but it was, until men dared the navigation of the high seas in the fifteenth century, the only portion of the huge peninsula which was accessible from without, through the well-known passes of the north-west. By those passes the Aryan conquerors swarmed into the plain, where in due time they developed the institution of the four original castes, now swelled to over two thousand. These four were the priests or Brahmans, the warriors or Rajputs, the agricultural class, and the Sadras, which last are presumed to have been the original conquered races. Of the early history of the Aryans little authentic is known ; but it must be noted that in the sixth century before Christ the sage, Gautama Buddha, was born in a kingdom on the Ganges, and became the founder of a religion which, though practically extinct in India, still reigns in Ceylon, Burma, Tibet, China and Siam. It may help us in our chronology to bear in mind that the death of Buddha occurred probably in 487 B.C., three years after the battle of Marathon.

A century and a half later, in 327 B.C., came the first European invasion of India by Alexander the Great. He penetrated no farther than to the Satlaj, the most easterly of the five rivers of the Panjab ; and after his death in 324 his work was utterly undone by a powerful native Government under one of the first of the great native rulers, Chandragupta. A century passed away, and there came a second Greek invasion from Bactria; but after two generations these strangers gave place to Indo-Parthian kings, who, about a hundred years later, were in turn swept away by nomad hordes from Central Asia. Then for three hundred years all is obscure, until there arose a second Chandragupta and a new native dynasty at the beginning of the fourth century of our era. The second of this line, Samudragupta, an enlightened monarch and a great administrator, formed the design of conquering all India, and did indeed penetrate almost to Cape Comorin, but was unable to hold the Dekhan, though he subdued Hindostan. Then about 450 A.D. arrived a fresh invasion from Central Asia; the native dynasty fell, and there followed a century of confusion, from which emerged in 606 another great native sovereign, Harsha, who after much hard fighting subdued Northern India, and essayed, but in vain, the conquest of the South. He died in 648, and India relapsed for three centuries into intestine confusion and anarchy.

Meanwhile a new power had arisen in Arabia. Mohammed had died in 632, bequeathing to the world a religion which, by its blending of devotional and military enthusiasm, was fated to affect the destinies of many lands, and above all of India. The aggressive Arabs, after a futile attempt to reach India by sea, finally invaded it at the beginning of the eighth century from Persia, and established themselves in Scinde. Two hundred years later a Turkish slave founded a separate kingdom in Afghanistan; and one of his descendants, the great Mahmoud, began in 999 a series of incursions, which took him farther and farther into Hindostan. His successors were supplanted by the rulers of a petty kingdom between Ghazni and Herat, one of whom, Mohammed Ghori, in 1176 entered upon a new course of raids, which ended finally in the establishment of a permanent Mohammedan kingdom, extending from Peshawar eastward to the sea.

The conquest, however, occupied nearly thirty years, and was not accomplished without hard fighting, not indeed at first without serious reverses. For out of the chaos which followed upon the death of Harsha had arisen the great Hindu power of the Rajput clans, whose territory stretched from the Rann of Cutch to Rohilkand, including, above all, the kingdoms of Kanauj and Gujarat. The days of their fame, distinguished by high pre-eminence in art, learning, and science, lasted for two centuries; but above all things the Rajputs were soldiers. These were the proud warriors, divided by countless jealousies, yet united always by religion and their code of honour, insubordinate in temper, yet obedient ever to the chief of the clan, who were the champions of Hinduism against Mohammedanism.

The greatest of these champions, Prithwi Raj, the hero of countless legends, had already made himself famous by the capture of Delhi in 1153, and by other exploits in love and war, when he was called upon to repel the Mussulman invaders. Brilliantly successful against them at first, he was presently deserted by fortune, and slain, together with his son, in a great battle in 1192. Delhi was captured in the following year; and before the close of the first decade of the thirteenth century the ascendancy of the Rajputs in India was overthrown, and that of the Mohammedans erected in its place. But the Hindu warrior clans maintained and still maintain their position about Ajmer; and the memory of that great struggle has never perished from among them.

The Mohammedans now established their headquarters at Delhi; but their kingdoms were not one but many, and, although the Kings of Delhi claimed suzerainty over all others of their faith, they were not always able to enforce it. Nevertheless, by the mere fact that they held Delhi itself, they were potential when not actual masters of India. For it was not mere chance which made that famous city the capital of Hindostan. Broad though the entrance to the plains of India may appear on the map when once the passes of Afghanistan are traversed, it is none the less narrowed at one point to a breadth of little more than one hundred miles between the mountains on the north and the desert on the south. Almost in the centre of that hundred miles stands Delhi; and it is there or within a radius of some fifty miles to north and south of it—between Panipat and Aligarh—that countless battles have been fought for the supremacy of India. It is in fact the key of the country; and it can hardly be taken in rear but by a nation which has command of the sea.

During the course of three centuries—1206 to 1526—from the reign of our King John to midway through the reign of King Henry the Eighth, thirty-four kings of five different houses held sway at Delhi, of whom no fewer than twelve were dethroned, assassinated or killed in action. They fought among themselves, they fought against other Mohammedan kings, they fought against revolting Hindus, and they fought against invading Tartars under Zinghis Khan. At the beginning of the fourteenth century the Tartars were finally driven back by King Ala-ud-din, who then conceived the project of conquering all India, and actually carried his raids almost to Cape Comorin. This great and famous sovereign died in 1316, when our King Edward the Second was on the throne; and then, as has too often happened in India, he was followed by a feeble successor, who brought the realm into confusion, and his own life to an ignominious end. The new dynasty lasted for less than eighty years, producing one great ruler, Firoz Shah, after whose death in 1388 the kingdom of Delhi fell to pieces. Thereupon a new invader appeared, Timur the Turki, who in a campaign of two years penetrated to Delhi and beyond it, and then withdrew, leaving the unhappy country in greater confusion than before. It would be wearisome even to give the number of the Mohammedan states, and the names of the men who ruled, or aspired to rule them; much more to dwell on the endless struggles between sovereigns, usurpers, rebels and adventurers, which signified desolation to the land and misery to the inhabitants. But all things come to an end; and in 1526 the Turkis, after many raids, finally invaded India in force under Timur's descendant Babar. The decisive battle was fought at Panipat; and with it began the age of the giants, when for nearly two hundred years strong man succeeded strong man upon the throne of Delhi, and made and consolidated the Mogul Empire.

Even so, however, that dynasty was not without its vicissitudes. Babar, a very great man, died in 1540. His successor, Humayun, while engaged in the conquest of the south, was recalled by a rebellion in the north, and being defeated in battle wandered in exile for fifteen years before he could recover his capital. But upon his death in 1556 he left a son, Akbar, who was one of the great rulers not of India only, but of the world. Akbar was confronted everywhere with rebellion, both of his co-religionists and of the Hindus, but after eleven years of hard fighting he crushed all his internal adversaries. Then turning from the work of restoring order to that of conquest he dealt out blows impartially upon Rajputs, revolting generals and fanatic Afghans, until by 1594 he had gathered all India north of the Narbada, from Kandahar to the Bay of Bengal, into a single Empire. He was proceeding with the conquest of the south, and had already reached Ahmednagar, when death overtook him in 1605, after a strenuous reign of just upon forty years. Akbar was not only a great conqueror but a great statesman. Bred in the most bigoted of all faiths he saw that India could be permanently unified only by the reconciliation of Hindus and Mohammedans; and to this end he spared no pains to favour the first, and to repress the stern and uncompromising spirit of the second. Finally, he essayed the bold experiment of piecing together the best elements of both religions, and launching the compound upon India as a new faith which should command the allegiance of all. To us who conceive of religious, political and social life as three things distinct and apart, such a policy may appear ridiculous; but in the East, where the three are one and inseparable, this heroic measure presents a different aspect. It is, however, manifest that, even under an autocrat of broad mind, imperious will, resolute character and the highest administrative genius, such a new creed must demand constant and careful nurture for a period exceeding the life of one man. The intellectual satisfaction of feeling that oneself is right, and that one's neighbour is wrong, appeals so strongly to poor mankind that militant intolerance, such as that of Islam, must always find readier welcome with the majority than a gospel of forbearance. Toleration has been the distinguishing mark of all the greatest rulers of India; and the greatest of them, because the most earnest striver to heal human differences, was Akbar.

His death was followed, as is the rule in the East, by a dispute over the succession, which after the usual war was decided in favour of his younger son Jahangir (1605–27), who was followed in turn by his eldest son Shah Jahan (1627–1658). Both were strong and capable sovereigns, but both were much troubled by rebellious subjects; and Shah Jahan, after a desperate struggle between his four sons, was finally deposed by the third of them, Aurangzeb. Neither Jahangir nor Shah Jahan made great progress in the Dekhan; and in the north-west, after bitter fighting, the Persians finally in 1653 established themselves in Kandahar, and severed it from the Empire. This was the beginning of the end. Shah Jahan's court was the most magnificent ever seen in India, and the buildings which he erected have made his name immortal; yet he died a prisoner in the fort of Agra, looking to the last at the Taj Mahal, the lovely tomb which he had raised over the body of the wife whom he had adored. This was in the year of the great fire of London, 1666. His successor, after three years' fighting, disposed of his three brothers; and then, reviving Mohammedan bigotry in its extremest form, he set himself to crush down alike the infidel Hindus and the two heretical Mohammedan kingdoms, Golconda and Bijapur, in the Dekhan. Oppressive persecution of the Hindus soon raised them up in fury. The Rajputs fought against him with desperate valour, and only after a most heroic resistance were at last brought down to sullen impotence. But both in the north and in the south Aurangzeb's mad intolerance called into being new champions of the old faith, who, from the lasting eminence which they attained in India, must receive more than passing attention.

The first of these were the Sikhs, a religious sect which traced its origin to Nanak, a pious Hindu born in the fifteenth century, who may be called the Calvin of Hinduism, inasmuch as he held that religion was a matter of the intellect rather than of the feelings. He preached the abolition of caste, the unity of the Godhead, and the need for holier and purer life; and he was followed by ten *Gurus* or apostles, whose succession ended in 1708 with Govind Singh. To the persecution of Aurangzeb the Sikhs could oppose only unfearing martyrdom; for the great leader who was to turn them into a powerful military state had not yet been born ; but the heart of such movements is of greater significance than the head ; and the heart of the Sikhs was already beating true and strong in the seventeenth century, against the time when the advent of a head should convert them into one of the great powers of India.

Meanwhile the task of resisting Aurangzeb called less for a saint than for a man of action ; and such a man appeared in the person of Sivaji Bonsla, the son of a chief of no great property in the neighbourhood of the Western Ghauts to the east of Bombay. Born in 1627—the year when George Villiers, Duke of Buckingham, led his abortive expedition to Rochelle —he was brought up at Puna, and early conceived the ambition of dispossessing the Mohammedans of the south, and setting up a Hindu kingdom in their stead. His men were hardy peasants from the mountains ; his horses, not less important than his men, were drawn from the valleys ; and with these he sallied forth to capture hill-fortresses, and to use them as bases for raids upon the surrounding country. Being a great military genius he rapidly achieved success ; and by 1664 had carried his incursions so far as to seize and sack the imperial city of Gujarat. This was a direct defiance to Aurangzeb, who sent an army to crush him, and succeeded in forcing him to surrender upon terms ; but the wily chief soon contrived to escape, and returning to the Dekhan quickly re-established and widened his ascendancy. He died in 1680, but he had already done his work in founding the power of the Marathas.

What the Marathas exactly were or are no one seems able accurately to define. They were not a caste, they were not a sect, they were not a nation; and, though some of them claim to be of Rajput origin, this pretension seems to be disposed of by anthropometric tests. Their name is taken from the territory of Maharashtra, and their language is called Marathi; but they are not the only inhabitants of that territory nor the only speakers of that tongue. In 1901 they numbered only five millions; and yet in the seventeenth century they ruined the armies of Aurangzeb, shattered the might of the Moguls and bade fair to become the masters of India. It is difficult therefore to predicate anything certain of them except that they were and are emphatically a power, and that they rose to that eminence wholly by the sword. Yet, though they were valiant warriors, their military organisation was loose enough; while their military tactics, if one may coin an expression, were of the offensive-elusive order. They swarmed out as great disorderly bodies of horse, devouring the country like locusts, carefully avoiding anything like a pitched battle, but hovering always about their enemy's flanks and communications, swift to see and to make profit of the slightest advantage, equally swift to perceive and to avoid any danger. Thus they wore out the Mogul armies, and broke the hearts of their generals by remaining always near enough to inflict much mischief, but always remote enough to suffer no harm. If they were suddenly compelled to assume the defensive, they had a perfect genius for choosing and occupying a position where they could resist attack; and woe to the army that retreated before them. Their leaders have always included some of the deepest and subtlest intellects in India; and yet their genius, so long as their ascendancy lasted, revealed itself as mainly destructive, and their instincts as wholly predatory. They levied tribute remorselessly, under pain of pillage, upon vast districts, and on condition of payment suffered them to escape famine and desolation. They showed, indeed, remarkable administrative talent in the collection of that tribute; but there their constructive work came to an end. It is therefore hard to see how India could have improved—how indeed it could have failed to deteriorate—under their mastery. The history of the country, so far as we have traced it, has been a continuous record of wars, revolts and intestine divisions; in the midst of which, at rare intervals of precarious repose, there had sprung up noble monuments of art and literature. There was nothing creative about the Marathas. Their reign, it is true, was short; but, even had it been prolonged, we can hardly conceive of the association of poetry or architecture with their name. For all their valiance and subtlety their rule was a blight rather than an influence. Once indeed, and in one particular, they imitated a foreign model in their own domain of war; and we must now examine where they found this model, and how it was turned to their own ruin.

III

From the conquest of Persia and Egypt by the followers of Mohammed until the sixteenth century, the sole line of communication between India and Europe had been by land through the passes of Afghanistan and Central Asia to the Black Sea and to Constantinople; but in 1492 Christopher Columbus, seeking the Indies by way of the Atlantic westward, discovered America; and in 1497 Vasco da Gama doubled the Cape of Good Hope, and cast anchor off Calicut in May 1498. Then came the Papal Bull of 1502 which divided the New World between Spain and Portugal, assigning the west to the former, and the east to the latter. Two great men, Almeida by valour against the fleets of the Sultan of Egypt, and Albuquerque by wise policy towards the Hindu natives, strengthened the hold of Portugal upon her new empire; and for a century, until annexation to Spain in 1580 gradually killed all enterprise in them, the Portuguese enjoyed a monopoly of Oriental commerce. But meantime the two great maritime powers of the future, the English and the Dutch, had arisen to contest with Spain her empire at every point; and their pioneers, busy since the beginning of the sixteenth century in attempting to find north-west and north-east passages to Asia, at last made their way round the Cape, the Englishman John Lancaster in 1591, and the Hollander Cornelius Houtman four years later. Companies to trade with the East Indies were speedily formed, that in England receiving its charter in 1600, and that in the Low Countries in 1602.

There was, however, a wide difference between the two companies. In Holland politics were commerce, and commerce was politics; and the States-General, though nominally distinguishing the Company from the State, virtually backed the adventure with all the weight and resources of the Republic. In England the Company was left severely to look after itself, the State being quite ready to take a share in the profits, but by no means disposed to partake in the risks. In truth it is hardly recognised that our East India Company was but the first of a long series of adventures of the same kind. The first half of the seventeenth century was more prolific in chartered companies than any period of our history. There was a regular mania for speculation in the New World; and King James the First granted away many hundreds of thousands of square miles, not only above the sea but under it, to a comparatively small number of "Undertakers," as they were called. Naturally there were many failures and even more quarrels among these companies; but their solid and visible results are the United States of America and the British Empire in India.

It need hardly be said that the Portuguese bitterly resented the intrusion of the Dutch and English upon their chosen field; and hard blows were exchanged between the rival parties, invariably to the disadvantage of the Portuguese. But though the two northern powers were always ready to combine against their common enemy, they were none the less furiously jealous of each other, and they pursued their commercial competition with the weapons not of trade but of war. Few ships went to sea unarmed in those days, so that a trading company was almost of necessity a militant association; and from fighting at sea to the attack of a factory by the seashore the step was very short. The Dutch, most practical and cold-blooded of nations, proved this in 1623 by seizing ten Englishmen and their native assistants at Amboyna in the Moluccas, and murdering every one of them after a mockery of a trial. This massacre, as it was called, caused furious indignation in England; but it was not until thirty years later that Cromwell took vengeance for it in the seven furious naval actions which marked the beginning of Dutch decay and of English predominance upon the seas. Meanwhile the East India Company had established factories at Surat in 1612, at Masulipatam in 1616, at Madras in 1640, and at Hoogly in 1651. Finally, in 1661 Bombay passed to the British Crown as part of the dowry of Charles the Second's queen, Catharine of Bragança, and was leased to the Company by the King for ten pounds.

Just three years later a new European competitor came upon the scene in the shape of the French Compagnie des Indes, founded by Colbert in 1664;[1] and in 1674 François Martin founded Pondicherry on the eastern coast and established the first French factory in Bengal at Chandernagore. It was just at this time that our countrymen were first brought into conflict with native enemies. In 1664 and 1670 the British only with difficulty held their own at Surat against the incursions of Sivaji; while in Bengal they suffered from the reaction of the wars of Aurangzeb and from the active oppression of his viceroy. In 1686 the Company initiated a new policy of reprisals against both Moguls and Marathas, and declared its intention to found "a large, well-grounded, sure English

[1] There are in the gardens of Government House, Calcutta, some brass cannon which bear the mark of the French East India Company in its early days. From constant cleaning with sand, however, the marks are in some cases almost obliterated, and in every case are in process of obliteration. Similar treatment has irretrievably damaged other beautifully ornamented guns, taken from Tipu Sahib and others, which are preserved in the same spot. Not a single Viceroy, apparently, has intervened to arrest the process of destruction, which for more than half a century has been going forward, and is still going forward, under their eyes.

dominion for all time to come." Their first operations ended in ignominious failure; and they were forced to fly from Bengal and to purchase their rights to return thither by an abject surrender and payment of a heavy fine to Aurangzeb. Nevertheless, in that same year, 1690, was witnessed the founding of Calcutta; while the nucleus of an European army had already been formed in Madras in 1644, and in Bombay in 1668. The first native troops of the Company's army had been enlisted, likewise in Bombay, in 1683-84.

Such was the position when in 1707 Aurangzeb died, a beaten and heart-broken man, at the age of ninety-one, leaving the Mogul Empire in ruins. Between that date and 1759 five Emperors ascended the throne of the Moguls with the empty title only of their great ancestors, while the Empire itself crumbled rapidly away. The viceroy of the Dekhan, the Nizam-ul-Mulk, established the independent dynasty which still reigns at Hyderabad; but even within his realm, the Carnatic, which bordered on the English and French settlements on the east coast, had become a semi-independent principality. Farther south a Hindu dynasty had established itself in Tanjore; and soldiers of fortune of various descriptions were setting themselves up as petty chieftains in hill-fortresses. In the north affairs were no better. Bengal had passed to one adventurer, Rohilkand to another, and Oudh was usurped by an official. Rajputs rebelled in one quarter, Sikhs in another. Every succession was disputed with arms; and amid all the vicissitudes of the various combatants the devastating flood of the Marathas rose higher and higher, till it threatened to overwhelm the whole of India. Moreover, as if these misfortunes were not sufficient, the fall of Aurangzeb's garrisons in Afghanistan allowed a Persian invader to penetrate the passes and to sack Delhi in 1737. Two years later an officer of his army, Ahmad Shah of the Abdali tribe of Afghans, seized Afghanistan, and from thence invaded and conquered the whole of the Western Panjab between 1748 and 1751. Never had India been in a more appalling welter of confusion, nor in more crying need of a master.

The struggle between the two aspirants to mastery had already begun. Its issue depended upon the command of the sea, for victory was bound to favour the side that could pour reinforcements into India regularly from Europe; but the fact seems to have been but dimly apprehended at the outset. On the scene of action everything appeared favourable to the French. A very able naval officer of that nation, Bertrand de la Bourdonnais, had in 1735 founded a naval base and arsenal at Mauritius; while in India itself two Governors of Pondicherry, Dumas and Dupleix, had instituted a policy of active interference with the internal affairs of the neighbouring native states; and Dumas had made such diplomatic intervention the more efficacious by creating an army of some seven thousand trained sepoys. These Frenchmen intended to play the part of statesmen in controlling the future of India, and they had an autocratic government at their back. The British, on the other hand, were still a trading company, independent of the Government; and their Governor at Madras was a man of mere ledgers and invoices, with, however, a quiet young clerk in his office named Robert Clive. France and England had come to blows over the Spanish Succession, and had opened the war which is remembered by the names of Dettingen, Fontenoy, Culloden, Roucoux and Lauffeldt. The news of the outbreak of hostilities reached India in 1744, at a time when no French fleet was on the coast; but the Nawab of the Carnatic informed the British at Madras that he intended to enforce neutrality within his province, and the English Governor meekly gave way. In July 1746 the fleets of the two nations met; and after an indecisive action the British Commodore sailed away with discreditable readiness, leaving the French free to land as many soldiers as they would. They accordingly laid siege to Madras, and in September forced it to capitulate. The Nawab attempted to intervene to enforce neutrality; but the French troops, readily facing odds of ten to one, swept his raw levies from the field without an effort. More than one writer of the seventeenth century had predicted that a small body of disciplined European troops would suffice to rout the most formidable of native armies; and now that prediction was verified. This incident assured supremacy in India to an European power.

The British settlements seemed now to be at the mercy of Dupleix, who had three thousand European troops at his disposal; but the tide was turned by the arrival of a British squadron with reinforcements; and instead of a British fort it was Pondicherry itself that was besieged, though most clumsily and unsuccessfully, by Admiral Boscawen. The operations, however, revealed the rise of a great British leader, Major Stringer Lawrence, who was not only a master of military manœuvre but a trainer of commanders. Simple and uneducated, for he could hardly write more than his name, he had none the less great insight into the characters of men, and finding a promising pupil in the gloomy and discontented clerk, Robert Clive, he took the latter's military education in hand and practically adopted him as a son.

The peace of Aix-la-Chapelle in 1748 brought the war of the Austrian Succession to an end, seemingly with no great advantage anywhere to either party, but really with the very solid result that France was left almost powerless at sea. Madras was restored to England in exchange for the French fort of Louisburg, to the huge indignation of the British colonists in North America, who had captured Louisburg with no assistance from British troops. Nevertheless, the British Government was right to make the exchange, for, as Admiral Saunders pointed out at the time, Louisburg was a source of weakness rather than strength to the French, being always at the mercy of the power that was superior at sea.

The rival companies in India meanwhile found it easy to continue the struggle, nominally as allies of native states but in reality as principals. Dupleix was anxious to make French influence supreme at the court not only of the Nawab of the Carnatic at Arcot, but also of the Viceroy of the Dekhan at Hyderabad; and the death of both potentates, with the inevitable result of a disputed succession, gave him the opportunity that he desired. The British naturally supported the candidates who were opposed to the French; but their best commander, Stringer Lawrence, had gone to England, and in his absence British military operations went sadly wrong. The contest centred around Trichinopoly; and in 1751 the situation was so desperate that it was only saved by a diversion made against Arcot by the young volunteer, Robert Clive. But at the end of that year Stringer Lawrence returned, and in action after action during 1752 and 1753 worsted the French before Trichinopoly. In 1754 Dupleix was recalled for gross misconduct in his office; and in January 1755 the contest in the Carnatic was brought to a close by a suspension of arms. The French should have had the better of the British, for, France and England being at peace, their fleets could not intervene; and in India itself Dupleix had enjoyed superiority of numbers, though his commanders were inferior to those of the British. Yet a step had been taken which ultimately assured the victory of the red-coats, for the British Government had initiated a new policy of sending the King's troops to assist those of the Company; and in September 1754 the first battalion arrived, the Thirty-ninth Foot, now the Dorsetshire Regiment—*Primus in Indis*—under the command of Colonel Eyre Coote.

But suddenly the centre of British interest was shifted to Bengal. That province in 1756 passed upon the death of Alivardi Khan to his adopted son Suraj-ud-Daula (Surajah Dowlah), a potentate of the most contemptible type. The Seven Years' War was on the point of breaking out in Europe; and the Governor at Calcutta, being warned of the fact, was setting his fort in order, when the Nawab chose to take offence at the action and marched upon the town. The tragedy of the Black Hole followed; and troops were hastily sent up from Madras under Clive, escorted by three ships of Admiral Watson's squadron, to recover Calcutta. This was done with little difficulty; but a French fleet and army were expected at Pondicherry; and it was essential to place Calcutta speedily beyond reach of danger from Suraj-ud-Daula, so that the ships and forces might return to Madras. Finding a disaffected party in the Nawab's own camp, Clive negotiated with the chief of them, Mir Jaffir, and with his help routed Suraj-ud-Daula's army at Plassey (June 23, 1757). He then set Mir Jaffir upon the Nawab's throne, appointing as Resident at his court a young man of twenty-five, named Warren Hastings, and himself became Resident at Calcutta, while the troops returned to Madras.

It was not, however, until April 1758 that the expected French armament arrived at Pondicherry under command of Count Lally de Tollendal. For a time superiority of numbers gave Lally some measure of success ; but towards the end of the year Clive made a diversion by sending an expedition under Colonel Forde of the Thirty-ninth against the French settlements in the Northern Sirkars. Forde, whose name is far too little known, fulfilled his mission brilliantly by defeating the Marquis de Conflans at Chundoor (Condore), and by the storm of Masulipatam—the latter a most daring feat of arms. Meanwhile the French fleet was driven off the coast by the British ; and the arrival of reinforcements from England reduced the inequality of numbers. For a moment there arose unexpected peril, owing to a wanton and unprovoked attempt of the Dutch from Java and Chinsura upon Calcutta ; but Clive faced the danger boldly, and at Badra on the 25th of

November 1759 Forde, with a force of inferior numbers, practically annihilated the Dutch troops in half an hour, and decided for ever the downfall of that nation in India. A few weeks later (Jan. 8, 1760) Coote, once again with inferior numbers, by brilliant manœuvring defeated Lally decisively at Wandewash; and a year later he received the surrender of Pondicherry. The first stage of the great struggle was over. It was now certain that if India was to pass under the rule of Europeans, those Europeans would be the British.

IV

Meanwhile internal confusion had increased, and the Mogul Empire was crumbling away more rapidly than ever. The Marathas had by this time organised themselves into their confederacy of five coequal parts under five principal chiefs. The degenerate descendants of Sivaji had long since been displaced, except in form, by an hereditary dynasty of mayors of the palace, who bore the title of Peshwa, with headquarters at Puna. The four remaining members were Sindia of Gwalior, Holkar of Indore, the Gaekwar of Baroda, and Bonsla of Nagpur; and although the five were constantly quarrelling among themselves, the confederacy at this moment was under the direction of Balaji Baji Rao, the ablest of all the Peshwas. After the capture of Delhi, Ahmad Shah Abdali had appointed a viceroy to administer his conquests, and had himself returned to Afghanistan. The Marathas in 1758 seized the moment to lay hold on Delhi, expel Ahmad Shah's garrison from Lahore, and establish Maratha domination in the Panjab. The action shows the high-water mark of the flood of Maratha conquest; but the intrepid horsemen had gone too far. The Mohammedans were not disposed to stand quietly by while a Hindu power of yesterday overthrew their rule in Northern India. In the winter of 1759–60 Ahmad Shah descended in his wrath from Afghanistan, recovered Lahore at a blow, fell upon Holkar and Sindia, who were ravaging the southern districts, and, smiting them heavily, one after the other, drove them away with great loss. He then occupied Delhi, and never paused upon his march south-eastward until he had pitched his camp upon the Ganges. The Peshwa, undismayed by these misfortunes, sent up a powerful army to retrieve them; and in January 1761 the two hosts met at Panipat. On each side the fighting men numbered over one hundred thousand, and the combat was long and stubborn; but the Marathas were at last defeated; and defeat in the circumstances almost signified annihilation, for the villagers turned savagely upon the plundering horsemen who for two years had ridden rough-shod over them. The disaster was the death of the great Peshwa; and the Marathas, though they recovered with singular rapidity, never again reached such a height of power as they had attained from 1758 until 1760. But the victor took no advantage of his triumph. The Afghans were anxious to carry home their booty, for the Persians were menacing their western frontiers; and thus it was that Ahmad Shah retired again to his own place, closing with a worthy majesty the long series of invasions of India from the north-west. In reality the Afghans and the Marathas were but rival vultures fighting over the carcase of the Mogul Empire; but the only result of their struggle was to exhaust themselves, and to leave Northern India as masterless as ever. So momentous were the events that occurred in the twelve months from the 22nd of January 1760 to the 29th of January 1761.

Unfortunately at this critical time the guiding hand of the master was withdrawn, for Clive went home in February 1760, leaving the supreme power in Bengal in the hands of the Company's clerks. These saw their opportunity for enriching themselves, and, being miserably paid and under no restraint of law or of honour, did not fail to seize it. The government and all responsibility for the expenses of administration lay nominally with Mir Jaffir, but his rule was wholly dependent upon British troops, which therefore held him at their mercy. He quickly chafed against the necessity of paying his masters; whereupon the Company's servants matured a plan for deposing him and setting up his finance-minister, Mir Kassim, in his place, in the hope that more willing submission would be found in a new puppet. At this juncture, however, there intervened a complication from without. The titular Emperor, Shah Alam, being an exile from Delhi, took refuge with the Nawab of Oudh, and with the latter's help threatened to enforce his claim to the sovereignty of Bengal. Major Caillaud marched forward with a small force to meet him ; but the Emperor contrived to out-manœuvre the British and to appear before Patna, which was only saved by a wonderful march and a most daring action conducted under the command of Captain Knox. The danger being over the Company's servants duly deposed Mir Jaffir, and installed Mir Kassim, insisting, however, on commercial privileges for their own advantage, which were so exorbitant as to exhaust Mir Kassim's patience very speedily. Therefore they displaced him in favour of their former puppet Mir Jaffir ; and Mir Kassim very justifiably sought redress with arms.

He was a dangerous enemy, for he possessed a certain number of regular troops trained after European fashion and commanded by an Alsatian, whose nickname, Sombre, had been corrupted by the natives into Sumroo. Moreover, the Company's servants had nothing ready, neither men nor arms nor supplies, nothing indeed excepting one marvellous commander, Major Thomas Adams. In July 1763 Adams began his campaign, fought one sharp action near Katwa on the 19th ; a second at Suti on the 2nd of August ; and a third, a crowning victory against odds of twenty to one, at Undwa Nala on the 5th of September. In despairing rage Mir Kassim ordered the massacre of all the British in Patna, an order which was faithfully executed by Sumroo, and fled to the camp of the Emperor Shah Alam and of his vizier the Nawab of Oudh. On the 6th of November Adams took Patna by storm, and then, worn out by hard work, he sickened, and died a few months later. A feeble and incompetent successor, Major Carnac, played for a while unsuccessfully with the united forces of the Allies ; but was soon displaced by a stronger man, Major Hector Munro. After first quelling a mutiny in his own army, Munro utterly overthrew the Emperor and his confederates on the 23rd of February 1764 at Buxar. The victory converted Shah Alam from an enemy into an ally ; and the army penetrating into Oudh captured in succession the commanding cities of Lucknow and Allahabad. Thus for the first time the British advanced beyond Bengal, and found themselves in contact with the new principalities created by sundry adventurers since the death of Aurangzeb—Mohammedan Pathans in Rohilkand, Mohammedan officers of the fallen Empire in Agra and Delhi, Hindu Jats in Bhurtpore. There was no stability in any of them. Any one of these states, rising under some leader of genius, might encroach upon the others, or, falling under some incompetent successor to an able man, might be swallowed up by the bold and ambitious owner of a few villages. In other words, they were dangerous neighbours which, as all experience of conquering nations has taught, can only be made safe by absorption into the system of the conquerors.

Fortunately at this moment Clive returned to India, and laid down clearly the policy of the Company. The first step was to take over the administration of Bengal, paying a definite tribute to the Emperor as his viceroy, and so to put an end to puppet Nawabs and to corrupt practices among the Company's servants. The second was to resist the temptation to annex Oudh, to reinstate the former ruler in it as a friend and ally, and so to establish what is called a buffer-state between the British in Bengal and the confusion in the north-west. Whatever was to come in the future, there was to be for the present an end of territorial expansion.

But in the south there were more dangerous neighbours than in the north. In addition to the presence of the Marathas, Madras was threatened by the rise of a Mohammedan soldier, Haidar Ali, who through sheer military genius had acquired the sovereignty of the Hindu principality of Mysore, and from that base was laying violent hands upon Southern India generally. His chief adversaries were the Nizam of Hyderabad, from whom he was constantly taking territory, and the Marathas, with whom he had fought many sharp actions. The Madras Government, in consideration of recovering from the Nizam the Northern Sirkars, from which the British had driven the French, had engaged themselves vaguely to support him in case of war; and Haidar by entering the territory of Hyderabad in 1767 obliged them to fulfil their pledges to the Nizam, which they did by sending an army towards Mysore. Very soon, however, both Nizam and Haidar turned against the British. The former enemy was quickly disposed of; but Haidar was not so easily beaten, and the Madras Council did their best by extreme imbecility to second him. There was indeed one British officer, Colonel Joseph Smith, whose very name sufficed to make Haidar tremble, and who, in spite of a thousand embarrassments put in his way by his masters, contrived always to beat the Indian chief in the field. But the Madras Council deliberately displaced him to make room for an incompetent nominee of their own; and the result was that in 1769 Haidar advanced to within five miles of Madras itself, and forced the Council to conclude an humiliating peace. Worse than this, Haidar had established friendly relations with the French, who were burning to recover their lost ground in India; and the British had hampered themselves not only by taking the Marathas into their pay, but by binding themselves to a defensive alliance with the Nizam, with Haidar Ali, and with the Marathas against any one or more of the three parties who should aggressively attack the other. The Marathas shortly afterwards did attack

Haidar, who appealed to the Madras Government for assistance and was refused it. From that moment he became the irreconcilable enemy of the British in India.

Meanwhile Parliament, after enquiring into Indian affairs, had passed in 1773 an act to reconstitute the Government of India, which, though it contained some wise provisions, was vitiated by one fatal blunder. Hitherto the three Presidencies had been coequal; but now a Governor-General and Council were set up in Bengal with general authority over Bombay and Madras also, which change in itself was eminently sensible. But unfortunately it was ordained not that the Governor-General should be supreme, but that he should be ruled by a majority of the Council, having himself no more than a casting vote in case the Council were equally divided. Nothing could have been worse devised for purposes of Asiatic government. The Governor-General, happily, was Warren Hastings, but his Council contained men who from personal spite laid themselves out to thwart him at every turn. Yet the times were most critical. England was entering upon the fatal quarrel with the American colonies, which was destined to turn the swords of half of Europe against her. In India the Maratha chiefs, without forsaking their original confederacy under the Peshwa, were just beginning to carve out for themselves independent sovereignties, and every year descended in predatory raids upon Oudh and Rohilkand. In

1773 the Nawab called upon the Rohillas and the British to aid him against the invaders; and the armies of all three in combination drove the Marathas back. When, however, the question of the cost of the war was raised, the Rohillas refused to pay to the Nawab the contribution which they had engaged themselves to discharge; and the Nawab therefore asked Hastings to join him in compelling them. Hastings consented; and thereupon followed the first Rohilla War, in which the Rohillas were utterly defeated by the British, and their territory annexed to Oudh for the consolidation of the buffer-state.

This was the only war initiated by Hastings, but in Bombay the President and Council, anxious as their peers to annex territory, entangled themselves in hostilities with the Marathas; and Hastings, while utterly condemning their folly, felt bound to support them. The war, for the most part miserably conducted, dragged on and on, the only redeeming feature being the storming of Gwalior, an almost inaccessible fortress, by Captain Popham. Then came bad news of disasters in America, of war with France, and of a coming effort of the French to recover what they had lost in India. Finally Haidar Ali, the Nizam and the Marathas formed a confederacy for the total expulsion of the British from India. The campaign against Haidar, directed by Hector Munro of Buxar, opened disastrously in 1780 with the complete destruction of a strong detachment of the British

Army. Sir Eyre Coote was then called to the command, and saved the situation by the victory of Porto Novo in 1781, and by further successes at Sholingur and Arni. The diplomacy of Warren Hastings broke up the confederacy, and Haidar Ali died at the end of 1782; but meanwhile French troops and a French fleet had arrived, and the war was carried on by Haidar's son, Tipu Sahib. Another British detachment was annihilated at Bednore. The French fleet under Suffren had the advantage of the British, and affairs were coming to an utterly disastrous issue after an obstinate action between the British and French armies at Gadalur, when the news of peace with France fortunately saved the British dominions in India. Humiliating treaties with the Marathas in 1782 and with Tipu Sahib in 1784 brought the struggle at last to an end. Hastings had been obliged to extort money from the Rajah of Benares and the Begums of Oudh in order to carry on the war at all; and but for his indomitable courage all would have been lost. The twenty years from 1764 to 1784 are the most dismal and discreditable of all Anglo-Indian history. Of the three Presidencies it is difficult to say which Council was the worst, Bombay and Madras for crookedness and folly, or Bengal from malignity of faction and personal spite.

Happily the fools have been forgotten, and the great man, Warren Hastings, is remembered. His enemies, as is well known, pursued him on his return to England, and contrived to work up against him the attack which is dignified by the name of his impeachment. A more infamous proceeding is not to be found in our history; infamous, not because there was no ground for enquiry into the administration of Hastings, but because, though it was conducted partly by honest but mistaken men, it was helped forward by politicians, who had not an atom of principle, and stooped to be the instruments of personal rancour not from any zeal for the right, but from sheer conceit of their own oratory.

V

It may be gathered that the position of the British in India at the close of the war of American Independence was none of the strongest; but fortunately a new power had arisen in the north to deliver them from their most pressing dangers. This was the Sikhs, whose organisation and enthusiasm had been so far quickened by persecution that they had by 1785 mastered the whole of the Panjab between the Jhelum and the Satlaj; where they formed at once a barrier against any new invasion from the north-western passes, and a dam against the flood, which was once again rising, of the Marathas. It was pretty certain that before long there must be a struggle between British and Marathas for the final mastery of India; for Sindia had not only reoccupied Delhi and Agra, but had actually called upon the East India Company to pay tribute for the tenure of Bengal. For the present, however, a policy of aggression was the last thing that was favoured either in England or at Calcutta. The British Parliament had been very busy with enquiry into Indian affairs, with the result that in 1784 and 1786 new India Bills had been passed by Pitt. Thereby the immediate Government in Calcutta was placed in the hands of a Governor-General, who was no longer merely a member of his Council with a casting vote, but was authorised upon extraordinary occasions to act upon his own responsibility, no matter what the opinions of his councillors. Simultaneously, superintendence of the civil, military and financial business of the Company in England was committed to six commissioners, nominated by the Crown, and known as the Board of Control. Thus the chief officials in India ceased to be answerable to the Company, and became answerable to Parliament, with the result that the standards of integrity and efficiency were rapidly raised, and many of the old abuses banished.

Lord Cornwallis was the first Governor-General appointed under the new system. He was a good soldier and an inflexibly upright man, but otherwise of little distinction; and he was hampered by a clause in the new India Act which forbade him to declare war except for the defence of British territory or of that of their allies. So fatuous an enactment practically bade the Governor-General sit still while his enemies completed their preparations for war; and Tipu Sahib, puffed up by his recent successes, did not fail to take advantage of the fact. Ultimately, in 1791, Cornwallis was obliged to take the field against him in person; and after two arduous campaigns Tipu was forced to sign a treaty which deprived him of half his territory and resources.

In 1793 began the long war with revolutionary France; and the last act of Cornwallis before he left India in that year was to seize the French settlements. He was succeeded by Sir John Shore, a cautious and feeble man, who allowed both the Marathas and Tipu to increase their strength at the expense of the Nizam, and by his weakness encouraged Tipu to court the alliance of the French. Meanwhile the Hindu power of the Marathas was gaining upon the Mohammedans in all quarters; and the five chiefs of the confederation had by this time practically established themselves as independent rulers; the most powerful of them, Sindia of Gwalior, being master of the old capital of the Mogul Empire. The control of the Peshwa over his subordinates had ceased; and these combative leaders were indiscriminately fighting each other, or any one else who might tempt their cupidity. The whole country was overrun by mercenary bands, ready to sell themselves to the highest bidder; and, in fact, those were the golden days of adventurers in India. Accordingly they swarmed thither not only from all parts of the Peninsula, but also from Europe. From the seventeenth century onward Europeans had resorted to the courts of Indian potentates as soldiers of fortune. Now they came in numbers, French, Italian and British, perhaps the most remarkable of them being George Thomas, an Irish sailor, who by rare courage and undoubted military skill became for a time a reigning prince with an army of ten thousand men. Indirectly these adventurers exerted an influence which was highly favourable to the British, for they persuaded the Indian chiefs to train their troops after the European model, or, in other words, to fight the British with their own weapons. Tipu Sahib succumbed to this temptation, as Haidar his father had succumbed before him; so likewise did Sindia, and the error was fatal to both of them.

At last, in 1798, came a new Governor-General, who from the first made it the foundation of his policy that Britain must be the paramount power in India, and reduce the prevailing anarchy to order. This was Richard, Lord Mornington, better known by his later title of Marquess Wellesley; and he was accompanied by his brother Arthur, a rather sheepish young man of twenty-nine, whom the Indian climate in a few months suddenly ripened to the full measure of an unsuspected genius. Tipu of Mysore, as the open ally of the French, was the first enemy with whom Mornington grappled; and in 1799 Seringapatam was stormed by General Harris, and Tipu was slain. It is noteworthy that in this campaign Arthur Wellesley held his first high command, and suffered his greatest failure, which might have wrecked any officer who had not the Governor-General for a brother. It is noteworthy also that, if Tipu had stuck to the old principle of reliance upon light cavalry only, instead of trusting to trained infantry after the European fashion, he might have evaded any decisive issue, and wearied out the British with an endless and unprofitable war. As things fell out he was destroyed, and his dynasty swept away; a menace which had hung over Southern India for a whole generation was removed; and the Carnatic and Tanjore were annexed by Lord Mornington to the British dominions.

The Governor-General's next step was to endeavour to restore the authority of the Peshwa over the confederate chiefs, and so to keep them not only from aggression against their neighbours but at peace with each other. The Peshwa readily signed a treaty of offensive and defensive alliance, but Sindia and Holkar refused to join in it, and it was soon discovered that Sindia was endeavouring to form a Maratha combination against the British. General Arthur Wellesley was accordingly set in motion against Sindia's dominions in the south, and General Lake against those in the north-west. Then followed the series of desperate actions which have immortalised the year 1803. Wellesley won the battles of Assaye and Argaum; Lake stormed Aligarh, captured Agra and gained the two signal victories of Delhi and Laswari. But the Marathas fought most nobly. Both at Assaye and Laswari their troops displayed a power of manœuvre which disconcerted the British commanders, while the Maratha gunners stood by their guns with heroic tenacity until they were slain by the bayonet. On the evening of Assaye the iron Wellesley, who had been miraculously calm all day, sat down and dropped asleep among the dead and dying, with his head on his knees, worn out with the exertions and anxiety of the day. Lake, when the battle of Laswari had at last been gained, wrote to Lord Wellesley that he had never been in so critical a position before, and hoped that he never would be again.

These victories shattered the strength and influence of Sindia; but Holkar, who had never abandoned the traditional tactics of the Marathas, was far more difficult to deal with. He nearly destroyed one of Lake's detachments under Colonel Monson, and, though subsequently defeated by this same Monson at Deig, led Lake a long chase almost to Attock before he was finally brought to terms.

Thus after three years of bitter fighting the great Maratha war came to an end in 1806; having gained for the British the imperial cities of Delhi and Agra with the contiguous tracts on both banks of the Jumna, and the entire country between the Jumna and the Ganges, together with the province of Cuttack. Thereby British territory was carried forward continuously from Bengal to the upper Jumna in the north, and from the presidency of Bengal to that of Madras in the south. Mornington also instituted the principle of subsidiary treaties, which provided that the native states which accepted them should keep no troops except those hired from the Anglo-Indian government; should not take up arms against each other but refer all disputes to British arbitration; should remain within the territorial limits imposed upon them; and should enter into no negotiations with foreign powers. Incidentally he earned the eternal gratitude of the Rajputs, the great fighting clans of India, in delivering them from extinction by the Marathas. Above all, as we have seen, he took possession of Delhi, the key of Northern India; and the object of all these vast designs and enterprises was to give the country, what it had never yet enjoyed, the blessing of peace.

Mornington's policy was in the highest sense imperial, but it had cost much money; and by 1805 both the Directors of the Company and the Board of Control were of opinion that he would be better at home. He returned, therefore, to be honoured with the title of Marquess Wellesley, but not with that to which, in his sublime conceit, he aspired, of Duke of India. He was succeeded by Lord Cornwallis, too commonplace a man to sympathise with Wellesley's masterful views of political supremacy and of keeping the peace in India. He thought that England should remain strictly within her own boundaries and not interfere with her neighbours ; but before he could carry his opinions into action he died, bequeathing them first to a temporary successor, Sir George Barlow, who is remembered chiefly by the fact that he goaded the officers of the Madras Army into open mutiny. Lord Minto, who presently superseded Barlow, endeavoured likewise to follow the precepts of Cornwallis and to avoid all foreign complications ; but being confronted with the schemes of Napoleon and Alexander for invasion of India, he was fain to send missions to Persia, Afghanistan and the Sikhs to secure his north-west frontier ; and to despatch expeditions to Mauritius and Java, which extinguished every French and Dutch settlement in the East. The quarrel between the two European potentates, and the invasion of Russia by Napoleon, released him from any further apprehension from the west ; and meanwhile he had the good sense to make a firm stand in another direction. A man of genius, Ranjit Singh, having reorganised the Sikhs as a military power, had united all the petty chieftainships of the Panjab into a great military despotism. In 1808 he was inclined to extend his frontier to south of the Satlaj; but desisted in consequence of representations from Lord Minto that England would not permit it. Checked thus on the south-eastern side, Ranjit Singh came to a friendly agreement with the British as to his south-eastern border, and took advantage of civil dissensions in Afghanistan to carry his sovereignty beyond the Indus and to annex Kashmir.

But though severely bitten with the doctrines of Cornwallis, Lord Minto found himself obliged once again to interfere beyond the British frontiers. True to his principle he had allowed Central India to take care of itself; and there had arisen in it bands of freebooters, some of which under a celebrated leader, Amir Khan, were finally united into a compact force of thirty thousand men. These bands were known as the Pindaris, but were mere brigands who overran all territories impartially, plundering and devastating not only with ruthlessness but with barbarous cruelty. This Amir Khan fastened himself upon Rajputana, which from internal strife and general weakness was powerless against him; and, in spite of Wellesley's effort for their salvation, the Rajputs were once more in danger of being eaten up. Minto was obliged to send an army to check Amir Khan's entry into the territory of England's allies, but he made no effort to extinguish the evil of these predatory bands altogether. The danger was the greater, for the Maratha leaders Sindia, Holkar and Bonsla were still chafing over their lost predominance, and might well look to the Pindaris as useful auxiliaries.

Happily, upon the departure of Lord Minto his place was taken by a true disciple of Wellesley and a very able soldier, General, Lord Hastings. Soon after his arrival, in 1814, his attention was claimed by the encroachments of the Gurkhas in Nipal who, having trained and equipped their men after the European fashion, conquered easily the local chiefs in the hills and descended upon the English territory in the plain. An expedition was sent to punish them under Sir Rollo Gillespie, a man who, if it were safe to fasten such a title upon a single individual, might be described as the bravest soldier that ever wore the red coat. He failed, however, at the outset, and was himself among the killed; nor was it until 1815 that Sir David Ochterlony reduced the Gurkhas to sue for peace, in return for which they ceded a long tract of the lower Himalayas, thus carrying the British frontier up to that of the Chinese Empire. This was the first of our many expeditions into the mountains in the north and north-west, and our first and last war with the Gurkhas, whose regiments have made so famous a name for themselves under the British flag.

Meanwhile the situation in Central India

grew worse and worse ; and the Pindaris, secretly abetted by the Maratha chiefs, made raids upon the presidencies both of Bengal and of Madras. The Rajput Raja of Jaipur, groaning under the oppressions of these robbers, appealed to the Governor-General for help ; and Lord Hastings decided that Central India must be reduced to order once for all. Sindia with some difficulty was overawed into co-operation with the British ; but the Peshwa, Bonsla and Holkar openly sided against them, only to meet with decisive repulses after hard fighting near Puna, in Nagpur and at Mehidpur. The Pindaris were hunted down by the British cavalry ; and their leader, Chitu, was driven into the jungle and there killed by a tiger. The Peshwa was deposed, his office extinguished, and most of his territory annexed.

The boundaries of the dominions of Sindia, Holkar and Bonsla were carefully laid down, and the predatory system of the Marathas was brought to an end. Furthermore, it was ordained that in every state in Central India the British Government should in future control all foreign relations, arbitrate in all disputes with neighbours, supervise generally through a Resident the domestic administration, and hold superior command of all subsidiary forces and contingents. Thus the peace of Central India was not only enforced for the present, but assured for the future ; and the policy of Lord Wellesley was carried to its appointed end. Few remember the merit of

Lord Hastings, either by that name, by his earlier title of Lord Moira, or by his earliest as Lord Rawdon, which he bore when he first won fame as a commander at the action of Hobkirk's Hill in the American War. As a politician at home he was a failure; as a military commander he lacked opportunity of distinction in his mature age; but he was none the less a great soldier and a great administrator, whose hand impressed itself permanently upon the future of India.

There were now but two points at which the frontier of India was threatened with disturbance, in the north-west by the Sikhs and in the north-east by the ruler of Burma. This last had been welded into a single kingdom by conquest while England was still busy over the subdual of Bengal; and the Burmese armies in 1823 carried their aggression so far to the south and west as to invade border-states which were under British protection. Lord Amherst, the Governor-General, therefore, sent an expedition to Rangoon, which, after a campaign of two years, dictated at Ava terms of peace, under which the British gained a safe frontier by the cession of Assam, Arakan and Tenasserim, and by the recognition of their protectorate over sundry minor states. But while the army was engaged in Burma, the throne of Bharatpur (Bhurtpore), a protected state, fell vacant, and was usurped by a pretender. Such usurpation was a direct menace to the peace of India, and Sir David Ochterlony, who was then Resident at Delhi, promptly assembled a considerable force to march against Bharatpur, and to vindicate the principles laid down by Hastings. So little, however, did Amherst understand his duty that he countermanded Ochterlony's preparations in terms of preposterous harshness. The veteran general, a man worth twenty Amhersts, thereupon resigned; but he was so much chagrined alike by his chief's departure from sound policy, and by the slight put upon himself, that he died shortly afterwards. However, Amherst after all was obliged to do himself what he had forbidden to Sir David; and the fortress of Bharatpur, which had foiled four successive assaults of the fiery Lake, fell before a systematic siege by Lord Combermere in 1826.

Then in 1828 came a new Governor-General, Lord William Bentinck, who combined with the office that of Commander-in-Chief also. As a soldier he had served with no great distinction in Spain and in Italy, and as an administrator he had been recalled from Madras in 1807 on account of his responsibility for the mutiny at Vellore; wherefore it is upon his later work in India that his reputation, unduly exalted by the fact that Macaulay wrote his epitaph, must be taken to rest. He is remembered chiefly for his abolition of the rite of *sati*, or widow-burning, and because he was the first Governor-General who made the material progress of the country his special care; and in virtue of these peculiar services he holds a just title to fame. On the other hand, his name is associated with certain acts of economy and false humanity which leave a terrible blot upon his memory. He blew up the celebrated great gun of Agra to make money out of the metal; he tried to sell the Taj Mahal; and, in order to save twenty thousand pounds, he nearly caused a mutiny among the British officers of the Bengal army, by cutting off, in direct breach of faith, one of their allowances. The Directors of the East India Company had pressed this last measure upon previous Governors-General, but every one had refused to take it; and its most mischievous result was that it lowered their officers in the eyes of the Sepoys, contributing not a little to create the spirit which brought about the Mutiny in 1857. Not content with this, Bentinck injured the discipline of the Sepoys still more by abolishing the punishment of the lash in native regiments, in the face of unanimous advice to the contrary both from Europeans and Indian officers.[1] Further, he threw to the winds the policy of Wellesley and Hastings, by abstaining, so far as possible, from intervention in the internal strife of protected states. In other words, he tried to abjure his responsibilities as constable for the maintenance of peace in India; allowing in the name of humanity full scope to disorder, which is only another name for human misery, until more than once even he at last found himself obliged to interfere. Lastly, it was Bentinck

[1] This measure was in fact revoked by his successors.

who was answerable at the very end of his term of office for the decree that made English the official language of India, and thereby held up the acquisition of a little superficial Western culture as the ideal to be attained by young Indians of talent. On the whole, excuse could be found for a Governor-General if he prayed that the record of his rule might be better than that of Bentinck.

Still during Lord William's term there was no war; very far otherwise was it with his successor Lord Auckland. After the fall of Napoleon Russia had resumed her march eastward, and very soon was pressing upon Persia. Though bound by a treaty of alliance to defend the Shah against aggression, England, in dismay at finding herself in contact with an European power, decided in 1828 to ask release from her obligations, and drew back her defensive frontier to Afghanistan. She thereupon became supremely interested in that country, where the sceptre, by a transition common in the East, had passed from Shah Shuja, the legitimate descendant of Ahmad Shah Abdali, to the prime minister, Dost Mohammed. Matters were brought to a crisis in 1837 by the advance of a Persian army on Herat; the Shah, who had ceded territory to Russia in the west, being anxious to compensate himself by encroachments to the east. Russia promptly offered assistance to Dost Mohammed, who, however, was much more inclined to throw himself upon

British protection. But Auckland received his overtures coldly ; and, though a British expedition to the Persian Gulf sufficed to raise the siege of Herat, yet the Governor-General determined to settle the Afghan question in another way by entering into a treaty with the Sikhs and with Shah Shuja to replace the latter on the throne. Accordingly, in 1838 a British force advanced to Kandahar, and Shah Shuja was restored with little difficulty.

The only means of maintaining his rule, however, was through a military occupation of Afghanistan by the British, and this, not less than the original invasion, was an undertaking of extreme danger. The base for the expedition was Scinde, a foreign country whose rulers, the Baluchi Amirs, were not too friendly to the British ; while on the flank of our communications was the Panjab, now organised into a great military power by the genius of Ranjit Singh, and exceedingly suspicious of our movements. The occupation was much resented by the free Afghan tribes, whose discontent in 1841 ripened into a general insurrection. The supplies of the British were cut off, and the troops were harassed by eternal petty fighting before the evacuation of Kabul, unwisely deferred until the winter, was finally carried out. The result, as is well known, was disastrous, for out of a total force of sixteen thousand men but one escaped. Lord Auckland, absolutely unnerved by a catastrophe unparalleled in the history of the British in

India, made no effort to retrieve their fallen fortunes; Lord Ellenborough, who succeeded him in February 1842, shrank equally from a task so formidable; and it was left to two British generals, Nott and Pollock, to advance upon their own responsibility from Kandahar and Jelalabad to Kabul, and to restore the reputation of the British arms by a final triumphant campaign.

Even so, however, the capital of Afghanistan was recaptured only to be speedily abandoned, together with every political object which Auckland's aggression had sought to attain. Moreover, the destruction of the British force at Kabul had dangerously shattered the prestige of the East India Company, and raised up a large crop of enemies. First the Amirs of Scinde, for violation of an unwelcome treaty which had been thrust upon them, were attacked by Sir Charles Napier, defeated in two great battles at Miani and Hyderabad, and compelled to cede to us Karachi and the estuary of the Indus. This was on the whole the most brilliant campaign ever fought by the British in India. Next the Sikh army, released from the iron discipline of Ranjit Singh in 1839, had become uncontrollable, while at the same time the army of Sindia had been augmented to dangerous dimensions and, owing to a contest over the guardianship of an infant ruler, might easily become an element of danger. Rightly perceiving the menace to the peace of India involved in the existence of these two masterless hordes, Ellenborough dealt first with the Marathas, who in two battles, Maharajpore and Panniar, fought on the same day (December 29, 1843), were reduced to powerlessness for mischief. But these masterful methods of anticipating and averting peril did not commend themselves to the Directors of the East India Company, and in 1844 Ellenborough was unceremoniously recalled.

His successor, Sir Henry Hardinge, a soldier of deserved reputation, found that Ellenborough's forebodings were well justified; for within less than six months after his arrival the Sikhs crossed the Satlaj into British territory (Dec. 1844). Then followed the severest fighting ever experienced by the British in India, for their General-in-Chief was unskilful and their enemy most gallant and steadfast. Four well-contested actions, Mudki, Ferozeshah, Aliwal and Sobraon, were necessary to bring the army of the Sikhs to reason. Hardinge thereupon confiscated all Sikh territory on the left bank of the Satlaj and the tract between that river and the Beas, exacted an indemnity of a million and a half, enforced the disbandment of many Sikh regiments, and, limiting the full number of their army to thirty-two thousand men, fondly imagined that he had given India permanent peace. In vain men of deeper insight urged the annexation of the Panjab, and the Government of Lahore predicted a second rising of the army against itself: Hardinge, not without reason, thought his armed force insufficient to execute a more thorough policy; so he did what he could and hoped for the best. All was still quiet when at the end of 1847 he made over the viceroyalty to his successor Lord Dalhousie.

Within three months after Hardinge's departure the peace was broken. Upon a trifling pretext the Sikhs again rose in insurrection, and, after a very bloody and indecisive action at Chilianwala, they were finally crushed by the victory of Gujrat. They had fought nobly, but had been ruined by their own indiscipline. Dalhousie, refusing to risk further trouble in the Panjab, annexed it; and its administration was refounded from the very base under the inspiration of Henry Lawrence, but under the actual rule of his brother John, aided by such young officers as John Nicholson and Herbert Edwardes. The like work is now in hand in the Soudan, where British officers are proving themselves worthy successors of their forerunners in the Panjab. The annexation brought the British frontier up to the foot of the Afghan hills, and made the conquerors responsible for checking any further invasions of India from the north-west. This was and is no trifling burden, even though recent events have tended somewhat to lighten it; for the task of punishing the raids of the predatory tribes in the mountains has been continuous and endless. The second Sikh campaign, however, was the last campaign of conquest to be fought within the bounds of India, for it assured the British their supremacy in the country.

Hardly had this most important object been accomplished in the north-west, when Dalhousie's attention was called to the south-east by the impracticable conduct of the government of Burma. A short campaign in 1852 sufficed to defeat the Burman armies; and the province of Pegu in Lower Burma, with the estuary of the Irawadi, was likewise annexed by the British, completing their hold on the entire coast-line of the Bay of Bengal. But Dalhousie did not stop at annexations by conquest. He was not only a Governor-General of Wellesley's type, who took it to be England's highest duty to maintain the peace of India, but he was also a typical Whig of the early nineteenth century, firmly convinced that British institutions were the last word in political wisdom, and quite satisfied that British rule was not only the best but the most acceptable that could be offered to every part of India. Hence, when the sovereignty of a native state lapsed through want of natural heirs to the reigning dynasty, he thought it not only expedient but morally binding upon him to disallow the adoption of an heir, and to take the state permanently into British possession. For this reason he annexed Satara, Jhansi, Nagpur, and some less important states. Finally, in 1856 he annexed Oudh upon the perfectly sufficient ground that the misgovernment of its rulers was insufferable, and in fact kept the entire state in a condition bordering upon anarchy.

There can be no question of the honesty of Dalhousie's plans and intentions for the good of India; but he had not sufficiently pondered Burke's saying, that most of the evils of this world arise from the efforts of one set of men to determine concerning the happiness of others. The failing was, and is, by no means confined to him; indeed there are signs that England herself is entering upon an era of compulsory happiness, which is without a precedent in her history. In India, however, Dalhousie's feverish haste and boundless self-confidence in the substitution of British for native ideas and prejudices begat suspicion and unrest. His eagerness to do away with misrule was construed as rapacity of power; and his zeal to abolish usages, which shocked his Western sensibility, was misinterpreted as a deep design to overthrow ancient custom and tradition. He brought, in fact, to a head all the discontent which had been bred by the mistakes, misconceptions and offences of every Englishman who had lived in India from the beginning of British rule. But it is due to him to add that he foresaw that trouble might come of some of his measures, until their good intent had been proved by experience, and that he asked, though in vain, for an increase of the British garrison to avert all peril meanwhile.

Now, however, the establishment of peace

through the length and breadth of India left the native army idle. In the course of a century the Sepoys, joined to the British, had met and vanquished every armed force in the land, and seeing their British officers steadily belittled both by the East India Company and by successive Commanders-in-Chief, the native soldiers thought that they themselves had accomplished everything and were invincible. An insult to their religious prejudices, which seems to have been fancied, though by them believed to be real, sufficed to make them break out in May 1857 into open mutiny and murder; and they were joined, as was natural, by all the bad characters and very many of the dissatisfied in India at large. The insurrection was, as has been well said, a wild fanatic outbreak; yet, viewed soberly at a distance of more than fifty years, its weakness and helplessness are the facts that show themselves in strongest relief. Though in more than one quarter British officials and officers blundered seriously, yet it can hardly be said that the issue was doubtful after the first two months, though the final restoration of peace and order was delayed, owing not a little to military mismanagement, until 1859.

Some months earlier, on the 1st of November 1858, it was announced by proclamation that the East India Company was abolished, and that the Government of India had been taken over by the Queen, with Lord Canning, the reigning Governor-General, for her first Viceroy. Incidentally the suppression of the mutiny had laid the uneasy ghosts of certain great names and offices which had long perished in substance from India. "The phantom of a Mogul Emperor and his Court vanished from Delhi; the last pretender to the honours of the Maratha Peshwa disappeared from Cawnpore." The East India Company, whose authority had been long threatened and continually weakened by successive Acts of Parliament, was finally extinguished. The British Crown assumed the unquestioned sovereignty of India; the new ruler, Queen Victoria, announced that she would always labour for the prosperity of her newly acquired dominions; and she faithfully kept her word.

VI

Since that time there has been unbroken internal peace in India. Dalhousie's policy of annexation was definitely repudiated in 1860, and all ruling chiefs received the Queen's assurance that, in default of natural heirs, successors chosen by adoption according to the law and custom of their families would be recognised and upheld by the British Government. Twice indeed the Government has intervened to depose rulers convicted of culpable misconduct or maladministration, but in each case the vacancy has been filled by another representative of the reigning family. So far indeed is the Crown from desiring to absorb native states that in 1881 it actually restored Mysore to the ancient Hindu family from which Haidar Ali had taken it in the eighteenth century, though the burden of reconquest had fallen wholly upon the British.

On the other hand, on the frontiers, and particularly in the north-west, there has been constant trouble with predatory tribes, and a long succession of expeditions. In 1863 the mountaineers about the Peshawar valley needed to be taught a stern lesson by what is known as the Umbeyla campaign. In 1864 it was necessary to send troops into Bhutan, a small state lying to east of Nipal, which, however, soon saw the advisability of submission, and has since given no trouble. In 1876 Baluchistan, whose unruly clans were constantly troubling the British border, was by successful diplomacy turned into a British protectorate; and two years later a similar result was brought about, principally by force of arms, in Afghanistan. In 1878 as a consequence of European complications, Russia sent an envoy to Kabul, who drew up a treaty of alliance with the Amir, Sher Ali, on the strength of which that potentate, in defiance of all warning, refused to receive a British mission. His territory was therefore invaded. The Amir fled; and after his death in 1879 his son Yakub Khan, in return for certain concessions, was set up by us as Amir, agreeing at the same time to admit the British envoy whom his father had excluded. Within three months that unfortunate gentleman was assassinated, and the whole country rose up in arms against Yakub Khan and his British allies. Not without difficulty and danger Kabul and Kandahar were held, but the outbreak seemed to be hopeless, for the Government of India had never contemplated the subdual of the whole country, and yet there appeared to be no prospect of an end to anarchy if the British garrisons were withdrawn. Happily at this moment came forward Abdur Rahman, nephew of a still earlier Amir, whom the Viceroy offered to accept as Yakub Khan's successor and to protect against foreign aggression. In 1880 the matter was finally settled, and the British troops were about to withdraw, when a younger son of Sher Ali, Ayub Khan, marched with an army from Herat, routed a British force which attempted to check him, and invested the British garrison at Kandahar. He was, however, presently attacked and defeated by Sir Frederick Roberts, who had marched from Kabul to the relief of Kandahar; and Abdur Rahman was left in charge of the country. Being a man of remarkable ability and indomitable will he soon established his authority on all sides, and put an end to the internal disorder which had distracted Afghanistan for generations. There was a critical moment in 1885 when a dispute about the frontier brought the Russians and Afghans into actual collision, and Russia and England to the verge of war; but hostilities were averted, and the border was demarcated by international agreement. Since then the convention of 1907 has still further improved relations between England and Russia, and, thanks to the removal of this long-standing cause of quarrel and to the firm rule of Abdur Rahman, Afghanistan for more than twenty years has been unusually quiet and prosperous. Upon the death of Abdur Rahman in 1901 his place was taken by his son, the present Amir, without a sign of any revolt or contest for the succession.

There was no further disturbance in the north-west until 1896, when the British protectorate was extended to the tribes on the western border of Kashmir. These rose and besieged the British garrison in Chitral, which was not rescued without hard fighting and a dangerous and difficult expedition. This protectorate brought the British frontier up to that of the Chinese Empire in Kashgar.

The next quarter in which there was trouble was Burma, where the King had not only maltreated British subjects, but was secretly favouring French interests in his country to the prejudice of the British. As he seemed deaf to all warnings, a British force marched to Mandalay in November 1885. Upper Burma was annexed, and after two years of hard work order was restored in the land. The tribes on the extreme east in due time became our tributaries; and on this side again we have come into contact with China.

Lastly, the expedition to Lhasa in 1903–4,

put an end, as was thought, to the encroachments of the last of our northern neighbours. But the situation was presently complicated by the expulsion of the Grand Lama from Tibet by Chinese troops, and has since been still further confounded by the return of the Grand Lama to his capital in consequence of the domestic troubles of China. Recent occurrences, indeed, have revived in great measure our anxieties not only in the north, but in the north-west; for with complete anarchy in Persia, and vast changes which may signify anarchy, or at least long intestine disturbance, in China, it is not easy to forecast where troubles may begin or end upon the Indian frontier.

So much for external affairs since 1860; let us now glance for a moment at internal progress within the same period. The first great administrative measures were the reconstitution of the Governor-General's Council for purposes of legislation in 1861; the enactment of the Penal Code and the Code of Criminal Procedure in the same year, and the passing of a succession of Acts to serve, as well as could be designed, in lieu of codification of the Civil Law. This great and essential preliminary work having been done for the foundation of a stable order, it remained to carry administrative reforms gradually into every department, and to endeavour by patience, tact, and understanding, to train the people of India to sympathy with the, to them, new idea of government by fixed law. Concurrently, education was promoted according to the ideas laid down by Lord William Bentinck, and consecrated by the approval of Lord Macaulay. Latterly Indians have been admitted more and more freely to high administrative and judicial offices; and a first step has been made towards representative institutions by the introduction of municipalities into all considerable towns, and of Legislative Councils first into the provinces and recently into the seat of supreme government.

Material enterprise has kept pace with administrative progress. Great public works have been undertaken; the country has been covered with a network of railways; and gigantic schemes of irrigation have made huge areas productive which were formerly sterile, already disarming the spectre of famine of some of its terrors, and bidding fair, with further development, to weaken it still more. With peace and order assured, with fertility enhanced, with improved means of transport from the interior to the sea, the wealth of the country has been augmented, the population has increased, and the habits of the people have been sensibly affected. Finally, the assumption by Queen Victoria of the title of Empress of India emphasised the incorporation of the great Peninsula into the British Empire, while her deep personal interest in Indian affairs brought home to all her Indian subjects that they were indeed the children of the Great White Queen.

Yet the administrative policy and actions of England, honestly and unselfishly designed for the good of India, have not borne the fruit which was hoped for. The results of higher education, in the Western sense, have not always fulfilled the hopes and aims of its advocates. It is true that this experience is by no means confined to India among British possessions, nor to British possessions in the world at large; but nevertheless the real end of education seems to be more dangerously misconceived in India than elsewhere, or at any rate the consequences of such misconception are peculiarly disturbing to Indian students. The truth perhaps is that there is much confusion of thought as to the meaning of the word education, for the term is used to cover two descriptions of training—that of the intellect and character for making a good citizen, and that of the hand, eye and brain for the making of a good craftsman. The latter is a means to an end, the former is an end in itself; but modern enthusiasts for so-called education have confounded these two things. They have breezily assumed that if a man be taught in theory to conduct himself fittingly as a social unit, all other things shall be added unto him; that, if he be trained in theory to exercise the suffrage, he will thereby be qualified to earn an honest living. In brief, they have forgotten that a full belly, and not a full brain is the vital condition of individual human life.

In former days in England the distinction between the two kinds of education was carefully observed ; and indeed it may be said that as a rule both kinds were rarely given to one man. The English gentleman, having higher civic duties imposed upon him than, as a rule, had the craftsman, trained himself to fulfil them by study of the laws of his country. The craftsman learned his craft through apprenticeship to a guild, and, having mastered it, could claim that he too had done his part as a good citizen ; even though private bounty had established many schools where the poorer children might learn at any rate to read, write and cipher. But the children of both rich and poor were brought up on perhaps the noblest brief code of citizenship ever drawn up by human hand—the exposition of one's duty towards one's neighbour in the Church Catechism. Hereby they were taught that the two great civic virtues are self-respect and self-sacrifice ; and this is a lesson which cannot be improved upon. Since then times have changed greatly. The right of voting at parliamentary elections has been given practically to every adult male ; and the obligation to learn how to read, write and cipher has been forced without cost to parents upon every child. Knowledge of the law has, for quite sufficient reasons, perished from among the gentry ; and knowledge of their duty towards their neighbour is perishing from among all classes. It seems to have been hoped that what is called a literary education would make good and more than make good all that has hereby been lost, for training the young to self-respect and self-sacrifice.

Now it must be observed that self-sacrifice has always been exacted in the form of taxation by every state, as well as in other forms, such as service on juries, in the militia, and so forth. With the more elaborate organisation of society, however, the tendency in England has been to make fewer and fewer claims upon the citizen; to encourage him, in fact, to think much of his rights and little of his duties. Other nations exact from all adult males a period of military training; England not only makes no such demand, but has swept away the old militia through which it was—perhaps still is—the law that every man must pass. British state education in the matter of self-sacrifice must therefore be set down as imperfect: let us now examine it in the matter of self-respect. The first step to self-respect is undoubtedly self-dependence; and it is probable that the old system which made the power to earn a livelihood the first point in the education of the mass of the people, was at least as good as the new. On the other hand, since the franchise has now been extended to all men, it is arguable that they should be trained to exercise that privilege aright; and that therefore the key to all knowledge should be placed impartially in the hands of all. Hence more and more time is given to delivering the rudiments of a literary education to children; and a still higher literary education is taken to be the ideal for those whom fortune has not compelled to work with their hands.

Yet literary education, the advantage of which I am not concerned to deny, is after all a luxury and hardly a necessity. At its highest it aims at imparting "the knowledge of the best that has been thought and said in the world," or what is often called culture; and, if such culture were more widely diffused, it would undoubtedly be the better for all of us. But much time, much labour and peculiar gifts are needed for its acquisition, and still more peculiar gifts for its rightful employment. It may perhaps be called the highest of all luxuries, too much despised by the rich, who can best afford to gain it; never perhaps so truly prized as by the honourable poor, who sometimes starve themselves to win it; but in any case a luxury of luxuries, enjoyable only by the few. Shepherds on different sides of the world are perhaps the most remarkable of its votaries. In Scotland there is the born shepherd, unmatched in his own business of tending sheep, but happy in the industry and devotion which has made him learn Shakespere by heart, and master thoroughly the history of ancient Greece and Rome. In Australia there is the young graduate of Oxford or Cambridge, an intelligent student and no mean scholar who, finding no work to do, has become a shepherd—and probably an indifferent shepherd—in Australia upon "five bob a day and his tucker," and consoles himself for a dreary outlook in life with his Homer and his Aeschylus.

These are men who use their literary education aright as an end in itself; but they are the exception. It is hard to see how they should be otherwise. In the first place, the State gives facilities for technical education to follow upon the earlier literary education; and technical education is simply a means to a commercial end. In the second place, parents, schoolmasters and tutors never cease to hold up to students the commercial as well as the intellectual value of a good degree at the University; while the State itself has made competitive examinations in literary subjects the means of ingress to the Civil Service. The truth is, that a great many students, unless they had a vague idea that culture would ultimately in some way provide them with a livelihood, would not pursue it at all; they would abandon it for more practical work, perhaps, though not certainly, to return to it later with joy. But few teachers have the heart to damp the ardour of an eager lad by telling him that his desperate struggles with two dead languages must be their own reward, and cannot stand between him and starvation. Hence when the time comes for the youth's entry in earnest upon the battlefield of life there is bitter disillusion and disappointment. There is not room for more than a very few in the ranks, already overcrowded, of the public service or of the learned professions ; and he must seek his bread elsewhere. The English-speaking world is wide ; he crosses the ocean to seek his fortune ; and after many humiliations he settles down to be a shepherd or a boundary-rider, happy or embittered according to his temperament, but sometimes broken-hearted, and always a little astonished.

In India the case of the student is still worse. It is difficult enough even for an European to assimilate with discrimination the best that has been thought and said in his world ; for in the first place there is considerable difference of opinion as to what is the best, and in the second, the best, unless rightly understood, may easily become the worst. The true value of education is to teach people to realise their own ignorance ; but no common knowledge is necessary to master this lesson, and no ordinary courage in the young to accept it as worth learning. Youth always craves for certainty, and finds it easiest to treat the knowledge, which flatters its own crude prejudices, as the best. In India the danger of haste and misunderstanding is multiplied an hundredfold. There public instruction is a new thing, and in its higher branches is based on foreign thought embodied in a foreign literature, while the intellects to which it is offered are singularly quick, subtle and voracious. What is its object? To train young men to good citizenship? But citizenship in the East is a very different thing to citizenship in the West. The most eloquent passages in English history and oratory are those devoted to conflict with Royal authority, the dethronement of Kings, and the conquest of what is called civil and religious liberty. The most famous of English legal enactments are those which strike at the power of the Crown and curb the domination of the priesthood. Pontiffs and autocrats have undoubtedly been responsible for much of the evil that has plagued the world, but they have also been responsible for much,—perhaps most—of the good that has improved it; and it may be questioned whether the Anglo-Saxon is not over prone to exalt resistance to authority as something in itself meritorious. In any case the classical incidents of English history do not furnish sound models for good citizenship in India. How should an intelligent Indian see any profit in such literary training if it is not to yield him a livelihood? But outside the public service and the legal and medical professions there is no demand for Indians of European education; and the number of candidates far exceeds the places that can possibly be found for them. The Indian cannot, like the Englishman, smother his disappointment and bury himself in the Colonies. The natural result is that the unsuccessful are bitterly discontented, that they cry out for the vote which they have been educated in theory to employ, and that they agitate for Society to be altered in order to fit their needs, because they find that Society in its present state offers no outlet for their accomplishments.

Again, the bare enforcement of the *pax Britannica*, though of infinite relief and benefit to the peasant, that is to say, to perhaps three hundred out of the three hundred and twenty millions, is galling to more ambitious spirits. The old medium of competition in India was the sword, and the country was the Paradise of adventurers. A soldier of genius at the head of a handful of villagers might carve out a kingdom and found a dynasty, enlisting the unhappy peasants, whose homesteads he had ruined, as his mercenaries. Then in due time the Court gathered about itself artists and craftsmen to build temples and palaces, to compose poems and histories, and to preserve those compositions in a beautiful script embellished with even more beautiful illuminations. The prosaic work of peace is not yet found to be equally inspiring; the railway and the canal, even though the canal may mean the difference between life and death to tens of thousands, awake no lyrics. All is quiet, but all is uninteresting. As a French critic said, the British Government is just, but it is not lovable.

To many of us at home this fact will seem strange and even mortifying. The British civilian's ideal of duty towards India is very high, and he labours honestly and conscientiously to fulfil it. The British military officer, being thrown daily and hourly with his Indian officers and men, is even more closely in touch with Indian thought and feeling than the civilian, and frequently makes the more successful administrator of the two. We know the names of men in both services whose deep interest in the Indians and sympathy with them has found expression in what may be termed the classic literature of British India, in the writings of Orme and Grant Duff, Henry Maine and Alfred Lyall among civilians, and of Mark Wilks and Meadows Taylor among soldiers. One soldier, John Nicholson, as is well known, is still worshipped by some Indians as a god. Moreover, we may confidently believe that there are men of this stamp always to be found among the British servants of the Indian Government. And yet that Government as a whole is to the inhabitants something distant and aloof; respected, indeed, as is the austere father of a family by his children, but not loved. It is often accused of trampling ruthlessly upon native custom; but one, who knew its excellences and its failings well, long ago vindicated it from this slander. "The interference of the British Government," he wrote, "has rarely taken the form of high-handed repression or contemptuous discouragement." On the contrary, he urged that since 1857 British administrators had been too nervous about altering native custom, alleging that the Indians are not so closely wedded to their usages as to be unwilling to surrender them for any tangible advantage. And this complaint is echoed by educated Indians at the present day, who appeal to the Government to come down from its high place and give the people a lead in certain social reforms; for if, say these writers, Government will not take the matter in hand, no one else will or can. There are, of course, two sides to such a question as this; and a man who is not intimately acquainted with India is wise to hesitate before he takes either the one or the other. Nevertheless, the defect of our administration seems to be that its functions are identified in the native mind chiefly with those of the constable and the engineer. The Government is just, but it is insufficiently human. Its benevolent element exists indeed, but has its dwelling-place in the heart of a White Queen or a White King many thousands of miles away across the sea.

VII

In 1906 His present Majesty, then Prince of Wales, visited India, together with his Princess, and was profoundly touched by the cordial welcome which he received in every quarter. On his return he was publicly entertained by the Lord Mayor of London at the Guildhall, and took occasion to appeal for a "little more sympathy" in the relations of the Indian Government with the Indian people. The native press caught up the phrase with joy and gratitude, and repeats it constantly to this day. But sympathy is a personal and not an official matter, a quality of the heart and not of the head, and therefore an attribute of a ruler and not of a Government. Hence the words of the Prince of Wales seemed after analysis to be rather a counsel of perfection. Within four years, however, the Prince, through the lamented death of his father, King Edward the Seventh, was suddenly called to the throne and to the headship of the British Empire. He then bethought himself of the words that he had spoken, and conceived at once an earnest desire to revisit India as King-Emperor. The idea, wholly his own, commended itself to his Ministers, and in his first speech to Parliament on the 6th of February 1911 His Majesty announced that he purposed to journey to India during the ensuing winter. The declaration caused the greatest surprise in England, and there was much difference of opinion as to the wisdom of this unprecedented step. Upon the whole, perhaps, the croakers were in the majority, partly no doubt because such a novelty as the King's visit to India had never occurred to more than ten in half a million of them; partly because prognostication of evil is generally rated a higher form of sagacity than anticipation of good. This was no more than was to be expected from human nature; but underlying these predictions of failure was a very sincere, though generally silent, apprehension for the King's safety. His Majesty, however, had no misgivings; and many gentlemen with great experience of India declined even to listen to gloomy forebodings of any kind.

Their Majesties were crowned in Westminster Abbey on the 22nd of June 1911, the anniversary of Queen Victoria's Diamond Jubilee; and long before that date the details of the ceremonies at Delhi were under incessant discussion, while the plan of the amphitheatre for the Durbar had been marked out on its full scale with flags in Windsor Home Park. After the Coronation followed the Royal progresses to Wales, Ireland and Scotland, and these had not long been over before the preparations for the voyage to India required attention. Their Majesties were able to enjoy a few weeks of well-earned rest at Balmoral; but the state of public affairs in the autumn, owing to the tension between France and Germany, the Railway Strike, and the war between Italy and Turkey, gave rise to constant rumours that the visit must be deferred. Nevertheless the date of departure was but very little later than that which had been first appointed.

At ten o'clock on the morning of the 11th of November, 1911, Their Majesties left Buckingham Palace with the Prince of Wales and Princess Mary, and drove by a circuitous route amid great crowds of people to Victoria Station. Nov. 11. There Queen Alexandra, Queen Maud, Princess Victoria and Prince Arthur of Connaught were waiting to accompany the King to Portsmouth; and many other members of the Royal Family, besides several of the Ministers, and of their Majesties' friends were assembled to bid them farewell. At 10.30 the Royal train left Victoria, and punctually at 12.30 ran alongside the jetty at Portsmouth. There the King, after inspecting the Guard of Honour, came aboard the *Medina*, together with the Queen, Queen Alexandra, the Queen of Norway, the Prince of Wales, Princess Mary, Princess Victoria, and Prince Arthur of Connaught. The captains of the escorting ships were then presented to the King by Sir Colin Keppel, after which they returned immediately to their commands. His Majesty's guests at luncheon, including the suite that was accompanying him to India, numbered in all fifty-three.

At a little after half-past two these guests took leave of Their Majesties and returned to the shore, Queen Mary supporting Queen Alexandra to the gangway. Three tugs came alongside to haul the *Medina* off from the jetty, and the great ship slowly got under way. By this time the weather had grown more threatening, the wind was blowing fairly hard from the south-west with every symptom of freshening, and the rain had begun to fall in angry stinging drops. Still, all adverse circumstances notwithstanding, the scene was a remarkable one. The bunting,

Nov. 11. with which every ship in the harbour was dressed, could hardly find time to be gay in its desperate striving against wind and rain; but the salute from the guns of the *Victory* could not but, from old association, be stately and solemn. Ashore, the strand on the side of Portsmouth was thronged by crowds of people, with and without umbrellas, all watching to see the last of the King, who was conspicuous upon the upper bridge. I read afterwards in the newspapers that they cheered loudly; but not a sound of it was to be heard on board. The last persons distinguishable on land were two military officers in full uniform who, with cloaks fluttering madly to leeward, brought their heels together, not without difficulty, and came to the salute.

The Admiralty yacht, *Irene*, with the First Lord on board, led the *Medina* to Spithead, where her escorting squadron of four cruisers was awaiting her, namely the *Cochrane*, *Defence*, *Argyll* and *Natal*, which took their places in the order named astern of her, in single line ahead. Presently the yacht drew away, having signalled a respectful message of farewell to Their Majesties; and an hour or so later eleven great ships appeared on the starboard bow, all, to the landsman's eye, in utter confusion. But presently the *Medina* altered course nearly a quarter of a circle, when as if by magic the seeming disorder disappeared, and the Home Fleet was discovered steaming in two parallel lines ahead; the starboard division consisting of the *Neptune* (flagship of Admiral Sir Francis Bridgeman), *Vanguard*, *Superb*, *St. Vincent* and *Collingwood*; the port division of the *Indomitable*, *Indefatigable*, *Invincible*, *Temeraire* and *Dreadnought*, with the *Gloucester* cruiser (to use a military phrase) on the flank. Into the gap between the two divisions entered the *Medina* and her escort, and the fifteen great ships, some of the most powerful war-vessels afloat, steamed away into the teeth of the increasing gale in three parallel lines, with the *Medina* leading, one and all in such perfect order that the whole seemed to be driven by a single engine. Darkness fell rapidly, the more rapidly as the weather grew steadily worse; and the ships of the Home Fleet could hardly be distinguished except by the signal-lights that flickered incessantly at their foremast-heads, showing that the perfection of orderly movement was no mechanical matter, but the fruit of practised skill and unintermittent vigilance. There are few things more striking to a landsman than the silent garrulity of a fleet at sea. To him, a mere passenger, everything seems to go on with monotonous smoothness; and only if admitted to a sight of the signal-logbook does he realise how incessant is the interchange of messages between ship and ship. Nov. 11.

Soon after night fell Sir Francis Bridgeman, having permission from the King to take his ships back to their anchorage, signalled to Their

Nov. 11. Majesties the Home Fleet's farewell; and at this point, when the *Medina* and her escort were for the first time left alone, it becomes time to say something of this vessel, and of those that sailed in her.

The *Medina* herself was in November 1911 the latest addition to the fleet of the Peninsular and Oriental Company, built of steel, with reciprocating engines and twin screws; and her burden, measured by the standard of the mercantile marine, is thirteen thousand tons.[1] Hired by the Admiralty to convey the King and Queen to India, she was commissioned, together with the four escorting cruisers, for particular service, and, when Their Majesties were not on board, carried the flag of Rear-Admiral Sir Colin Keppel, who commanded the whole squadron. Sir Colin's flag-captain was Captain Chatfield; and the ship's full complement was thirty-two officers and three hundred and sixty petty officers and men of the Royal Navy, over and above four officers and two hundred and six non-commissioned officers and men of the Royal Marines, including the band of the Royal Marine Artillery. The total number of souls of all classes and denominations on board the ship was seven hundred and thirty-three.

Built to accommodate about six hundred and fifty passengers of all classes, it may be guessed that the *Medina* afforded ample space for the King and Queen and their suite of twenty-two

[1] Eighteen thousand, Admiralty measurement.

MISS BARING. DUCHESS OF DEVONSHIRE. COUNTESS OF SHAFTESBURY.

THE QUEEN AND HER LADIES.

To face page 85.

persons. She possesses a great many decks, Nov. 11.
called by sundry arbitrary names, of which it must suffice to say that the uppermost was occupied by the officers of the ship, the next by the junior members, and the third by the senior members of the suite; Their Majesties' cabins being forward on the same deck with the senior members, but separated from most of them by the entire length of an immense saloon. This proved to be a bad arrangement. The cabins of Their Majesties and of the ladies and gentlemen who were near them were so far forward as to be very trying in a seaway, though in other respects they were luxurious. No pains, however, had been spared to ensure the comfort of all; and, to speak only for myself, I can say that I have in other voyages in distant seas shared with seven other persons a smaller space than was in the *Medina* assigned to me alone. Being old enough to remember that thirty years ago subaltern officers were forced to be content with a hammock in the lower troop-deck of the old Indian troop-ships, and having seen "the pandemonium" (as it was called) with the troops actually in it, I am glad to think that the enormous increase in the size of ships has brought augmented comfort to many thousands.

The suite consisted of the Duchess of Devonshire, Mistress of the Robes; Lady Shaftesbury, Lady of the Bedchamber; Miss Venetia Baring, Maid of Honour; and Lord Shaftesbury, Lord Chamberlain, in attendance upon the Queen.

Nov. 11. In attendance upon the King were H.S.H. the Duke of Teck, personal Aide-de-Camp; Lord Crewe, Secretary of State for India; Lord Durham, Lord High Steward; Lord Annaly, Lord-in-Waiting; Lord Stamfordham, Private Secretary; Lieutenant-general Sir Horace Smith-Dorrien, Aide-de-Camp General; Sir Derek Keppel, Master of the Household; Captain Godfrey Faussett and Commander Sir Charles Cust, Majors Lord Charles Fitzmaurice and Wigram, Equerries; Major-general Sir Stuart Beatson, Extra Equerry; Lieutenant-colonel Sir Havelock Charles, late of the Indian Medical Service, Serjeant Surgeon; Sir Edward Henry, Chief of the Metropolitan Police, and Extra Equerry; Sir James Dunlop Smith, Political Officer; Mr. Frank Lucas of the India Office, private secretary to Lord Crewe; Mr. Jacomb Hood, the official artist; and the present writer. Of the above-named gentlemen all but three had visited India before, as travellers or on duty; and five had spent a good part of their lives there. No fewer than thirteen had begun life in the Army or Navy, or are still serving in one or the other, of whom eight had seen active service in the field; and strangely enough there were among them representatives of the Household Cavalry, Cavalry of the Line, Indian Cavalry, Artillery, Foot Guards, and Infantry of the Line. Taking the whole body together there were few portions of the British Empire, to say nothing of foreign countries, which were not known to one or other of them at first hand, and few campaigns of the past thirty years in which one or other of them had not taken a share. There were only two who had travelled less than thirty thousand miles, and only three who had travelled less than fifty thousand miles by sea; while one, not a naval officer, had traversed over two hundred thousand miles. Nov. 12.

The wind continued to freshen; and after rounding Ushant, early in the morning of the 12th, the *Medina* encountered a full gale from the south-west. In order to reach Gibraltar at the appointed time the Admiral increased speed to seventeen knots; and thereupon matters became uncomfortable. The huge bulk of the *Medina* seemed to promise that she would be comparatively still in any sea; but driven against the long rollers of the Atlantic she was sufficiently lively, and pitched heavily. At every plunge she took in green seas over her bows, while the flying spray drenched her from stem to stern. Considering that most of the people in her were old travellers or sea-faring men, the amount of sea-sickness was astonishing. Officers, men and passengers, all suffered alike, the men perhaps most severely of all. Doubtless this was due in part to the fact that their quarters were very far forward, where the motion of the ship was felt at its worst; but the truth is that the British sailor of these days so rarely leaves home-waters that he has little experience of long heavy seas. Thirty years

Nov. 12. ago a naval officer twenty-one years of age had probably served in at least three different foreign stations; now it is a common thing to find officers of still longer standing who have never travelled so far even as Gibraltar. Be that as it may, the number of seamen prostrate was extraordinary; and the attendance of the passengers at meals was very scanty. The cruisers astern thought that the *Medina* was making bad weather of it, and we certainly thought the same of them. Low in freeboard and weighed down forward by huge guns, the cruisers took the water over their bows in tons; and at every plunge they were hidden to their topmast-heads by clouds of spray—a very grand sight. Nevertheless they suffered little harm. In the morning the *Argyll's* torpedo-netting broke loose, and she dropped out of the line to secure it, the *Natal* standing by her to give assistance. All day the gale continued, and in the course of the night a heavy sea struck the *Medina* amidships, broke the window of a cabin on the second deck, tore down all the fittings of the electric light, and flooded the cabin itself. Had any one been sleeping there he would have been unpleasantly awakened, but, as it happened, there was no one, the place having been set apart as a writing-room for myself. I am bound to say that the first aspect of the cabin after the mishap filled me with dismay; but fortunately little of my stuff had been unpacked, the trunks were waterproof, and the damage done was trifling.

By daylight of the 13th the gale had greatly moderated, the sea had gone down, it was brighter and warmer, the passengers were reappearing one after another, and altogether it was pleasant cruising. Another twenty-four hours brought still greater improvement; and at a little past eight in the morning of the 14th we were off Cape St. Vincent, steaming over the waters where Sir John Jervis fought his memorable action of the 14th of February 1797. Even now, when Captain Mahan's books have been in our hands for nearly twenty years, we have hardly done full justice to the great commander, who in the sixth year of a war of almost uninterrupted failure boldly attacked twenty-one ships with twelve, because "England had great need of a victory at that moment." Meanwhile, however, the wind continued always dead in our teeth, checking our way, and making it impossible to reach Gibraltar at half-past four, which was the appointed time. It was therefore necessary to cancel all previous arrangements; and in the forenoon the Admiral sent the four cruisers forward at a speed of nineteen knots, so that they might have the more time to coal, and thus save delay in the departure on the morrow. They left us accordingly; and after one of the most glorious sunsets that I ever beheld we steamed into Gibraltar, guided by the search-lights of the Atlantic fleet, which was anchored in two lines outside the mole. Nov. 13.

Nov. 15. The town was a blaze of illumination, which forbade all sight of the Rock itself; and hardly was the *Medina's* anchor down at a little before nine o'clock than a flotilla of steam-launches swarmed out all round her, playing their little search-lights in all directions, and sparkling like fireflies. The fleet knows how to keep watch over the Sailor King.

Dawn of the 15th revealed the Rock in all its majesty, with the curious zigzag walls which mark the remains of the old fortifications, and the modern guns stark against the sky-line. Over against us lay the King's Bastion, its glory departed, if indeed the glory can ever depart from such a relic. For here it was that stout old Eliott strode up and down in the thick of the French and Spanish shot during the long night of the 13th and 14th of September 1782, until day dawned at last and showed the enemy discomfited. Within it, too, there is the grave of General Robert Boyd, the engineer who designed the bastion; who was Eliott's second in command during the famous siege; who urged upon him the use of red-hot shot against the French floating batteries; and who finally begged that he might be buried on the spot which he had defended so well. In the King's Bastion, accordingly, he lies, too much forgotten by the thousands of Englishmen who week after week pass and repass Gibraltar, without a thought for those who kept the flag flying on the summit through some of the darkest years of recent English history. Nov. 15.

At eight o'clock the ten ships of the Atlantic fleet fired a salute; and two hours later the chief officers of the garrison and the fleet came on board to pay their duty to the King,—the Governor, Sir Archibald Hunter and his staff; Vice-Admiral Sir John Jellicoe; Rear-Admirals Cradock and Burney; Captains Hopwood, Sinclair, Ward, Prendergast, Sheppard, Chapman, Kemp, Hodges, Grant and Heaton Ellis, all of the Atlantic fleet; and Rear-Admiral Pelham, Admiral Superintendent of the Dockyard. The Spanish Governors of Cadiz and Algeçiras, the captain of His Spanish Majesty's ship, *Principe Regente*, the captain of the Portuguese warship, *Adamaster*, and the foreign consuls were also received by His Majesty.

The escorting cruisers, having completed their coaling, steamed out shortly afterwards; and at a little past eleven the *Medina* followed them, every ship of the Atlantic fleet saluting, with her seamen lining the decks and her marines on the superstructures. The King, always in his uniform as Admiral of the Fleet, was on the bridge of the *Medina*, and as she steamed past the fleet the men gave him three cheers, ship after ship, the marines holding their white helmets high aloft in their left hands. It was a fine sight, for disciplined men are always a fine sight; and when they cheer from their hearts it is an inspiriting sound. Within an

Nov. 15-20. hour the *Medina* had overhauled the cruisers and taken her place at the head of the line; and thus ended the King's outward visit to Gibraltar, so far abridged, owing to the inevitable delay caused by foul winds, as to be practically deferred until the return journey.

Beautiful weather followed Their Majesties on their passage through the Mediterranean; and the whole party, being recovered from sea-sickness, settled down to the regular routine of life at sea—breakfast at 8.30, luncheon at 1.0, dinner at 7.30, and the band at all hours. The prayers, which are read daily (except on Saturdays) in the King's ships, were regularly attended by Their Majesties; and on Sunday mornings (excepting during the gale in the Bay of Biscay) Divine Service was held on deck by the chaplain. Early in the voyage the King expressed his desire, though he did not make it his command, that such members of the suite and their servants as required it, should be revaccinated. To so wise a measure there were no conscientious objectors; and for a day or two Sir Havelock Charles and the naval surgeons were besieged by a crowd of patients.[1] On the night of the 19th the Admiral reduced speed to thirteen knots, so as to avoid too early an arrival at Port Said. About four in the afternoon of the 20th, the two rearmost of the cruisers came up on the *Medina's* port quarter, and in

[1] It may be mentioned that at least one visitor at the Durbar—an American gentleman—caught small-pox and died at Delhi on the very day when the camp was broken up.

this new formation the squadron steamed up to the anchorage. Nov. 20.

It was now ascertained that one of the colliers appointed to bring coal to the squadron had gone ashore some eighty miles from Port Said, and that in consequence fresh arrangements for coaling must be made. It was therefore decided that three of the cruisers should be sent forward to Aden to coal there, and that the *Argyll*, after coaling at Port Said, should form the *Medina's* sole escort to Aden. The sun went down in gorgeous colours behind the low land and palm trees before us; and at about six in the evening the *Medina* picked up her moorings opposite to the Custom House and about a hundred yards from it. The entire town was illuminated, making a very pretty effect, which was heightened by the reflection of the lamps in the water. Shortly afterwards Lord Kitchener came on board with his staff, followed by the Sirdar and by General Maxwell; all of whom having been received by the King went ashore, returning later to dine with Their Majesties.

In the midst of all the hubbub by land and water the *Argyll* came up into the narrow passage, all crowded with shipping, where the *Medina* lay, her vast bulk creeping on silently and very slowly like a huge grey ghost. It seemed almost incredible that so powerful an engine of destruction should be so noiseless, and her appearance suggested astonishing possibilities of surprise against an unwary enemy, if there should arise

Nov. 21. such another master of that difficult art as the famous Dundonald.

All night the process of coaling the *Medina* went forward, with extraordinarily little sound and disturbance considering the circumstances; and dawn revealed great activity in the camp of a British battalion which lay a few hundred yards distant from the ship. That activity was presently explained by the appearance of a guard of honour of the Scots Guards, and of a second guard of the Seventh Egyptian battalion, before the Custom House. The Egyptians were fine men, well set-up; and in their uniform of dark grey-blue, red tarboosh and white Zouave gaiters, they looked uncommonly smart. At half-past ten His Highness the Khedive, wearing Egyptian uniform and the star and ribbon of the Bath, came on board, attended by his brother, Prince Mehemet Ali, his Prime Minister, and the two British Ministers of Finance and the Interior. H.I.H. Prince Zia-ed-Din, son of the Sultan of Turkey, attended by the Turkish Grand Master of the Ceremonies, arrived at the same time. Lord Kitchener, the Sirdar, and General Maxwell had already preceded them; and the Governor of Suez, Kiamil Pasha, and the principal officials of the Suez Canal Company also came on board. The King, who wore the uniform of an Admiral of the Fleet, and the ribbon and star of the Medjidieh Order, received their Highnesses in the drawing-room above the dining saloon, where Kiamil Pasha read aloud a letter of welcome to His Majesty from the Sultan in Turkish, of which the Master of the Ceremonies read a translation in French. The King then replied in English. Shortly afterwards the King returned the Khedive's visit on board His Highness's yacht, which was lying close by, and the King and Khedive then inspected the two guards of honour. At one o'clock His Highness, Kiamil Pasha and the whole of the visitors of the morning returned to the *Medina* for luncheon, and at a little before three His Highness took leave. No one could fail to remark the very cordial bearing of the Khedive towards Lord Kitchener, bearing witness to the good relations which evidently reigned between the head of the Egyptian State and the British Consul-General. Nov. 21.

Late in the afternoon the Queen went ashore privately, and most of the suite also went ashore upon their own account. To the present writer, who had not visited Egypt since 1878, the change in the appearance of the natives was startling. Their bearing was independent and self-respectful, and their physical condition greatly improved; while the number of the blind, of the one-eyed, and of those marked with small-pox was reduced beyond belief. It was difficult to credit that these were the same people which one had seen sometimes working in chains in the fields, sometimes trussed like fowls and carried away to Cairo as refractory conscripts, nearly always abject and cowering. One must not draw hasty conclusions from superficial

Nov. 22. observation, but, even after all that one has heard and read of the benefits that Egypt has derived from British direction of her Government, I confess that I was amazed at the transformation which had been accomplished within thirty years. One change, however, though doubtless welcome to a section of Englishmen, seemed to me deplorable, namely the substitution of vulgar Manchester goods for the older cotton garments, woven and dyed at home, which formerly clothed the Egyptian peasant.

The Royal dinner-party in the evening included Lord Kitchener, the Sirdar, Admiral Gamble, and Captains Culme Seymour, Tothill, Moubray, and Tyrrwhitt of His Majesty's ships *Argyll*, *Lancaster*, *Suffolk* and *Bacchante*, of which ships the three last were lying at Port Said when the *Medina* came in. After dinner there was a display of fireworks given by the Suez Canal Company; and as water was not lacking to reflect the blaze, which is of the essence of a successful show of fireworks, the effect was extremely beautiful.

The *Medina* weighed anchor at 6 A.M. on the 22nd November, and shortly afterwards entered the Suez Canal. The Khedive had taken every precaution for the safety and honour of his Royal guest during the passage. At every kilometre-post stood a sentry; and patrols of the Egyptian camel-corps or of Bedaween followed the ship throughout on both banks, relieving each other from time to time. Sometimes a group of fifteen or twenty Bedaween would assemble together in their picturesque robes of black and white, fire their muskets in salute, and trot alongside for a few hundred yards. Hardly less picturesque were the men of the Egyptian camel-corps in khaki coat, tarboosh and putties, mauve-grey breeches, brown bandoliers and brown goat-skin saddles; a beautiful combination of greys and browns which admirably sets off their jet-black faces for purposes of parade, and yet makes for the extreme of invisibility on active service. Curiously enough the actual speed of one of the camels was just that of the ship; and this animal kept his station exactly off a certain point of the starboard quarter for fully six miles. But the most remarkable feat of all was that of an Austrian officer of the Egyptian gendarmerie, who followed the ship from Port Said to the lakes without a moment's halt. He was well mounted, changing horses about every ten miles, and moved generally at a trot with an occasional break into a canter, but sat always bolt upright without rising in his stirrups. He crossed Lake Timsah in a steam-launch, and on reaching the other side mounted a camel which was waiting for him, when he continued his trot until he reached the Bitter Lakes, forty-seven miles from his starting-point, and could go no farther. I watched him constantly, and I could not see that he displayed the slightest symptom of fatigue, for he sat erect and soldierlike from beginning to end. Nov. 22.

Nov. 23–27. At Ismailia, where Sir Garnet Wolseley landed in 1882, the whole population was on the banks; and when the *Medina* reached Suez at seven in the evening the entire front of the canal was lined with people, bands were playing, and the town was ablaze with rockets and illuminations. One party of Englishmen, apparently at the Club, gave three tremendous cheers; and when Their Majesties showed themselves on deck, a stentorian voice cried out "One cheer more for their coming up," which evoked a final prodigious roar. We did not stop at Suez, however, but only slowed down to take on board some telegrams, and proceeded onwards down the Red Sea.

VIII

And now for the first time the three flags borne by a royal yacht—Admiralty flag at the fore, Royal standard at the main, and the Union Jack of an Admiral of the Fleet at the mizzen—were seen east of the Mediterranean; and it seemed a pity that there was but one escorting cruiser to do honour to the occasion. In the Red Sea we were lucky in encountering calm weather and no oppressive heat. Indeed at sunset on the 25th we ran into heavy squalls of rain, lit up by an incessant flicker of blue sheet-lightning, which not only was better than any display of fireworks, but also considerably reduced the temperature. At one in the morning of the 27th we passed Perim, and at a little after nine the *Argyll* went ahead to join the remaining cruisers at Aden. An hour and a half later the *Medina* dropped her anchor in Aden harbour, amid a thunder of salutes from the four cruisers of the escort and from the *Royal Arthur*, which, together with three destroyers, was awaiting Their Majesties' arrival. Each of the large ships fired one hundred and one guns, for we were now within the territory of the Indian Empire, where salutes of twenty-one guns are given to native princes, and are no longer sufficient for the King-Emperor and the Queen-Empress. Nov. 27.

Aden is generally known in England as the abomination of desolation, and it is not difficult to believe that it is a dreary quarter for a garrison. Nevertheless, for all their aridity, its cinder-coloured peaks and mountains are singularly wild and grand; while the ancient lines of fortifications, wall within wall, invest it with some halo of romance. Probably, however, Aden has never in the whole of its history presented such an aspect as it did on the 27th of November 1911. The five men-of-war in the harbour were all dressed with bunting; the entire foreshore was hung with festoons of gay colours; the houses were brightly decorated, and the native population in a hundred gaudy hues were clustered like bees upon the lower slopes. Towering above them the cold grey-

Nov. 27. purple mountains looked down with a certain kindly condescension upon the swarming humanity below. The weather was for Aden decidedly cool; the sunshine was frequently broken by clouds; and heavy showers during the past forty-eight hours had imparted to the place generally an unwonted savour of freshness.

Soon after the *Medina's* arrival the Resident, Major-general John Bell, came on board with his staff and was received by His Majesty, who conferred on him the second class of the Victorian Order, and knighted him there and then. At half-past three Their Majesties went ashore, whither the bulk of their suite had already preceded them, the King in the white uniform of an Admiral of the Fleet with the ribbon and star of the Order of the Star of India and the star of the Bath; and the Queen in pale-blue silk. A pavilion had been erected by the landing-stage, where the Resident and Lady Bell, with the members of the staff and the leading officials, were waiting to receive them. On the left of Their Majesties, as they landed, was drawn up the Aden troop of Native Cavalry, principally Sikhs, in khaki uniform with red girdles and turbans of khaki, blue and yellow; a very smart body of men and in one respect unique, inasmuch as the front rank was composed of lancers mounted on Arab horses, and the rear-rank of riflemen mounted on camels. In front stood a guard of honour of the Lincolnshire Regiment, a fine body of men in white, with the King's colour—

evidently a very old one—still showing the former regimental number Ten. The Resident having presented the leading officials and their ladies to the King and Queen, Their Majesties drove off, followed by their suite, in five more carriages, to the bronze statue of Queen Victoria, which is the most conspicuous object on the small area of flat ground that faces the harbour. Nov. 27

On its own limited scale this short progress was probably one of the strangest ever made by a British sovereign. In the first place the van of the escort was composed of horsemen and the rear of camel-men; and in the second it is probably for once a literal truth to say that the entire population was out to see the procession. The entire population of Aden, to be sure, is not very large, though far larger than I, for one, had imagined; but it is very decidedly mixed. Within the course of half a mile it was easy to distinguish at a glance Sikhs, Pathans, Bengalis, Parsis, Somalis, Arabs, Negroes, Jews, Greeks, Levantines—what not; and, since the principal street has for the most part houses upon one side only, there was plenty of room for all the men and children by the roadside and for the maturer ladies on the house-tops. The variety of colour was not so great as, say, in Rajputana, but two or three very young ladies in gorgeous gowns of magenta silk made a bright touch here and there, contrasting strongly with the white which was worn by most of the spectators and with the copper skins of a certain number who had little

Nov. 27. clothing of any kind. The route was lined by a body of Sikh infantry, and here for the first time we heard the English words of command delivered by native officers and non-commissioned officers, curiously combining the foreign accent with the traditional vigour and intonation of the British drill-sergeant—"Sacund Sekshan, slo-p-e arms." The procession trotted briskly on, the camels keeping their distance in rear of the Royal carriage with admirable accuracy, and producing a most imposing effect; and finally, when the Victoria Memorial was reached, they formed line to the left with a precision that the Life Guards themselves might have envied. These may seem to be small things, but they make all the difference to the success or failure of a pageant.

Adjoining the Victoria Memorial a pavilion, which was really a large tent, had been erected; and with excellent judgment Indian stuffs and Indian dyes had been selected for the decoration of the roof. The native taste, while not shrinking from strong colours upon occasion, delights especially in pale and tender tints, than which none look more beautiful under the Eastern sun. The roof of the tent at Aden was in broad stripes of pale yellow and rose-madder, which gave sufficient dignity to the interior and yet was cool and restful to the eye. The carpet was of the commonplace red which the official mind—quite unnecessarily in the East at any rate—appears to regard as inseparable from any royal function, and at the far end were two carved thrones heavily gilt and upholstered in crimson velvet. To these thrones Their Majesties then walked in procession between a great throng of the more distinguished inhabitants. A Parsi gentleman, Mr. Cowasji Dinshaw, read an address of welcome, to which His Majesty read a reply, not failing among other things to commend the happy choice of the place of his reception at the foot of Queen Victoria's statue. The Resident then presented the foremost of the native gentlemen to the King, and, the ceremony being over, Their Majesties drove to the Residency, some two or three miles distant, on an eminence overlooking the sea. It is noteworthy that the latter part of the route was lined by the Fifty-second company of Garrison Artillery, which had saluted His Majesty when Prince of Wales from Colombo in 1901 and from Madras in 1906, and had on this same morning fired the first salute ever paid on East Indian Territory to the King-Emperor in person. Nov. 27.

At the Residency Their Majesties drank tea, and after conversation with the guests who had been honoured with an invitation to meet them, took their leave soon after five and returned to the *Medina*. As their launch moved off from the quay the foreshore and all the principal buildings burst suddenly into a blaze of illumination, making an extremely pretty and striking end to a very successful day. The rain, though often threatening, happily held off; but, as the

Nov. 28– Dec. 1. sun fell low, the wind became positively cold. It was something to have felt the want of a great-coat at Aden.

On the 28th the *Medina* entered the Indian Ocean, which was pleasantly cooler than the Red Sea; and, as we were now drawing near our destination, Sir Havelock Charles took occasion to give a short lecture both to the suite and to the servants, laying down a few simple rules for the preservation of health in India. Knowing India, as a medical man, by heart, he succeeded so well in impressing his lessons upon them that none but trifling cases of sickness occurred among them throughout the whole of the visit to the East. It was, however, difficult to realise that a few days more would find us at Delhi, until on the night of the 29th the *Defence* transmitted the following wireless telegram, which had just been received direct from the Mogul capital over a distance of sixteen hundred miles: "Marconi Wireless Telegraph Company, Fort, Delhi, beg to offer their most loyal greetings on His Majesty's approach to India." If all wireless telegrams received during the voyage had been of the like innocent tenour, the King would have enjoyed more repose in the course of it than he did.

For the rest, the last three days at sea, the 29th of November to the 1st of December, were in part taken up by sports among the ship's company. There was not—indeed there could hardly be—much variety from the usual pro-

THE KING. THE QUEEN.

WATCHING A SPAR-AND-PILLOW FIGHT.

To face page 104.

MAJOR PHILLIPS, R.M A.

A SPAR-AND-PILLOW FIGHT.

To face page 105.

gramme of obstacle-races, three-legged races, potato-races and so on; but there was one form of contest which possessed an irresistible fascination both for combatants and onlookers, that namely in which two men sit astride of a greased spar, which they are forbidden to touch with their hands, and strike at each other with pillows until one or other falls off the spar into a sail suspended below. The number of aspirants to fame in this particular field was extraordinary. Marines, bluejackets, officers, even to the Captain himself, members of the King's suite, their servants, the photographer and the barber, all came down to try their fortune amid breathless excitement and shouts of laughter from every soul in the ship who was not on duty. Lord Annaly after a strenuous conflict was defeated but not disgraced by Lord Shaftesbury; Captain Godfrey Faussett vanquished a bluejacket, but was overthrown by the Fleet-Surgeon, a most dangerous opponent. Soon it became apparent that Major Phillips of the Marine Artillery, a gentleman of herculean strength, and not less skilled in parrying with his left hand than in striking with his right, was superior to all rivals; and after three battles, which can only be described as Homeric, he finally swept the Fleet-Surgeon's legs from under him, and was hailed as victor among the officers. A private of his corps won the same distinction among the men.

Nov. 28–Dec. 1.

In the evening the Queen presented prizes to

Dec. 1. the winners; but the passengers secured very few of these trophies; and indeed their credit was only saved by one of the King's footmen, an old Coldstreamer and the most powerful man on the ship, who vanquished all rivals in the gentle art of cock-fighting. Nearly every prize fell to the marines; and in truth the marine is a wonderful person. The press is fond of holding up the bluejacket as a handy man; but in these days the epithet should be transferred to the marine. On the 1st of December, the last day of the voyage out, there was a concert on board. The suite could produce in Lord Shaftesbury a trained singer who naturally eclipsed all other performers; but setting him aside, the marines had matters all their own way. One of them was a sufficiently accomplished vocalist to be accompanied by the band, while several others played an astonishing number of instruments and played them in tune. The credit of the bluejackets was mainly saved by the proficiency, in a sister art, of Mr. Staples the boatswain, who danced a hornpipe quite admirably. Their Majesties were of course present; and so passed away the last evening of real freedom which they were to enjoy for some weeks.

Early in the morning of the 2nd of December the low land and palms of Bombay were seen; and at about ten o'clock the *Medina* and her escort anchored about two miles from the shore in a dead calm and rather oppressive heat. Three-quarters of an hour later the

CAPTAIN CHATFIELD. THE KING.

WATCHING THE SPORTS ON H.M.S. *MEDINA.*

To face page 106.

Viceroy[1] came on board to wait upon the King; Dec. 2. presently followed by the Governor of Bombay, Sir George Clarke. The Commander-in-Chief of the East India Squadron, whose flagship the *Highflyer* was lying in the harbour, and other officials followed; and the Viceroy with his staff remained to luncheon. At half-past three the greater number of the suite went ashore to be ready to receive Their Majesties, who shortly afterwards left the ship and steamed, amid a salute of one hundred and one guns, to the landing-place at the Apollo Bandar. The King-Emperor wore the white uniform of an Admiral of the Fleet, with the ribbon and star of the Star of India, and the Queen-Empress wore on her dress the star and the ribbon of the Garter, the latter fastened on the shoulder by a brooch of a single row of diamonds and clasped below by a diamond George. The Viceroy and the whole of the Imperial suite were in full-dress white uniform. At the pavilion the principal officials of the Bombay Government and Corporation and the foreign consuls, in all about forty gentlemen, were presented by Sir George Clarke to His Majesty; after which a procession was formed, and Their Majesties advanced a distance of about one hundred yards to a second and smaller pavilion, where two thrones upon a dais had been prepared for them.

[1] Singularly enough, among the King's suite there were no fewer than three gentlemen who had been school-fellows of Lord Hardinge at Harrow, two of whom had also been his fellow-undergraduates at Trinity College, Cambridge.

Dec. 2. Over against the pavilion an amphitheatre had been made ready for the accommodation of several hundred spectators who, it is to be feared, must have suffered not a little from the fierce and unusual heat of the day. All, however, rose and cheered enthusiastically as Their Majesties took their places; and then Sir Pherozsha Mehta, President of the Bombay Municipal Corporation, stepped forward and read an address welcoming Their Majesties to India, vindicating the right of Bombay, as part of the dowry of Queen Katharine of Bragança, to be the first to welcome them, and recalling the fact that this was not the first time that Bombay had had the honour of entertaining them. His Majesty having received the address in the silver casket which had been given to him with it, Sir Pherozsha presented to him the members of the Corporation.

Then to the great surprise, as was afterwards discovered, of the majority of the spectators, the King-Emperor delivered his reply in a loud clear voice, which could be heard by every one of them. Catching up at once the note which had been struck by the Corporation, "I can heartily respond," said His Majesty, "that I feel myself no stranger in your beautiful city"; and proceeded next to speak of his earnest desire, as soon as he found himself called to the Throne, to revisit his good subjects in India. Ignoring all accepted traditions of etiquette, the audience broke in again and again with loud applause,

THE RECEPTION AT BOMBAY.

To face page 108.

which culminated in a great outburst of cheering at the close. Their Majesties then entered the carriage prepared for them, and started forth, the suite following in six more carriages, to drive in procession round the city. Dec. 2.

The troops that took part in the procession were the Seventh Dragoon Guards and Y Battery of the Royal Horse Artillery in advance; the Governor's bodyguard of Lancers in scarlet and gold forming the immediate escort of the Imperial carriage, and King George's own regiment of the Twenty-sixth Lancers, in French grey with dark-blue turbans, the rearguard. But in India it is not, as in England, the troops that supply the bulk of the colour in the pageant. Much care had been devoted to the decoration of the streets of the European quarter with arches, masts and festoons, and the effect was decidedly better than I have ever seen in London. The Indian sun may have been partly responsible for this, but not wholly. On one or two buildings there was a bold and successful scheme of colour; but in adorning their houses the Europeans too often bound themselves to the slavery of English decoration—trophies of European flags and even worse displays of crude and tasteless colour. It is strange that the British in India cannot make better use of the native materials and dyes, which can hardly be dearer, and are certainly much more beautiful, than those of the West. Fortunately the eye was distracted by the far more lovely decoration

Dec. 2. presented by the people themselves. The crowd was immense, and the variety of shades indescribable—here a group of men in rich dark-red turbans, with perhaps one of vivid grass green flaming among them; there a group of children, wide-eyed and open-mouthed, with one or two little maids in blazing crimson silk huddled into their midst; there again a body of Parsi ladies in simple gowns of the palest pink, blue or dove-colour, draped on one side with light transparent muslin in graceful folds, which made the delicate hues more dainty still. There was no rest for the eye in the ever-changing feast of colour.

But most striking of all was the scene in the quaint irregular buildings and narrow streets of the native town. There is no appearance of wealth in the houses, the stucco being often decayed and fortunately rarely repainted; but there are quaint wooden stairways, balconies and loggias, which the wealthy owners had beautified with the best and simplest of all street-decorations by simply throwing over them rugs and carpets, or occasionally a great sheet of rich dark silk shot with gold. The houses were crammed with spectators. The housetops and the highest stories were occupied chiefly by peeping women, nearly all of whom displayed at least a scrap of costly red material; the lower windows were simply packed with tier upon tier of heads—I counted over thirty in one of no extraordinary size—and even the steep narrow scraps of verandah over the native shops were swarming with men and boys. In the East it is not considered respectful to make even a joyful noise in the presence of the great; yet the native inhabitants of Bombay upon this occasion cheered loudly and continuously, and in fact gave Their Majesties an enthusiastic reception. Dec. 2.

The entire route measured about six miles, which was traversed at a slow trot, the procession returning through the suburbs and round Malabar Point to the Apollo Bandar. Here the King inspected the guard of honour of the Norfolk Regiment, and then returned to the ship, which was reached at a little before six o'clock. The sun went down in a gorgeous blaze of orange and scarlet, against which the palms on the low spit of Malabar Point showed black as ink. For a short time the temperature fell slightly, but soon rose again, and the thermometer, even in the King's cabin, stood at eighty-five degrees. In the evening Their Majesties gave a state dinner on board the *Medina*, at which fifty-four guests, including the suite, were present; but, though the dinner was held on deck, the heat was such as to make full-dress European uniform very trying to wear. None the less the Queen, who was wearing a white dress embroidered with gold, never looked better than on that evening; and the guests soon discovered that the temperature made no difference to the welcome accorded to them by their Royal hosts.

Dec. 3. On the morning of Sunday the 3rd Their Majesties attended Divine Service as usual on board; but the day was no idle one for the King or for his Secretaries, for over six hundred telegrams of welcome had been received from different persons and societies in India since the *Medina* had dropped anchor in Bombay, and all required an answer. In the afternoon Their Majesties honoured the Governor of Bombay with their presence at luncheon at Government House, and in the evening attended Divine Service in the Cathedral. The weather was hotter than ever, and the Bishop of Bombay who preached the sermon, wisely ascended the pulpit in his rochet only, though the building was kept fairly cool by electric fans. Later on Their Majesties gave a second official dinner on board the *Medina*, under even more trying conditions than on the previous day, the heat being more intense and the air perfectly still. This was a misfortune which could not have been anticipated at the time of year. Perhaps the only one of the guests on either evening who felt himself not only in comfort but in luxury was the Captain of H.M.S. *Fox*, who, after months of service in prevention of "gun-running" in the Persian Gulf at a temperature of one hundred and ten degrees, found the eighty-five degrees of Bombay very pleasantly cool. It was a good lesson for any of us who were inclined to complain, for the work in the *Fox* signified not merely existence, in itself sufficiently trying, in the Persian Gulf, but incessant watchfulness and hard labour for all on board, with many a difficult diplomatic problem for the commander in addition. For the rest, Bombay, being illuminated on both of these nights, presented a most beautiful appearance when looked on from the sea. Dec. 4.

On the 4th of December Their Majesties left the *Medina* soon after nine o'clock, landed at the Apollo Bandar at half-past nine and drove, with their suite in attendance, to a children's fête in the grounds adjoining the Bombay Gymkhana Building. Here in an open space some twenty-six thousand children had been drawn up in a large semicircle, over against the centre of which was a dais for the King and Queen. As Their Majesties drove up at a quarter to ten, four selected groups of children, belonging to European, Urdu, Gujarati and Marathi schools, sang each two verses of the National Anthem in their own tongue. The bare fact is a lesson to those who talk glibly about the "Indian people." Twenty-six thousand children is not a very great many; yet to gather that number together as representatives of the Presidency of Bombay it was necessary to include the speakers of three different tongues (or four if we include the Europeans), each of them with its own literature and its own written character, and one of them—Marathi—with three principal dialects, and sub-dialects innumerable. However, to return to our main narrative, it was

Dec. 4. curious to note the difficulty which the Indian children evidently found in singing a western melody in the major mode. To them it was obviously a noise, compounded of strange intervals, with an over-monotonous rhythm; and the cause was soon sufficiently apparent.

Immediately after the children had fallen silent at the close of their singing, some fifty to a hundred Gujarati girls performed a Gurbi or rhythmic dance and song—one might rather call it a prayer, for the ceremony is of a religious character—for behoof of Their Majesties. They formed two concentric circles, the older girls wearing simple, loose-flowing gowns, mostly of very pale pink, blue or orange, varied occasionally by the mixture of two pale colours or by vivid magenta or still more vivid green, and relieved in nearly every case by a scarf of transparent white muslin. Many of the younger children unfortunately wore European clothes, which, being white, were comparatively harmless, but were too frequently marred by atrocious European button-boots reaching to mid-calf. The dance consisted of rhythmic waving of raised arms, rhythmic clapping of hands, and curious interlacing movements of the performers in the two circles. The language of the song was Gujarati; and the music, of course in the minor mode, was not only curious but effective. The rhythm, however, was very difficult to seize; duple, triple and quintuple time being each of them easily perceptible by the ear, but no one of them continued for long consecutively. The dance was extremely graceful and impressive, being carried out in a religious spirit without a trace of self-consciousness on the part of the performers. At its close Their Majesties drove through the heart of the semicircle, where a way had been left clear, so that all the children might see them, and the young people, both white and brown, shouted themselves hoarse with delight. Their Majesties then inspected some historic exhibits in the old Bombay exhibition hard by, and returned to the *Medina* soon after eleven o'clock. Dec. 3-5.

Owing to the number of the King's suite, an advanced party of nine gentlemen[1] was sent forward to Delhi on the evening of the 3rd. The total length of the journey was nine hundred and eighty-two miles, and, thanks to those who were charged with the care of us, we made the journey of thirty-six hours with all possible comfort. But India is the land of dust, and it is impossible to travel there by rail in the dry season without realising that fact to the full. The route lay by Baroda, which took us through a dreary and monotonous country, but incidentally through the famous Mokandara pass, the scene of the military blunder which led to the destruction of Monson's detachment in 1804. The most singular point about railway travel in India

[1] Prince George of Battenberg (midshipman on H.M.S. *Cochrane*), Lord Annaly, Lord C. Fitzmaurice, Lt.-Gen. Sir H. Smith Dorrien, Maj.-Gen. Sir Stuart Beatson, Sir J. Dunlop Smith, Mr. Jacomb Hood, Major Ashburner, Mr. Fortescue.

Dec. 5. is that one rarely, if ever, sees a town. There are not, relatively speaking, many towns in India; and stations are, for good reasons, as a rule situated two or three miles from them. Hence one seems to traverse an interminable land of jungle and villages. The changes of temperature also were trying, varying in our carriage from eighty degrees by day to forty-eight or lower by night. However, this was a matter concerning which we had been amply warned; and soon after eight o'clock on the morning of the 5th of December we arrived at the Kingsway station at Delhi, whence motors conveyed us to our camp.

Certainly the first sight of the great canvas city, covering in all twenty-five square miles, was very wonderful, and all the more so when we saw the trim grass lawns which marked the camps of the greater officials, and remembered that a year ago this was a mere brown waste. The King-Emperor's camp lay at the extreme edge, being in the form of a huge semicircle, with the arc facing towards the remaining camps, and the base formed by the road to Delhi city. Opposite the central point of this arc was a large open space with a tall flag-staff, and over against this staff lay three huge reception-tents, facing almost west, with the Viceroy's camp to the left or north, and the King-Emperor's, with the circuit-house behind it, on the right or south. A circuit-house, it must be explained, is a residence kept up, somewhat like the judges' lodges in England, for the reception of the

THE KING-EMPEROR'S CAMP, DELHI.

To face page 116.

THE VICEROY. THE KING-EMPEROR. DUKE OF TECK.

THE ARRIVAL AT SELIMGARH BASTION.

To face page 117.

Viceroy or of minor great officials when on tour. The Viceroy's staff was encamped round the curve of the semicircle to the north, and Their Majesties' round the corresponding curve to the south. Dec. 7.

At ten o'clock on the morning of the 7th Their Majesties arrived at the Selimgarh station upon a detached bastion of the great fort of Delhi, where the Viceroy, Lady Hardinge, the leading officials of India and several Indian princes were assembled to receive them. Among these last was the Maharaja of Udaipur, the Ruling Chief in Waiting and the representative of the bluest blood in India, an elderly prince dressed in a flowing gown of white satin edged with gold; Sir Pratap Singh and the Maharaja of Bikaner, the former in the white frock and sky-blue turban of the Imperial Cadet Corps, and the latter in the beautiful uniform of his own Camel Corps. As Their Majesties alighted, the guns of the fort opened a salute of one hundred and one guns, twice broken and finally concluded by a *feu de joie* from the troops in the plain without. Within the bastion, ringed about by the pink sandstone of the walls, was drawn up a guard of honour of the second battalion of the Berkshire Regiment, with the remainder of the battalion in rear; the rest of the space being filled by selected men from every corps in the Native Army and representative sections from every corps present at Delhi, with three squadrons of the Thirtieth Native Lancers, part mounted

Dec. 7. and part dismounted, in rear of all. The great space was thus worthily filled, and presented a fine mass of colour, topped by the bright points and waving pennons of the lances. After the presentation of several high officials in a pavilion which had been erected on the platform, the King inspected the guard of honour, and observing four representative veterans, one English and three Indian, just outside the right of the line, stepped aside to shake hands with each and ask them as to the campaigns where they had won their medals. The old fellows drew themselves up and saluted after the fashion of their youth, with the hand parallel to the horizon, remembering bygone times. They will not readily forget this day.

A procession was then formed with the heralds at its head, followed by the staffs of the Viceroy and the King-Emperor; and Their Majesties advanced over the crenellated bridge that spans the moat, between a line of men drawn from each of the King's own regiments; then entering the inner courtyard they turned sharp to the right, where a large tent had been set up for the formal reception of the native princes by the King. It was perhaps a pity that the Dewan-i-am, or public hall of audience of Shah Jahan, which was likewise within the fort, had not been selected for this ceremony. It is true that the original tent designed for the purpose, the Bahawalpur State "Shamiana," was so superb that it might well have been worthy of the occasion;

but this had perished by fire on the 5th, and the new tent hastily improvised to take its place, though in no degree mean, appeared small and low, strait and dark. The great open space of the courtyard, with a splendid regiment of native lancers drawn up in hollow square, and four companies of British and native infantry, seemed to dwarf it still more; but there was no help for it. The staff parted to right and left at the entrance. Their Majesties, advancing up the centre, took their seats upon the thrones erected for them; and the ceremony of presentation began. Dec. 7.

First came the Nizam of Hyderabad in plain black with yellow mitre-like head-dress, then the Gaekwar of Baroda, the Maharajas of Mysore and Kashmir, and the rest of the Ruling Chiefs in succession according to territorial arrangement; but it will be more convenient to speak in detail of this homage when we come to the repetition of it on a greater scale at the Durbar. The presentations ended, His Majesty mounted his horse, and a procession, or rather three processions, were formed, first that of the principal British officials in carriages with their escorts and bodyguards; then that of the King-Emperor; and lastly that of the Ruling Indian Chiefs. In the King's procession twenty-eight officers of the King's staff led the way; then came the Viceroy's bodyguard, gigantic lancers in scarlet and gold; then three non-commissioned officers of the First and Second Life Guards and

Dec. 7. Blues, in cuirasses and brazen helmets, the Duke of Teck, two equerries, and finally the King-Emperor, with the Viceroy and Lord Crewe immediately behind him. The Queen followed in a carriage drawn by six horses, conspicuous by the huge golden fan and crimson and gold umbrella held over her by the Indian attendants; then came the Imperial Cadet Corps; and lastly the remainder of the suite in five carriages, with a rearguard of native lancers. A salute of one hundred and one salvos announced the departure of the procession for what was described as the State entry into Delhi.

Every yard of the route was crammed with spectators; and where, as in the progress round the Jama Masjid, there was an architectural setting to the crowd, the scene was most striking. The sky overhead was cloudless, and the white marble domes of the great mosque fairly flamed above the dull pink sandstone of the walls. Below it the turbans of the people made a nodding flower-bed of every shade of blue and green and every variety of brown, tawny, yellow and orange. In more than one place members of some school or college had been grouped together, making a sheet of blue or pink or yellow; but such colours are better scattered than massed. In the main street, the once famous Chandni Chauk, the diversity of colour in the dress of the spectators was even more pleasing against the background of rather unkempt white houses; but it was painful to notice that a few occupants had decorated their balconies with some of the vilest colours produced by Manchester. The whole body of the spectators, Europeans only excepted, was silent after the Oriental fashion; but the truth must be told outright that the King-Emperor was not recognised as he passed. He alone wore the uniform of a Field-Marshal, but this does not to a native eye differ materially from that of a general or staff-officer; while the ribbon of the Star of India, which he wore over his tunic, was also to be seen over the shoulders of every great official present. Again, our military head-dresses, from the helmet to the bear-skin, entirely conceal the face when the lip-chain is down, and this is doubly true of the white helmet, necessarily wide and overshadowing, of the British Army in India. His Majesty's equerries could hear the spectators murmuring as they passed that the King was not there; and when the Queen followed, marked out conspicuously by the gorgeous fan and umbrella, the natives noticed that she was alone, and decided that His Majesty was not present. Dec. 7.

There was a certain irony in the situation; for the King had deliberately chosen to ride a horse instead of an elephant, as had been done by Lord Curzon in 1902, so that he might more easily be seen of the people. Critics were ready immediately after the event with a score of recommendations as to what should have been preferred. The King ought to have worn a special dress; he ought to have ridden an

Dec. 7. elephant; he ought to have driven with the Queen; he ought to have ridden a horse with a Royal Standard before him; he ought to have had four, eight, a dozen standards all round him. "Malignant officialism," such was the phrase, had deliberately destroyed the pageant. In consideration of all this it must be remembered that the troops formed the most essential part of the pageant; that indeed there can be no true pageant without disciplined men; that in the last resort everything in India depends upon the British soldier—a fact which the Indian civil officials nowadays appear not always to remember—and that in such a huge concourse of soldiers, British and native, lining the route and taking part in the procession, it was fitting and right that the King should appear in the uniform which distinguished him at once as their chief and as one of themselves. From an Oriental point of view probably the ideal arrangement would have been that the King-Emperor should have ridden a horse, and that the Governors and Lieutenant-Governors, instead of riding in carriages, each with his own petty escort to indicate his comparative insignificance, should have walked afoot in a body surrounding him; and it was perhaps unfortunate that the climate makes such a thing impossible. Nothing could have exalted both His Majesty and those high officers so truly in the Indian mind; and the latter would have gained rather than lost honour by such an act of voluntary self-abasement. The Indian takes no account in the Sovereign's presence of his deputies, much less of Ministers of State, Parliaments and the like appendages. His attention fastens itself for better or worse wholly upon the person of the Sovereign ; and in comparison with him all other officials are as nothing. Plainly, therefore, on any future occasion the person of the King should be notably distinguished. Should he ride—and a chief who is a man, a soldier, and a horseman is very dear to the greatest of the Indian Princes—a standard should be borne before him, and a host of native attendants with Imperial insignia should be about him. Should His Majesty drive in the same carriage with the Queen, they should be surrounded with the like pomp and circumstance. Dec. 17.

After leaving the city the procession halted at a pavilion on the summit of the historic ridge on the way to the camp, where were assembled representatives of British India, that is to say, Members of the Imperial and Provincial Legislative Councils, the Judges and other high officers. Here the Hon. Mr. Jenkins, the Vice-President of the Governor-General's Legislative Council, read a short address of welcome and loyalty to the King-Emperor, which was then handed to His Majesty on a silver tray. His Majesty read his reply as usual in a loud tone, which could be heard by all present. At about half-past twelve the Imperial camp was reached, and here was drawn up a quadruple guard of honour, one of bluejackets, one of Marine Artillery, one of the

Dec. 7. Royal Fusiliers and one of the 130th Baluchis, this last the King's own regiment, picturesquely dressed in green coats and loose cherry-coloured knickerbockers. The whole formed a magnificent body of men; and the contrast was great from the broad sturdy bluejackets on the right of the line to the lean slender Pathans, long-haired, hawk-eyed and hawk-nosed, on the left. There was little to choose between the four companies when they saluted, but the Marines showed just the slight superiority over the rest which made perfection. Presently the guards filed away, and revealed the person of Sergeant Trotter of the King's company of the Grenadier Guards, standing solitary in his bearskin at attention by the flag-staff, an unrehearsed effect which, owing to the huge stature and disciplined bearing of the Sergeant, was sufficiently impressive.

In the afternoon the King held his first reception of the Ruling Chiefs individually, giving to each one of them an audience of at least ten minutes, and welcoming them as his friends. The Queen, whose interest in historic buildings is inexhaustible, with the Viceroy, her ladies, and a few gentlemen in attendance, paid a visit to Shah Jahan's palace, built in 1638–48, within the fort of Delhi. This volume is not a guide-book and no place for a description of the famous building, which in extent, and many would contend in beauty also, far outdoes any palace in Europe. But Her Majesty, and others who had visited the place before, were amazed at the improvements which, under the impulse of Lord Curzon, had been effected through the sweeping away of modern excrescences, the restoration of gardens, fountains, watercourses and grass-plats,—in a word, the general rehabilitation of order, amenity and good taste. The British are by no means solely responsible for the debasement of some of the noblest buildings in India; but it is incontestable that it was a British Governor-General, a sentimental Whig and an arch-Philistine, who proposed to sell the Taj Mahal; so that it is not surprising if officers boldly erected coarse partition-walls and carved out spaces from the gems of Oriental architecture in order to make an orderly-room or an ordnance-store. Dec. 8.

On the morning of the 8th the King continued his reception of the Ruling Chiefs; and the Queen, attended by a small party of the suite, visited the Kutab Minar, the Mosque of Kutab-ud-din, and the tomb of Ala-ud-din, buildings which date from the twelfth to the fourteenth centuries of the Christian era, and preserve the memories of far older Delhis than the present. In the afternoon, soon after three o'clock, Their Majesties drove, under escort of a squadron of the Tenth Hussars and a squadron of native cavalry, to lay the first stone of the memorial to the late King Edward the Seventh. The site of this memorial, which will ultimately take the form of a bronze equestrian statue, is

Dec. 8. well chosen, being in a garden which stands on a slight eminence in the open space between the Jama Masjid and the fort; and a huge crowd of Indians filled a series of stands running down from the Jama Masjid to the scene of the ceremony. Here a pavilion had been erected; and the way from the entrance of the garden to this pavilion was lined by guards of honour of the Gordon Highlanders and the Second Gurkha Rifles, both of them King Edward's own regiments. The ceremony itself was brief enough. The Viceroy read an address setting forth that the cost of the memorial was to be defrayed by subscription, which had been contributed by "thousands and thousands" of loyal subjects of all ranks and conditions in India, testifying to their love and reverence for the ruler whom they had lost. His Majesty replied in a few feeling words, and with due ceremony laid the first stone. A salute of one hundred and one guns was then fired; Their Majesties drove off, and all was over. But for the vast throng of Indians present one would have thought that the function was one that would hardly have appealed to them. There were no masonic rites, in which many might have joined, yet they watched the brief spectacle by tens of thousands.

In the evening Their Majesties gave a state dinner to one hundred and six guests, including the Viceroy and Lady Hardinge, six Indian Princes and several members of the Viceroy's

Council. The banqueting tent offended against the elements of sanitary science in the matter of ventilation; and it must here be added, as a warning for future occasions, that being very long, very narrow and low, it presented neither a dignified nor an inviting appearance. The reception-tent beside it, to which Their Majesties and their guests withdrew after dinner, was less open to such reproach, except in respect of ventilation, being both lofty and spacious; while the roof, in broad stripes of pale blue and white, was, though somewhat paltry, at least pleasing and restful to the eye. Dec. 9.

On the morning of the 9th the King held his third reception of Ruling Chiefs; and the Queen likewise received a number of Indian ladies who came to present an address of welcome and a historic jewel and necklace to Her Majesty. The address, having been read by Lady Hardinge, and the presentation having been made by H.H. the Maharani of Patiala, the Queen read her reply of thanks, which was then interpreted in Urdu, after which the whole of the ladies were presented to Her Majesty. In the afternoon Their Majesties drove to the polo-ground, arriving there at half-past three, just at half time, in the middle of two matches between the King's Dragoon Guards and Bhopal upon one ground, and between the Inniskilling Dragoons and Kishengarh upon another. These matches were semi-final ties, for the final decision of which, as the day's work proved, the

Dec. 9. Inniskillings and the King's Dragoon Guards, both of them fine teams, were destined to meet again. The ground was thronged with private soldiers, both British and native; and it was pleasant to see a tall British red-coat take up an excited little Gurkha on his back to enable him to witness a thrilling moment in the game. But beyond the polo-ground was another field, where a football-match was going forward between the Lancashire Fusiliers and the Border Regiment, with an even greater crowd, composed chiefly of private soldiers. To this the King presently made his way, walking across the polo-ground attended by the Viceroy and by his staff-in-waiting. The visit to the polo being informal, His Majesty wore a simple grey suit with a grey topee and broad gold puggaree; the Viceroy was as simply dressed; and the whole proceeding came upon the soldiers, as indeed upon every one else, as a surprise. However, on recognising their visitor they made a rush to see His Majesty enter the stand with roars of delighted cheering. The sound naturally increased the crowd, and when, after watching the match for half an hour, the King went back to rejoin the Queen, it was only with the greatest difficulty that he was able to pass through the masses of enthusiastic, shouting men.

In the evening Their Majesties attended a torchlight tattoo on the polo-ground, of which it is unnecessary to say more than that, owing to the extremely heavy work thrown upon the troops at Delhi, it was impossible for them to find time to prepare a really effective display of that kind. At Calcutta, as we shall see, the case was different, and the spectacle was very fine. But at Delhi the men were on duty every day lining the streets; they were turned out very early, some ventured to think unnecessarily early; they had long marches to make from their own camps; they were out in the sun during the fiercest heat of the day; and, though the oiling of most of the roads about the camp delivered them from a certain amount of dust, yet it did not deliver them from all; while finally, owing to the long distances to be traversed, they frequently did not get back to their tents until late. In such circumstances the preparation of the elaborate manœuvres which go to make an effective tattoo was out of the question. The parade, therefore, was necessarily too simple to be really striking. Dec. 10.

On Sunday the 10th of December Divine Service was held at Jagatpur Island, on the far side of the Military Camp, eight thousand British troops being present. Although the King and Queen attended, all arrangements were of the simplest, three small shelters for Their Majesties and for the clergy alone testifying to the fact that some ceremony was going forward. The clergy and the massed bands with a body of singers selected from the troops were placed upon a slight eminence at the edge of the congregation, with the natural result that both

Dec. 10. voices and music reached the mass of the troops indistinctly, and after an interval. It seemed a pity that the men had not been grouped around the clergy and bands as a centre. The service was admirably intoned in unison by Archdeacon Nicholas and the Rev. W. Foster. The Bishop of Lahore read the prayers slowly and earnestly, in a voice that could be heard by all; and the Bishop of Madras likewise made his sermon reach the ears of at least the majority of those present. But the soldiers would not sing. In fact the British soldier at best will rarely sing more than two or three hymns, and those unfortunately not of the highest quality; while unless he is brought into a proper frame of mind (which is difficult when he considers himself to be more or less on duty) and unless he is well supported by a band close to him, he will not sing at all. The element of a great body of sound was therefore wanting to this huge congregation; and its absence was a disappointment to many. On the other hand, the approach to the site of the ceremony through the military camp had a grandeur that was all its own—a huge brown dead flat plain, covered with little humble tents and streaked with bodies of troops, moving, both mounted and on foot, in all directions. It presented a fine contrast to our own luxurious camp with its great marquees, fringed with palms, its broad drives and refreshing grass-plats, its bustling orderlies and chuprassies gorgeous in scarlet and gold. At one point could be seen a swarm of little Gurkhas climbing about the decayed walls of a ruined building from mere schoolboys' love of adventure, and grinning over the pleasure of it. One could hardly believe that they were ready to march, fully equipped for service in the field, within twenty-four hours, and to give a good account of themselves against any enemy. Dec. 11.

The morning of Monday the 11th witnessed what was perhaps the prettiest and most perfect of all the pageants that were crowded into the eventful eight days at Delhi, namely the presentation of colours to seven battalions of British infantry on the polo-ground. The ground was, of course, perfectly flat, though reasonably green for India in the dry season; and the seven battalions, each of them in quarter-column with fixed bayonets, were drawn up in a hollow square. On the left, as one faced the interior of the square, stood the Northumberland Fusiliers and the Durham Light Infantry; in the centre the Black Watch, Seaforth Highlanders and Gordon Highlanders; and on the right the Highland Light Infantry and the Connaught Rangers.[1] The Scottish Borderers were to have received new colours at the same time, but could not be brought to Delhi owing to an outbreak of cholera.[2] Thus two English battalions formed

[1] To give them their old numbers in succession the battalions were the 1/5th, 68th, 73rd, 72nd, 93rd, 71st and 88th.

[2] Here it must be remarked that it was only by unremitting vigilance and care that the awful spectre of cholera was kept at a distance. At Bombay the King's suite was to have been provided with Indian servants. Half of these servants could not come, owing to an outbreak of

Dec. 11. one side of the square; three kilted battalions the second side; and a Scots battalion in trews and an Irish battalion the third side, with the massed pipes in rear of the Black Watch, and the massed drums and bugles in rear of the Gordons.

Before the King's arrival parties marched out from each battalion and built up a small pyramid of drums, those of the Connaught Rangers solitary in front, those of the two English battalions next behind them, and those of the four Scottish battalions in rear of all, the drums thus arranged being in the form of a triangle with the apex towards the saluting point. The new colours were laid crosswise upon the drums, and a guard of two sergeants and a colour-sergeant was left over each. The clergy then advanced and grouped themselves near the drums, the Bishop of Lahore and the chaplains of the English Church in front of the English battalions: Father Gentilli, the Roman Catholic Archbishop of Agra and his chaplains over against them; and the six Presbyterian ministers in their black gowns in front of the kilted battalions and at right angles to their brethren of England and of Rome; each one of the clerical parties moving with as stately precision as if they had been themselves soldiers. Presently the King at the

cholera in their district, and I was told that two of them had actually died in Bombay that morning. At Delhi other servants were provided, but some of them were again withdrawn from the same cause. All this was rightly kept very quiet; but from these circumstances the reader may judge of the anxiety and trouble which was thrown upon those who were responsible for such matters.

head of a very large staff rode on to the parade-ground and into the hollow square; and the five thousand men, acting under an admirable word of command, presented arms as one man. Then with the same perfect unity the five thousand bayonets flew up together and came down to the "slope," and the King rode round the hollow square to inspect the troops. The inspection over, His Majesty rode to the saluting point and dismounted; and the sergeants guarding the new colours marched back to join their battalions. Dec. 11.

Then Bishop Lefroy came forward to the English drums and read the prayers of consecration, slowly and impressively in a penetrating voice which must have been audible not only to the troops but to most of the spectators. After him the six Presbyterian ministers came forward to do the like for the Scottish colours; and lastly the Roman Catholic Archbishop of Agra, vested with cope and mitre, read the prayers of his church and sprinkled the colours of the Connaught Rangers with holy water. Each group of the clergy retired in rear of His Majesty when its work was done, and then the commanding officer, the two senior Majors, and the two senior subalterns of each battalion advanced to the drums; the Majors took up the new colours, and the parties advanced in three columns towards the King and halted. The massed bands played a slow march, and each party in succession marched in slow time to the King, who took the colours from the

Dec. 11. Majors and handed them to the kneeling subalterns. Each party having received its colours moved back in slow time to its drums, and the commanding officers again advancing took each of them in succession a written address from the hand of the King.

It is usual in presenting colours for the Sovereign to address the battalion that receives them by word of mouth, but, this being impossible on so large a parade, His Majesty substituted a written address signed with his own hand—no unwelcome novelty, for the document can be framed and hung up in the mess-room as a perpetual memorial of the occasion. The opening exhortation was the same for all; but at the close were a few special words for each corps. The Northumberland Fusiliers were reminded specially of St. Lucia in 1778; the Durham Light Infantry of their latest feat at Vaal Krantz more than a century later; the Black Watch of their share in the old campaigns of India; the Seaforths of a yet longer list of Indian honours; the Gordons of the great name which they have made greater during every successive campaign during the past century; the Highland Light Infantry of the defence of Gibraltar and the action of Porto Novo; and the Connaught Rangers of their superb behaviour at Bussaco. It is true that the very names of these great feats of arms are absolutely unknown to an overwhelming majority of the British nation, who make money out of East Indian and colonial trade without remembering who gained that trade for them; but regiments happily never forget such deeds and rejoice to find that others too have kept them in mind. Dec. 11.

Having received their addresses, the commanding officers, always moving at slow march, rejoined the colour-parties, and amid a great roll of drums the colour-parties advanced each towards its own battalion; upon which the seven battalions as one man presented arms to their new colours. Then came the singularly pathetic incident which is inevitable at this ceremony—"Old colours, march off." The bands struck up "Auld Lang Syne," and the subalterns bearing the old colours marched slowly from their places in the centre of battalions across the front and round the flank to the rear, where the old colours, some of them mere ragged ends of silk at the end of a staff, were veiled in their cases, to be seen no more on parade. Finally the troops again presented arms, and the new colours were borne to the place of the old and let fly, while the band played "God Save the King." His Majesty then remounted his horse, the seven battalions, removing their helmets, gave him three cheers, and the ceremony was over.

All who witnessed the parade—and there were officers present of very many years' service—agreed that it was the most perfect thing of the kind that they had ever seen. An inspection of a brigade of Guards in Hyde Park by the Duke

Dec. 11. of Cambridge thirty years ago was a sight not easily to be forgotten ; but in these days, when parade movements are rightly held to be of little account, such a display is very rare. But it must not be thought that such perfection in mere manual movement of arms is valuable for spectacular purposes only ; for, as every military man knows, it is indicative of the greater unity that is produced by good discipline. A rather curious example of discipline in another form came under my immediate notice on (I think) this same day. The pavilion of the polo-ground was reserved for such spectators only as had been provided with a ticket ; and two sentries of the Gordon Highlanders were posted at the entrance to see that none but ticket-holders were admitted. Among others the Adjutant-General of the army in India presented himself, advancing in full uniform with many decorations, so that there could be no mistake as to his rank or as to his claim to be present. He was stopped by the sentry and required to produce his ticket. By accident or mishap he had none, and was proceeding to explain, when the sentry cut him short with "Beg pardon, sir, but my orders are to admit no one without a ticket," to which unanswerable statement the Adjutant-General, being responsible for the discipline of the army, cheerfully bowed his head, and fetched a wide compass to seek legitimate entrance elsewhere.

From the British regiments the King-Emperor rode next to two Indian battalions, the

Eighteenth Infantry and the Ninetieth Panjabis, to which he presented colours with the same formalities, omitting the consecration. His Majesty then proceeded to the veterans and holders of the Order of British India, who were present to the number of eight hundred and eighty, thirty of them being Europeans. As he passed down the line he said a few words to each of the Europeans, giving particular attention to Major Allum of the old Bengal Horse Artillery, who is eighty-four years of age, and was wearing two medals of earlier date than the Mutiny. Two more veterans—Mr. Thitton and Mr. James Roots, the latter of whom wears the Victoria Cross—also received special notice, both from the King and the Queen. Among the Indian soldiers were many grand old fellows, notably a father and a son, the one seventy-eight, the other fifty-eight years old, both of them late of the Twenty-third Sikhs, and both wearing five or six medals. One younger man explained to the King that he had received twenty-two wounds in Chitral, showing some of them as he spoke, but added proudly that he had killed two of the enemy. Altogether the King devoted a full hour to these gallant old men, the Queen following him closely in her carriage; and never was an hour better spent. Even from an ordinary European the Indian officer or soldier rates no compliment so highly as a glance at his medals and a salute paid to them, from which it may be guessed that the appreciation of the King-Emperor and the Dec. 11.

Dec. 12. Queen-Empress was received as the highest of honours and gratifications.

In the afternoon Their Majesties again visited the polo-ground to witness the final contest for the championship of the Delhi Durbar Polo Tournament, between the King's Dragoon Guards and the Inniskillings. After a very fine and hard-fought game the Inniskillings were victorious; whereupon both teams were summoned to the pavilion and presented to Their Majesties, the Inniskillings also receiving the cup from the hand of the Queen.

IX

And now Tuesday the 12th day of December was come, the great day around which all other events of the Imperial visit were centred, and for which preparations had been going forward for many months. The general arrangements were entrusted to a Committee, of which Sir John Hewett was the chief and the leading spirit; and it may be well first to take account of these and of the many difficulties which confronted the Committee in getting ready for the ceremony.

It was early decided by the King that the Durbar must not be held in any building, no matter how superb its intrinsic magnificence or how interesting its historic associations, but in the open air, so that it might be witnessed by

ROYAL PAVILION.

THE DURBAR—THE ARENA AND SPECTATORS' MOUND FROM THE TOP OF THE STAND.

To face page 139.

the greatest possible number of spectators of all races and conditions. The ground does not naturally lend itself to the convenience of spectators, Delhi being situated on a level plain with no eminence near it except the famous ridge, which is only sixty feet high and ill-suited for any such purpose. His Majesty therefore urged that a semicircle should be marked out in the plain ; that the outer circumference should be raised into a mound, so as to afford room for fifty or seventy thousand spectators ; that at the centre of the semicircle there should be erected a pavilion, high enough to enable Their Majesties to be seen from all points of the amphitheatre ; and that the stands for the Indian Princes and for privileged spectators should likewise be curved about the Royal pavilion for the same object. Dec. 12.

Upon this plan the ground was laid out. From the Royal pavilion as a centre a semicircle with a radius of about two hundred and forty yards was marked out to the north, and a mound was erected round the circumference for spectators. All round the base of the mound ran a processional road, so that Their Majesties could drive under the very eyes of the onlookers. A broad road also led from the pavilion due north, called the central road, and two more due east and west, called the east and west vistas respectively, all of them designed to open a clear view of Their Majesties from every quarter.

From the same centre of the Royal pavilion,

Dec. 12. but on the opposite side to the mound, a circular road was marked out on a radius of about one hundred and twenty yards; and round the southern margin of this road was erected a huge stand with seating accommodation for some ten thousand spectators, and with closed apartments up above for the great Indian ladies. Southward from the Royal pavilion ran a paved way leading to a second royal canopy called by the native name (which I shall retain for convenience) of the Shamiana, which abutted immediately upon the stand above mentioned.

The general plan having been decided, the formation of the mound and the sowing of the arena with grass became a question of labour, severe and trying enough no doubt in itself, but still comparatively speaking simple; and the problem now was to work out the remaining details. It was here that the Committee's difficulties began, and they were very many and great. It was plain that the body of the spectacle at the Durbar must be furnished by soldiers; and it was therefore rightly decided that the main space of the arena must be filled with troops. But the great mass of the King's soldiers are dressed in scarlet, and though I should be the last to say a word against the historic red coat, which is now approaching the age of three centuries, it must be confessed that it does not look its best under the Indian sun. It is hard, crude and glaring, and there is no escape from the fact. The Indian army, of course, affords a greater variety of colour than the British. Dec. 12. There is plenty of khaki, which looks far better in India than in England, often blended with turbans of blue, green or orange ; and there are regiments of cavalry in light blue, yellow, and other less difficult colours. Still the prevailing tone, even with twenty thousand troops massed within the arena, was bound to be scarlet, and the only thing that could be done was to blend the scarlet well with other less glaring colours.

To accomplish this, as well as to make the troops within the amphitheatre visible, it was necessary that the arena should be terraced, for it is obvious that, if it were left at its original unbroken level, not one tenth part of the soldiers could be seen. This terracing could be accomplished in two ways. The first was to raise the earth from the circumference towards the centre, so that the Royal pavilion would have risen as the highest point, above tier upon tier of troops, and above successive waves of colour. This would have been highly effective ; and though no doubt there would have been some difficulty in adjusting this arrangement to the smaller space to south of the greater semicircle, yet this need not have proved insuperable. On the other hand, it would have been possible to terrace the arena from the centre outwards, so that it should rise in continuous tiers up to the extreme circumference at the spectators' mound. This would have been both less effective and more costly than the other, for it would have involved

Dec. 12. the raising both of the spectators' mound, and therefore of the Royal pavilion also, to much greater height. However, whether these difficulties of terracing were invincible or not, no attempt was made to overcome them. The body of the arena was left at its original dead level, and hence for the vast majority of the beholders three-quarters of the troops contributed in no degree whatever to the spectacle.

Another point must also be noticed. With excellent judgment the Committee left a gap in the north centre of the spectators' mound, so that there should be a vista of Their Majesties upon their thrones from north, east and west ; but none the less the effect of the mound was such as to make a hard unbroken straight line against the horizon. By unhappy mischance no trees grew anywhere near the amphitheatre to break this line, and it was of course impossible to plant trees of sufficient size for the purpose. It must be added that no attempt was made to break it by artificial decoration. If the experience of the past is to be used for the profit of the future, this hard line should be noted with a view to possible amendment.

As regards the minor details, the architecture selected for the stand and for the pavilion was rightly Oriental in its general character. The stand, however, presented a compromise between East and West, for it had a steep sloping roof, a thing so rarely seen in the East that the tiny Oriental cupolas with which it was liberally

THE DURBAR—DISTANT VIEW OF THE ROYAL PAVILION AND THE SPECTATORS' MOUND.

To face page 143.

sprinkled could not disguise its foreign character. Dec. 12.
Moreover, this sloping roof, being abruptly cut off at the ends, presented an appearance so far from Oriental as to recall painful visions of a grand stand at Ascot. As the roof was not occupied by spectators, this unhappy effect might have been avoided, and should be avoided at any future durbar.

The Royal pavilion rose from a broad base in three tiers, ascended by broad stairways, to a central structure supported by four slender columns and surmounted by a huge gilt bulbous dome. This dome rose out of a kind of balustrade of gilt fretted work with four small domes at the four corners, beneath which extended a kind of gilt verandah, and beyond this a canopy of crimson velvet with a broad straight fringe of crimson and gold. The canopy was carried out as far as to the second tier of the pavilion, upon which it was supported by a number of thin gilded iron poles. These very slight supports were necessary, lest the view of the interior of the pavilion should be obstructed; but at a short distance they gave the impression that the heavy dome and canopy were resting upon nothing, and the more so inasmuch as the bulbous dome, which is typical of late Mohammedan architecture, seems even in the finest buildings to weigh very heavily on the substructure and to threaten to crush it. It may therefore be doubted whether the dome and its adjuncts would not have been better of white, picked out with gold; the

Dec. 12. canopy itself of white, or of some pale colour, embroidered in gold; and the straight fringe (which was not beautiful) made lighter by being broken up.

Indeed it may be questioned whether too slavish an adherence to crimson as the Royal colour, even though it was in some sort the Imperial colour of the Moghuls, be not a mistake. The canopy over the Shamiana and the embroidered mat at its foot might well have been, as they were, of crimson and gold; but the carpet round the foot of the stand and that leading from the Shamiana to the pavilion were of the commonplace red baize which is, perhaps, most generally associated with weddings at churches in the west end of London. The colour is not a good red, and at the foot of the stand made a very poor background for the rich dresses of the Indian Princes. But it was still worse on the paved way which led to the pavilion. There were officers in one shade of scarlet to walk on it; soldiers in a slightly different shade of scarlet all round it; Their Majesties' Indian attendants in a deeper and nobler shade of scarlet to stand by it; the Imperial trains of rich purple to be held up against it; and the deep crimson of the pavilion's canopy to overhang it; and the miserable baize swore vigorously and irreconcilably with one and all of them. Moreover, its appearance was lamentably mean and paltry. A decent border would have done something to redeem it, but even this was wanting. Indeed to me it seemed that the circumstances positively demanded a pale tint both in this carpet and in the canopy of the pavilion. The Shamiana lay in shade, screened by the grand stand. The paved way and the pavilion lay out in the full glare of the Indian sun. Their Majesties were to march from the first, where they could hardly be seen by the spectators on the mound, to the second, where they were in full view. The transition from the homage of the Princes, which was practically hidden, to the homage of the whole people, which was in the full light of day, should have been marked by a change of hue; and it must be repeated that the Indian dyers excel in the production of pale and tender colours.[1] Dec. 12.

So much must be said for the preparations, in order that the reader may imagine the setting of the scene in which the King-Emperor and the Queen-Empress were to play their most difficult part of the central figures. The morning of the 12th, to the general relief, broke fine and cloudless. On the two previous days the sky had become overcast, and the evening temperature

[1] Objections may of course be raised to the foregoing criticisms on the ground of expense; but a glance at the distribution of the funds would seem sufficient refutation. According to figures supplied to me, the cost of the Government of India's camp—60 people—for the week was 500,000 rupees; the expenditure on four persons alone out of those 60 was 22,000 rupees; the grant for the whole of the head-quarter camp of the army, 160 people, was 25,000 rupees. From this it would seem to be a legitimate conclusion that if the leading civilians of India had meted out to themselves the allowance which they thought sufficient for the leading soldiers, there would have been more money to spare for the proper decoration of the amphitheatre on the great occasion, perhaps the greatest in the history of India, of the 12th of December 1911.

Dec. 12. had risen, both of them signs of coming rain which were accentuated by gloomy forecasts from the Meteorological Office at Simla. All misgivings were happily set at rest at dawn of the 12th. Long before that, the air had been alive with the song of bugles and trumpets, with the braying of bands, the roll of drums and the tramp of marching troops. By nine o'clock the royal escort was beginning to form; a battery of Horse Artillery was halted in the avenue of the King-Emperor's camp, with its guns and harness looking fit to be placed on a lady's dressing-table; and the three huge non-commissioned officers of the Household Cavalry, with cuirasses flaming in the sun, were seeking their horses. At half-past ten such of the suite as were not in personal attendance began to leave camp in motors for the amphitheatre, which, owing to the excellent arrangements of the police, was reached within a quarter of an hour. By that time the spectators' mound was already more than three parts full, and presented generally a huge dark mass of black and white, dotted with the red tunics of British soldiers who, with inexhaustible patience and good temper, mingled with a certain peremptoriness of manner, were guiding people into their seats. On one side of the central gap broad bands of yellow, white, green and blue showed the presence of some college or similar institution. On the other, a still happier mixture of turbans of every imaginable hue gave the appearance of a giant bed of flowers. Round

THE MAHARAJA OF BIKANER AND THEIR IMPERIAL MAJESTIES' PAGES.

To face page 147.

the base of the stand most of the principal officials and of the Ruling Chiefs were already assembled; and grouped on the steps of the Shamiana were Their Majesties' pages, ten in number, all of them either themselves Princes or the descendants of Princes.[1] They were charmingly dressed, no two of them alike, in the usual long-skirted cassock of white or pale-coloured silk, buttoned to the waist, with turbans of another pale shade or of orange, shot with gold, jewelled swords, priceless necklaces and armlets of precious stones, and a brooch of the King-Emperor's initials in diamonds—the gift of His Majesty—fastened in their turbans. They varied in age from fourteen to six; but the centre of all their attention at the moment was the Lord High Steward, gorgeous in gold lace and the collar of the Garter, who was blandly explaining, amid shouts of laughter, that the true use of his long wand of office was to whip little boys at durbars. Dec. 12.

The arena was already full of troops, beautifully turned out, but a little too monotonously scarlet. There was abundance of variety if it

[1] The King-Emperor's pages :—
(1) His Highness The Maharaja of Jodhpur.
(2) His Highness The Maharaja of Bharatpur.
(3) The Maharaj Kunwar of Bikaner.
(4) Maharaj Kumar Himmat Singh of Idar.
(5) Bhanwar Vir Singh of Orchha.
(6) Sahibzada Muhammad Wahid-uz-Zafar Khan of Bhopal.

Queen-Empress's pages :—
The Thakur of Palitana.
Maharaj Kumar Gulab Singh of Rewa.
Kumar Mandhata Singh of Sailana.
Kumar Ramchandra Singh of Sailana.

Dec. 12. could have been seen; but only the waving pennons of the lancers, green, blue and white above their heads, softened the glare of the red, though the prominent place assigned to the Hundred and Thirtieth Baluchis in their green and crimson also gave a little relief. The guards of honour were furnished by bluejackets, Royal Marines, the Black Watch, and by the Fifty-third regiment of Native Infantry, this last being specially chosen for the honour, because it is recruited from every part of India. Dressed in khaki with touches of bright orange in their turbans, they made a remarkable foil to the scarlet doublets and dark kilts of the Black Watch.

The first episode was the entry of the Veterans, who were loudly cheered, though a repetition of the pathetic scene at Lord Curzon's durbar was not to be expected. On that occasion their entry was new and a surprise; now it was looked for, and people were prepared. The massed bands played "See the conquering hero comes"; and then one realised how nobly Handel's music, no matter how much hackneyed, can sound on a great occasion. At half-past eleven the Viceroy and Lady Hardinge arrived with their escort, and the massed bands played the march which he had selected for himself during the King's visit, most fortunately that from *Scipio*, again by Handel. Thus, so far as music was concerned, the day was opened with dignity.

His Majesty meanwhile had begun the day

characteristically with holding a Council ; for, no matter what may be going forward, the King is never free from the routine of business. At half-past eleven Their Majesties left the camp in an open landau drawn by four horses, with two Indian attendants behind them, carrying the crimson umbrella embroidered in gold and the huge gold fan-like sunshade which belong to their Imperial rank. Both were arrayed in Royal attire ; the King in the raiment of white satin which he wore at the Coronation in Westminster Abbey, with robes of purple velvet bound with gold, and wearing further his Imperial crown, which was one great sheet of diamonds, the collar of the Garter, and the star of the Order of the Star of India in diamonds. The Queen was dressed in white embroidered with gold, with a robe of purple, a circlet of emeralds and diamonds on her head, and the Orders of the Garter and of the Crown of India. For their escort the Tenth Hussars, V Battery of Horse Artillery, and the Bodyguard rode in front of the carriage; General Rimington, Sir Pratap Singh, and two equerries alongside it ; and the Imperial Cadet Corps and Eighteenth Indian Lancers in rear. Over and above these the Third battalion of the King's Royal Rifle Corps, and the First Ghurkha Rifles, awaited them, also as part of the escort, at the south-eastern corner of the amphitheatre. Dec. 12.

Just before noon Their Majesties reached this entrance, their arrival being heralded by a salute of one hundred and one guns. The whole of

Dec. 12. the vast assemblage rose to its feet; and the procession, reducing its pace to a walk, passed amid the salaams of the Indians and the cheers of the Europeans, round the eastern half of the spectators' mound and thence down the central road. Here the Tenth Hussars and the battery turned out of the route, while the Bodyguard, the Royal carriage and the Imperial Cadet Corps—let me call it the Noble Guard for brevity—proceeded down the eastern side of the circular road to the Shamiana. The steady array of the blue-clad hussars; the less compact but not less perfect order of the Horse Artillery, in their bright yellow-embroidered jackets; the tall stature and dignified bearing of the Bodyguard, all scarlet and gold; the gleaming helmets and cuirasses of the three Lifeguardsmen; the huge crimson umbrella and golden fan which marked the Royal carriage; the scarlet tunic of General Rimington and the spotless white of the veteran Sir Pratap Singh, followed by the gleaming white frocks, sky-blue turbans and glittering aigrettes of the Noble Guard—all this long parti-coloured procession winding its devious way half seen above the immovable forest of turbans, helmets, bayonets and lance-pennons, presented a spectacle of amazing majesty and grandeur. Nothing could have been better conceived or more admirably executed.

Arrived at the Shamiana the King and Queen alighted, the Viceroy coming forward to receive them; the pages gathered up the long purple

THE SHAMIANA—DELHI DURBAR.

To face page 151.

trains; and Their Majesties, standing for a moment before their thrones on the dais, bowed right and left to the huge ring of spectators in the stand, and then took their seats with their pages grouped on the steps before them. The Viceroy then seated himself with Lady Hardinge, Lord Crewe and the Lord High Steward on the lower stages of the dais to the right of the King; the Duke of Teck, the Duchess of Devonshire, Lord Shaftesbury and Miss Baring occupying the corresponding place to the left of the Queen. The remainder of Their Majesties' suite and the Viceroy's staff were behind them on both sides; and the Noble Guard, which had dismounted, was seated in rear of all. It must be added that for the first time in British history members of the corps of Gentlemen-at-arms and of the Scottish Archers were in waiting simultaneously upon the King upon this unique occasion; and that among all the thousands of soldiers of the King's own regiments, the Royal bodyguard of England, represented by four men, held its place of honour; a mounted Lifeguardsman being stationed at the northern, eastern and western faces of the Royal pavilion, and the solitary sergeant of the Grenadier Guards half-way up the steps on the southern face. But perhaps the most striking figures of all were Their Majesties' Indian attendants, fourteen of them carrying maces, and the remaining four the fans of yaks' tails and of peacocks' feathers, which are the eastern emblems of royalty. All were dressed in long scarlet Dec. 12.

Dec. 12. gowns covered with gold embroidery, and wore white turbans striped with gold about their heads; but there was no mistaking these grand grey warriors for anything but old soldiers, even if the row of medals upon their breasts had not proclaimed the fact aloud. Immensely proud of their office, they never for a moment took their eyes off their sacred charge, while from time to time a whisk of the yak's tail or a sudden lunge of the peacock's feathers, aimed at imaginary insects, proclaimed alike their readiness and their vigilance. They were grey, as I have said, and their natural force was abated with age, but any one approaching the King-Emperor with evil intent would have reached him only over their dead bodies.

All being ready, Sir Henry McMahon, as Master of the Ceremonies, asked His Majesty's permission to open the Durbar, which being granted, the massed bands by the pavilion sounded a noble flourish of trumpets culminating in a mighty roll of drums. Then His Majesty rose, the whole assembly, of course, rising with him, and read slowly and clearly a short speech expressive of his desire to announce the ceremony of his Coronation in person to his subjects in India. "To all present," His Majesty ended, raising his voice and glancing round the sea of upturned faces, "feudatories and subjects, I tender my loving greetings." A purely Oriental audience would have received such an allocution with a silent obeisance; but the leaven of Euro-

THE KING-EMPEROR'S CHOBDARS.

To face page 152.

peans in the stands was large, and the English, being too self-conscious to express satisfaction by mute gesture, broke into loud cheers. Oriental taste showed at this moment to advantage. Dec. 12.

Then the Viceroy came forward to do homage, bowing low thrice as he approached the throne, and finally kneeling to kiss His Majesty's hand, a distinction confined to him alone. To Lord Hardinge succeeded the members of his Executive Council; and then followed the Ruling Chiefs of Hyderabad, Baroda, Mysore, Kashmir, Rajputana, Central India, Baluchistan, Sikkim and Bhutan, led by the Nizam, who was dressed entirely in black but for his yellow mitre-like head-dress, his simple dignity enhancing the respect of his obeisance. After them came the Chief-Justice and Judges of the High Court, and the Viceroy's Legislative Council; and then in succession the Governors and Lieutenant-Governors of Madras, Bombay, Bengal, the Panjab, Burma and Eastern Bengal and Assam, and the Chief Commissioners of the Central and North-West Frontier Provinces; followed in each case, first by their Executive Councils, next by the Ruling Chiefs in relation with their Governments, and lastly by the representatives of their provinces.

The entire ceremony occupied a full hour, and was not only often extremely picturesque, but, to those who know anything of the history of India, of surpassing interest. The British officials, for the most part in staid blue uniforms

Dec. 12. with little adornment, quietly and unpretendingly made the military salute and passed almost unnoticed; though now and again attention was arrested by a giant such as Sir Charles Bayley, the Governor of Eastern Bengal and Assam, or by a Hercules, such as Sir George Roos-Keppel, who, for all his civil uniform, bore the unmistakable brand of the soldier and the fighting man, ready to wring the life out of an opponent at any moment, and able by sheer personal prowess to overawe an angry mob of the wildest tribes on the marches. No one would have suspected that the quiet, low-voiced Master of the Ceremonies himself is most at home on the Baluchi Frontier, where he has made his reputation as a patient, tenacious and successful diplomatist. But all eyes were naturally reserved for the Indian Princes, resplendent in gorgeous robes, hung with priceless jewels, and employing every variety of salutation. Very many used the gesture of throwing earth on the head once or oftener; others simply bowed, sometimes over their hands placed palm to palm, sometimes over their tendered swords. The Rajput chiefs almost without exception laid their swords first at the feet of the King-Emperor, and then of the Queen-Empress, with deep obeisance; and not the least striking of these was the young Maharaja of Jodhpur, who, together with another of the Imperial pages, left his place by the throne for a moment to do homage. The Begum of Bhopal, veiled from crown to heel in

H.H. THE BEGUM OF BHOPAL LEAVING THE ROYAL RECEPTION TENT.

To face page 158.

cloth of gold, made her reverence with a stately gravity which impressed the beholders not a little. The little Maharaja of Bharatpur, quite a child, bore himself with childish naturalness and grace. Then occasionally the ordinary course would be broken by the homage of one of the Noble Guard, who, with moustache curling up to his eyes, and sky-blue turban low over his forehead, marched upright as a dart to his place, halted with heels together, pressed the scabbard of his curved sword to his side, and saluted with the conscious pride of a soldier of the King-Emperor. Most reverential of all were the chiefs of Bhutan and of Sikkim, who, after bowing profoundly and throwing earth by gesture seven times on their heads, drew from their breasts two white shawls, such as they use only to drape the most sacred images of their gods, spread them before the King and Queen, and finally raising their quaint caps from their heads, passed on. Their homage was a solemn religious ceremony. One chief only marred the proceedings for a moment by a laboured ungainliness of bearing which lent itself to misinterpretation. It was a pity, for Indian Princes do not generally need lessons in deportment; and it may be hoped that after this occurrence no further lessons will be necessary. Dec. 12

Incidentally the Durbar afforded curious illustrations of the past history of India. The greatest of the chiefs were the latest, the Nizam and the Marathas having no more lengthy pedi-

Dec. 12. grees of sovereignty to show than have the English themselves in India. There was, however, a goodly company of the old proud families and of the heads of the fighting clans which, even after repeated defeats, had defied the Moguls in the plenitude of their power, and with unquenchable pride and independence even rejected alliances with them by marriage. These were they who laid their swords at the feet of Their Majesties, remembering that Lord Mornington and Lord Hastings had saved them from utter extinction at the hands of the Marathas. They had ruled India once and, if their brains had been commensurate with their bravery, would have ruled it for longer. Very noticeable, on the other hand, were the absence of any Bengali chiefs enjoying independent relations with the central Government, and the very small number, no more than two, of those who stood in the like relation to the Government of Bengal. For the Bengali is the converse of the Rajput, a thinking man rather than a fighting man, who surrenders his outward independence with little ado, trusting, not without justification from past history, that his intellect will give him the greater sovereignty which belongs to those who govern the Governors.

For the rest it would be impossible to describe the richness and variety of colour displayed by the dresses of the native princes. The head-dresses alone would require several pages, from the voluminous turban of Kashmir to the small golden jewelled cap (I know not how else to describe it) of Travancore, and the pagoda-like structures of Burma. In the surroundings and against the infelicitous background selected by the Committee, one costume of white shot with gold, with a broad girdle and turban of bright green silk, was perhaps the most effective; but taken as a body nothing could exceed the group of the Imperial pages. Dec. 12.

At length the homage was over. Few if any of those who saw it could have found it tedious, and, if they did, the monotony was broken by the applause with which the different personages were greeted as they advanced to the throne. Such applause perhaps suggested rather prize-giving than reverence, but the instincts of the public meeting are strong in Englishmen; and, if cheers were out of place, it may at least be pleaded that they were more freely bestowed upon the Indian Princes than upon the European gentlemen. The last outburst died away. The fourteen mace-bearers faced about and formed in column, two and two, on the paved way; and the Lord High Steward and the Queen-Empress's Lord Chamberlain presently took their places behind them. The King and Queen rose; the pages gathered up the purple trains; the massed bands blared out a march; and the whole assemblage sprang to its feet. Then with joined hands and measured step Their Majesties moved slowly up the paved way towards the Royal pavilion. Immediately before them and facing towards

Dec. 12. them walked Lord Durham and Lord Shaftesbury, with the mace-bearers in front of all. Immediately behind them marched the four remaining Indian attendants; then after an interval the Viceroy, Lady Hardinge, the Duke of Teck, Lord Crewe and the Duchess of Devonshire; and after a second interval the remainder of the suite and the Viceroy's staff, four abreast, in all nearly fifty persons. At the foot of the pavilion the mace-bearers halted, and turning right and left lined the way on each side; and Their Majesties, slowly ascending the steps to the highest stage, took their seats on two gorgeous thrones, with their four Indian attendants behind, and the pages grouped before them. On the stage next below them the Viceroy, Lady Hardinge, Lord Crewe and Lord Durham stood upon the King's (or eastern) side; the Duke of Teck, the Duchess of Devonshire, Lady Shaftesbury and Miss Baring upon the Queen's side; while the remainder of the suite divided themselves between the two sides of the lowest stage.

The scene at this moment was extremely fine. As a matter of spectacular effect the lower tiers of the pavilion might perhaps with advantage have been more thickly covered, while some Oriental dresses would have brought a welcome relief of soft colour to the hard blue and scarlet of the uniforms. Still the presence of the Maharaja of Bikaner and of Sir Pratap Singh gave at any rate a touch of white and sky blue;

THE DURBAR—THE ROYAL PAVILION.

To face page 158.

and on the Queen's side the three ladies—the Duchess of Devonshire in creamy white, Lady Shaftesbury in buff with a pale-pink sunshade, and Miss Baring, tall and graceful, in pale blue—provided just what was needed. But this was merely a question of the setting, for all eyes were rightly fixed on the topmost stage, where Their Majesties sat, all white and gold against the rich purple and creamy ermine of their trains, with the soft-coloured robes of the pages grouped about their feet. And this was beautiful as well as imposing. Dec. 12.

The massed bands again sounded a superb flourish of trumpets, with a thundering roll of drums: a shrill fanfare answered them from without the amphitheatre, and the trumpeters advanced on horseback to the north entrance of the central road, with the two heralds, Brigadier-General Peyton and the Hon. Malik Umar Hyat Khan, in tabards, at their head. The trumpeters numbered twenty-four, drawn in equal numbers from British and Indian cavalry regiments, with one drummer from the Thirteenth Hussars. They were dressed in the crimson and gold worn by the State trumpeters at home, the British wearing white helmets, and the natives white and gold turbans; and all were of course mounted on white horses. Arrived before the entrance to the central road at the cut through the spectators' mound, they halted and blew a second fanfare. Then advancing up the central road to the Royal

Dec. 12. pavilion the drummer again spread his arms wide, and at his signal the flourish was repeated a third time.

Then the chief herald rode up before the pavilion and read the King-Emperor's proclamation, announcing, in effect, that the solemnity of his Coronation had been celebrated in Westminster Abbey on the 22nd of June, and that it was his wish and desire to make this known in person to all his loving subjects in India. "Now" (ran the closing words), "We do by this Our Royal Proclamation make announcement thereof, and extend to all Our officers and to all Princes, Chiefs and Peoples now at Delhi Our Royal and Imperial Greeting, and assure them of the deep affection with which We regard Our Indian Empire, the welfare and prosperity of which are, and ever will be, Our constant concern." The Indian herald then repeated the Proclamation in Urdu, in tones which, though less deep and powerful than General Peyton's, were more penetrating and carried much farther. "God Save the King-Emperor," cried the shrill voice in Urdu ; and the drummer once more opened his arms wide for a last flourish of trumpets. The supreme moment was come. The bugler of the commanding General sounded a note ; the troops presented arms ; and with a crash the massed bands burst into the National Anthem. The last note was hardly silent when a battery of artillery at the north end of the amphitheatre fired the first salvo of six guns, which was repeated by a second battery to west, and a third to east, the salute passing round and round in the same order until thirty-four salvos had been fired. Then came a faint sound as of rending paper, which died away into a faint mutter and swelled again into an angry snarl, as the *feu de joie* of the troops that lined the roads sped away for three miles from the amphitheatre to the King's Camp, and rushed back from thence to the amphitheatre again. The bands once more played the opening bars of the National Anthem; the batteries fired three more salvos; and the same procedure was followed until one hundred and one salvos and three *feux de joie* had been completed. Dec. 12.

Throughout this time, full fifteen minutes, the whole of the great congregation remained silent and motionless. The sun, high in the heavens, beat down fiercely upon all within the amphitheatre—upon all except the King-Emperor and the Queen-Empress, who stood, even as the rest, erect and still in all the pomp and glitter of robes and crown, under the shadow of the canopy. They alone, being seen of all men, could command at a glance of the eye the huge concourse of men that encircled them. At their feet in long curved concentric lines stood great ranks of disciplined soldiers, standing patiently, in contempt of all muscular strain, with presented arms—light little English townsmen from London, Birmingham, Sheffield, Durham and fifty other cities; heavier country lads from Berkshire, from the Midlands and from Northumberland; solemn

Dec. 12. Highlanders from Banff and Aberdeen; sturdy bluejackets from Hants and Devon; lean, eager-eyed Pathans from the north-west; bearded Sikhs with the steel quoits glittering round their turbans; tall Rajputs with traditions of centuries of fighting behind them; Dogras, Panjabis, Marathas, and last, and least in stature though by no means least in fighting power, battalion on battalion of short Mongolian Gurkhas. At the head of them all an officer in high command sat on his horse before the pavilion, through salvo after salvo, with his hand glued to his helmet; a little to his rear stood the solitary gigantic Guardsman, equally with hand held fast to his bearskin. For this mingled host of many ranks and many races and many tongues was united into one by the bond of discipline as soldiers of the King. Let men revile as they will the noble profession of arms; it will always form the strongest of human brotherhoods, for military discipline is the organised abnegation of self.

And beyond these ranks of scarlet and blue and yellow and khaki lay the vast ring of the peoples, no mere *claque* of the populace of Delhi, but a great assembly gathered together from every part of India. It would be difficult to say how many languages and dialects were used as mother-tongues within the small compass of those two semicircles that day, certainly not fewer than twelve, and quite possibly more than twenty; but not a voice was heard among them. The huge mass of spectators stood silent and awe-struck, gazing at the two resplendent figures beneath the golden dome, with thoughts that were presently to be revealed in a manner for which no one had looked. And through boom after boom of the cannon Their Majesties gazed upon the great throng before them, with simple, tranquil dignity and, though deeply moved, with perfect outward calm. One would have said, and said truly, that they were present as earnest and devout leaders and partakers in a great religious celebration. It was indeed the reverential spirit in which they regarded the ceremony that brought them into sympathy with the feelings of the large majority of the spectators about them.[1] None who saw them during that long salute will speedily forget the sight; and those, I think, who were privileged to stand near the Queen will never quite lose the vision of her noble bearing as, with head slightly thrown back, she stood out in majestic gentleness against the radiant grey-blue of the Indian sky.

The tension had become almost unbearable when the last sound of the salute died away, and the bugle sang out three quiet notes: "Slope arms"; "Order arms." The supreme moment was over; and after another preliminary blast from the trumpeters the Viceroy, by the King-

[1] A Madras Brahman, a very successful pleader both in British and Hyderabad courts and in sympathy with the India Congress, turned with tears in his eyes to an English friend at the close of the Durbar, and said, "This is what I have always dreamed the procession of a God must be. If the Bengalis give any more trouble, they will get no support from any other province in India."

Dec. 12. Emperor's order, stepped forward and read a proclamation of boons to be conferred in honour of the occasion. These may be summarised shortly as increased expenditure on education; grant of half a month's pay to all non-commissioned officers and soldiers and to minor civil officials; concession of additional privileges in the matter of honours and rewards to native officers, and release of certain criminals and of poor persons imprisoned for debt. Then after yet another preliminary flourish of trumpets the chief herald stood up to his full height in his stirrups and, doffing his helmet, called for three cheers for the King-Emperor, and three more for the Queen-Empress; and with this final roar of sound the ceremony at the pavilion came to an end. The trumpeters galloped away to a new station, and Their Majesties descending, returned hand in hand to the Shamiana to the worthy music of German's Coronation March, in like procession as they had advanced from it.

There the trumpeters sounded another fanfare, and then to the general surprise, for the official programme gave no hint of such a thing, His Majesty rose, holding a paper in his hand. With clear voice and just emphasis he announced that the capital of India would be transferred from Calcutta to Delhi, and that a Governorship would be created for the Presidency of Bengal, a new Lieutenant-Governorship for Behar, Chota-Nagpur and Orissa, and a Commissionership, as before, for Assam, with a general redistribution of boundaries. In other words, Lord Curzon's partition of Bengal, which had caused so much agitation, was revised, and a new and different partition projected. Admirably delivered though this announcement was, no human voice could have reached more than a small portion of the spectators in the stand ; and the news flew from the centre to both flanks with a buzz as of passing bees. But the trumpeters now blew their last fanfare, and galloped out of the arena. The Master of the Ceremonies received permission to close the Durbar, the massed bands again played the National Anthem, all present rising to their feet and singing with the bands ; and Their Majesties, re-entering their carriage, drove off amid loud cheers and a last salute of one hundred and one guns in the same order as that of their arrival, only taking this time the road along the western corner of the amphitheatre. The Viceroy followed next, and after him the members of the Imperial suite. And then, when all seemed to be over, came the most impressive scene of all. The people rushed down by thousands from the mound to the Royal pavilion on which Their Majesties had sat, and prostrating themselves, pressed their foreheads against the marble steps. Soon, as the crush became too great, they were fain to touch the pavilion with their hands and press their fingers to their foreheads, content with this, so only they could pay their homage to the one supreme ruler of all India. For the East has Dec. 12.

Dec. 12. not yet lost the ancient habit of exalting their Emperor above all human kind, a habit which the West, with its Divus Julius and Sanctus Carolus, formerly shared, and perhaps may yet again share, with them. So strong is the impulse in men to deify the power which keeps them in discipline and order, and thus brings to them the divine blessing of peace.

In the evening Their Majesties gave a State dinner in the banqueting tent to one hundred and seventy-three guests, no light addition to a heavy day's work; but every one was cheerful and of good heart on that evening after the brilliant success of the Durbar. It may fairly be said that everything passed off without the slightest hitch or mishap. That the preliminary arrangements might possibly have been somewhat improved, many were disposed to agree; but as regards the actual transaction of the ceremony in every detail from beginning to end there were not two opinions. The filling and emptying of the huge amphitheatre was accomplished without the slightest difficulty, and the patience and gentleness of the police, both British and native, were beyond praise. The appearance of the troops was faultless; the massed bands played their part admirably, alike in whiling away for the spectators the tedious hours of waiting, and also in accompanying the most solemn moments of the ceremony. The selection of music was, on the whole, good, and the flourish of trumpets and drums magnificent.

The trumpeters likewise did themselves credit. Dec. 12. The fanfare composed for them was stately and stirring; they played it exceedingly well; and their appearance, with its alternation of white faces and brown, of white helmets and gorgeous turbans, was well fitted to the spectacle at large. There were, it is true, critics who objected to the headlong speed at which they galloped round the circular road, half of them on the east side and half on the west, when the time came for them to change stations. But though there was certainly high speed, there was no disorder; the men kept their distances admirably; they had their horses perfectly in hand; and they rode particularly well. Further, it must be acknowledged that their movements filled up very suitably the short pauses that necessarily intervened between different stages of the ceremonial. But by general consent the success of the Durbar was ascribed, above all, to the sympathetic bearing and perfect dignity of Their Majesties.

X

On the morning of the 13th the King-Emperor was on horseback before eight o'clock, riding through the camps of the naval contingent and of the Infantry brigades which had worked so hard for him on every day of his stay. At eleven o'clock he presented the Albert medal

Dec. 13. to ten officers and sergeants of the Indian Ordnance Corps, who had distinguished themselves by conspicuous gallantry in saving life after the explosion of cordite at Hyderabad and Ferozpur in 1906. He then held a levee of the officers of the Volunteers, of the Indian officers of the Imperial Army, and of the Imperial service troops of the native princes, touching the swords which they tendered to him according to the graceful custom of India. He then accepted addresses from deputations from the Presidency of Madras and the municipality of Delhi, while the Queen-Empress received one hundred and twenty ladies of the families of the Ruling Chiefs. In the King-Emperor's camp that morning all functions seemed to be of minor importance after the Durbar, and yet in those very hours there was taking place at Delhi the most remarkable ceremony of all.

It had been arranged that three separate processions of Hindus, Jains, Mohammedans and Sikhs should start early in the morning by three different routes, and, after offering prayer for the King-Emperor each in their own congregations, should proceed, the chiefs to the fort of Delhi and the remainder to the plain beneath it, where all should meet and together make their common supplication to the Most High. The earliest of these processions started at half-past six in the morning, and before nine o'clock a vast crowd was assembled at the fort. I personally was unable to see more than the Sikhs, and among them chiefly the followers of the Maharaja of Patiala. These included wild horsemen, some clad in orange, with breastplate, matchlock, lance and shield; others similarly armed, but dressed in blue, with ring upon ring of steel encircling their high caps; foot-soldiers similarly attired; gorgeously caparisoned horses, and two elephants, upon one of which was seated the High Priest. Every Sikh soldier of the British Army who could be spared was present; and the aspect of the Maharaja and his suite, all with yellow garlands about their necks, showed that this was no common occasion. They had already visited the shrine in the Chandni Chauk of Guru Teg Bahadur, who in 1675, when dying in torment at the hands of Aurangzeb, had flung at the fanatical Emperor this prophecy—"I behold coming from across the ocean a race of men, who will spread peace and justice, and root out tyranny and oppression." Before this shrine they had uttered the following thanksgiving: "By Thy Mercy, O God, his words have proved true; for the British Government, which confers happiness on its subjects, has been established in India. We Sikhs of the Gurus in the midst of our happiness and rejoicing to-day specially render Thee our humble thanks that our beloved Emperor has come to the City where our holy Guru, the Bestower of Salvation, uttered this fateful prophecy, in order to place the crown of many realms upon his head. O Eternal God, may this peaceful and just Sovereignty ever Dec. 13.

Dec. 13. endure, and may the Emperor George, and his gracious Consort, Queen Mary, abide in happiness, and may the Empire extend and prosper." At the shrine Sir Louis Dane, Lieutenant-Governor of the Panjab, had met them, a welcome guest, and joined in their wishes for the welfare of the King-Emperor and of the Khalsa. Presently these gaily dressed warriors began to move down from the fort to the plain below, following the High Priest on the elephant. There hundreds of the King's Sikh soldiers joined them and, massing themselves together, watched at a little distance, while some scores of yellow turbans swarmed round the High Priest's elephant, repeating with endless iteration a plaintive chant[1] to the accompaniment of drums and tambourines.

Meanwhile the Mohammedans had met in vast numbers in the Jama Masjid, and since early morning the most famous preachers of their faith in Upper India had discoursed to them of the value and virtue of loyalty. From the Sikhs Sir Louis Dane passed to this mosque, where, after listening for some time to the address of a learned Maulvi from Lucknow, he was begged by the leading men to say a few words, which request was confirmed by the entire assembly. He therefore spoke briefly, thanking them and joining in their prayers for the prosperity of the King-Emperor who on the preceding day had

[1] Curiously enough this chant was identical with the first six notes of Sullivan's air "Prithee, pretty maiden" in *Patience*.

restored the glories of Delhi by making it again the capital of India. That a Christian should deliver an address, which was itself in the nature of a sermon, to thirty thousand Mohammedans in a mosque by their own invitation, is a fact which sounds almost incredible; yet so it was; and the vast congregation not only heard him with eager respect, but greeted the conclusion of the exhortation with fervent shouts of "Amin." Dec. 13.

The Hindus likewise were holding their religious service—an oblation with sacrifice—under the auspices of the Maharaja of Darbhanga and the Sanatam Dharm Mahamandal upon the traditional site by the Jumna where Yudisthira (as related in the Mahabharata) performed his oblation and horse-sacrifice when he was crowned Emperor of all India.

Finally the whole of the processions met under the walls of the fort, immediately facing the historic balcony where the Mogul Emperors were wont to show themselves to the people. The British Governors and Lieutenant-Governors, and the Ruling Chiefs thereupon descended from the fort where they had met together, and took their appointed places, the British officials in the centre of all, and the Ruling Chiefs at the head of the groups formed by the leaders of their religions. A gun was then fired as a signal from the Selimgarh bastion, and all present offered up united thanksgivings for the success of the great solemnity of the Coronation, and prayers for the King-Emperor and the Royal Family. The

Dec. 13. Imam of the Jama Masjid led the Mohammedan prayers, two Pandits those of the Hindus; two Granthis those of the Sikhs; and the Archbishop of Simla read a prayer to the little body of British officials. To any one who knows aught of the history of India the spectacle was almost staggering in its impressiveness. In that country religious differences are accentuated by the fact that religious observance governs the minutest details of daily social life; yet Christian Englishmen—descendants of the men who had fought savagely to rescue the Holy Sepulchre from the followers of Islam—Hindus, Jains, Sikhs and Mohammedans by a common impulse laid aside all prejudice and crushed down all intolerance in order to unite in one heartfelt prayer for the King-Emperor. For the first time they felt that they were possessed by a sentiment common to them all, and so paramount as to dominate all the impulses bred by divergence of creed, dissimilarity of custom and rivalry of race—the sentiment of loyalty to one sovereign. That Sovereign was no longer a mere legend to them. He had come over the sea many thousand miles to visit them; they had seen him with their eyes; he was even then near them, and in a few hours would be in the fort actually moving in their midst. The white men from overseas bowed down to him even as they themselves; under his rule, as past years had shown, all might live, if they would, in peace—in peace after endless centuries of war and devastation.

Therefore were they met together to give God thanks. Dec. 13.

In the afternoon Their Majesties drove to the fort and there held a garden-party—a name too paltry for the reception of many hundreds of guests in such surroundings as the beautiful buildings of Shah Jahan's palace and the stately and peaceful gardens which connect them together. Even these, however, formed not the most remarkable feature of the occasion. A great national festival had been organised by Sir Louis Dane for this day, and the plain between the eastern wall of the fort and the Jumna was thronged by a vast assembly of half a million people, all waiting to defile past the King-Emperor. The spectacle was one that bewildered the oldest inhabitants, whether native or English, of India. Scattered about in open spaces were to be seen groups of entertainers; in one place a handful of jugglers; in another a musical ride of green-clad lancers from some Indian Prince's contingent; in another a war-dance of wild warriors with sword and shield; in a fourth a group of lightly-clad sowars, leaping to and from their steeds at full gallop and performing other feats of horsemanship. But these were mere islands in a vast sea of brown faces and many-coloured turbans. To prevent dangerous crushing, barriers had been erected at intervals leading on to two broad ways, like racecourses, which met below Shah Jahan's balcony already mentioned, and there parted right and left

Dec. 13. parallel to the wall of the fort. Within these barriers the people had been assembled in parties according to the several districts from which they came; and, as many of them had taken a distinguishing colour, one could see looking down upon them fringe after fringe of white, backed by great blocks of yellow and red and green and blue in every imaginable shade. At the outermost edge of each lay a thin line of khaki topped with the turbans of red and blue which distinguish the Panjab police.

In due time Their Majesties appeared at the historic balcony. The King had come to the garden-party in the undress uniform of a field-marshal and the Queen in a plain mauve morning dress; but they had determined not to disappoint the expectations of the people, and, before they showed themselves, they had put on their robes of purple and ermine, the Imperial crown and the tiara worn at the Durbar. They stepped into the balcony without sound of trumpets to herald their coming, and their appearance was therefore not recognised by all of the onlookers simultaneously. The buzz of voices suddenly died down, giving place for a few seconds to a low hum; and then tens of thousands of arms leapt into the air and the hum swelled from front to rear and from flank to flank into one mighty shout of wonder and acclaim. The balcony, however, being small, Their Majesties left it and took their seats upon two thrones on the ramparts where, with their

THEIR MAJESTIES AT THE NATIONAL FESTIVAL.

To face page 174.

THEIR MAJESTIES AT THE NATIONAL FESTIVAL.

To face page 175.

pages grouped around them, they remained in full view of all for nearly an hour. Presently the foremost string of khaki police shrivelled up quietly into a knot, and the first great masses of colour moved forward to defile past the King-Emperor. The effect was indescribably beautiful. The hard blocks of yellow dissolved into a soft confusion of yellow and white, and streamed away on one hand with the varied hues of a flight of canaries. The rigid masses of blue and green and red melted into a wave of mingled colour, and flowed away to the other hand as though they had been floating feathers from a parrot's wing. Company after company was released in due time by the patient police to add their volume to the flood, until for a full mile in length and half a mile in depth the plain was inundated with one great sea of colour, which moved and halted, eddied and swayed, deepened and lightened with ever new combinations, until the eye turned from it in sheer bewilderment and amaze. And so the defile continued with increasing shouts of acclaim, until at last there arose a kind of wail, and the one or two hundred thousand who were still crowded before the thrones stretched out their hands in appeal. The King and Queen had risen and were withdrawing themselves from sight. Their Majesties did not reach the camp until nearly six o'clock, concluding the day as usual with a dinner-party to ninety-seven guests. Dec. 13.

On the morning of the 14th Their Majesties

Dec. 14. motored to the village of Dahirpur, where the King-Emperor mounted his charger to review the troops, which were drawn up in two lines to receive him under the command of General Sir O'Moore Creagh. The total strength of the force was close upon forty-nine thousand men, of which rather more than sixteen thousand, including officers of native regiments, were British, and the remainder Indian officers and soldiers of the King's army and of the Imperial Service Corps. After the usual Royal salutes the troops marched past, the Horse Artillery in line of batteries, and the cavalry by brigades in brigade-mass, at the walk; and the infantry by brigades in line of quarter-columns. The infantry being for the most part brigaded as if for active service, that is to say with one British to every three Indian battalions, the march past was not so perfect to the eye as it might have been had the brigades been composed of homogeneous units, such as Gurkhas or Highlanders; but on the other hand its interest was enormously increased by the mingling of the soldiers of both nations, and by the knowledge that it was in this order that they would take the field. Perhaps, however, the most gratifying sight of all was the Imperial Service troops, which made an astonishingly fine display. Of the cavalry the Bhopal Lancers had perhaps rather the best appearance in the walk past: but it was difficult to choose between the different contingents, whether in cavalry or

THE REVIEW AT DELHI.

To face page 176.

AN INDIAN CAMEL CORPS.

To face page 177.

infantry. A word must be said, too, in praise of the European Volunteers, and in particular of a composite battalion of infantry, over eight hundred men strong, which had been raked together from all quarters, many of the men paying their own travelling expenses. They marched past with a steadiness and a swing which did them much credit. Dec. 14.

The Indian chiefs generally led their cavalry past in person, and by no means always as amateurs. Few men can handle a brigade of cavalry or of infantry better than the Maharaja of Gwalior, who was conspicuous in his uniform of a British Major-general. The Maharaja of Bikaner, again, is at home both with his infantry and his camel-corps. But the leaders that attracted the most attention were naturally the young Princes. The Maharaja of Jodhpur, one of the Queen's pages, rode at the head of his lancers. As he reached the saluting point his horse swerved away from the waving plumes of the King and his staff; and it was pretty to see how this young soldier, without taking his eyes for a moment off the King, and without apparent movement of a muscle, brought the animal square to the front again and completed his salute. A still younger officer, the child Maharaja of Bahawalpur, led his camel-corps past, himself riding a camel in front of a grave and trusty trooper. Dressed in full uniform of khaki with gold-embroidered skirts the little fellow boldly faced the King-Emperor at the

Dec. 14. saluting point, threw out a baby's right arm to its full length, and with perfect correctness and time in every motion brought down his tiny sword to the salute. Seventy or eighty years hence, it may be, he will be conspicuous as the only survivor of the many gallant gentlemen who rode past King George on that day.

The Horse Artillery then galloped past by batteries and the cavalry by regiments, in line; and, as is so common in the British Army, the effect was too often spoiled by excessive speed. In both batteries one gun was at least a length in rear of the rest; and its drivers could be seen punishing their horses, not because the animals were sluggish, but because the highest speed of a slow team is not so rapid as that of a fast team. All of the British regiments, except the King's Dragoon Guards, galloped too fast, and consequently were in very ragged order; and their example led most of the Indian cavalry astray, though the Ninth and Tenth Indian Lancers were an exception. The Imperial Service Cavalry mostly followed the lead of the British, though the Patiala Lancers held their horses well in hand until close upon the saluting point, when a shrill whistle from a veteran Indian officer sent them flying past like a whirlwind. Considering that British Generals first endeavoured to check this tendency to headlong speed one hundred and fifty years ago, it seems a pity that they should not have succeeded yet. The parade ended with an advance in review order, which was exceptionally magnificent and impressive; and altogether the military display was extremely successful. Dec. 14.

In the evening at half-past nine the King held an investiture in the largest of his reception-tents. It must, I fear, be remarked that the decorations of the tent were not worthy of such an occasion, which indeed demanded something more magnificent than stripes of light blue and white in cheap materials. However, nothing better had been provided; and the tent, just as it was, was packed with from three to four thousand ladies and gentlemen. The first candidate for investiture was the Queen-Empress who, dressed in pale blue, made a graceful obeisance, knelt before the King, and was invested with the Order of the Star of India. Her Majesty then kissed His Majesty's hand, received his kiss on her cheek, and took her seat on the throne by his side robed, with the happiest and most becoming effect, in the light-blue mantle of the Order. The remaining candidates, of whom there were a very large number, then came forward one after another, and the ceremony was about half-completed, when suddenly the fire-alarm was heard without, and a strong smell of burning became evident to every one. The electric light at the same time flickered up and down, threatening to go out at every moment, and continued to do so for two or three minutes. Presently some one cried out "*Fire*," and two or three hundred people rose to their feet. The

Dec. 14. officials who were taking part in the Investiture pursued their functions with perfect calmness and indifference; the Queen, who has a peculiar horror of fire, sat motionless and apparently unconcerned; and His Majesty continued to throw ribbons over heads and to pin stars to breasts as if he had been at St. James's. Nevertheless, the assembly was within a hair's-breadth of a panic, and might have succumbed to it, had not some gentleman in the body of the tent sternly growled out "Sit down," whereupon the timid reluctantly resumed their seats. Presently the light became steady; and confidence being restored, the ceremony came successfully to an end.

The danger, however, had been real and great. The tent of Lord Crewe's private secretary, not above one hundred yards away, had caught fire, and from thence to the reception-tent there was one continuous spread of canvas. Happily there was no wind, and the fire-picquets had immediately cut the ropes of the adjoining tents, so that the conflagration spread no farther. Three hundred men were on duty round the reception-tent with orders to cut away the sides instantly if anything should go wrong, but even so a panic must have led to a great catastrophe; and this warning is one which should not be neglected in future. It is not safe to pack people by the thousand into a single tent in the midst of a great camp. Mr. Lucas's tent was burning for about three minutes, and after that brief space he was left literally with nothing except the civil uniform which he wore on his back. Tin trunks with the whole of their contents had vanished as if they had been made of wax, and only the corners of a stout leather portmanteau had made some little resistance to the fierce heat and flame. It must be added that no man could have accepted so trying a misfortune with more perfect cheerfulness and good temper that did Mr. Lucas. Dec. 15.

On the morning of the 15th at ten o'clock Their Majesties drove to the avenue of the Indian Government's camp to lay the first stone of the new capital city of Delhi. By dint of working day and night the Public Works Department had raised a wall seven feet high upon solid foundations, and over this wall were hung two huge blocks of dressed stone. The ceremony was extremely simple, and those that attended it were necessarily few, since there was no space for more. A small but very beautiful tent had been erected hard by, where Their Majesties upon arrival were received by the Viceroy and the members of the Executive Council; a guard of honour of the Gordon Highlanders being drawn up in the avenue. The Viceroy then addressed a short allocution to the King-Emperor, dwelling upon the importance and advantages of the change of capital, and announcing at the close that the Maharaja of Gwalior had expressed his intention of presenting a statue of the King-Emperor to

Dec. 15. the new city. His Majesty, having made a brief reply, advanced to lay the first stone, after which the Queen came forward and laid the second stone. The heralds, British and Indian, then proclaimed the fact with a flourish of trumpets; Sir Louis Dane called for three cheers for Their Majesties; and the brief ceremony was over. The change of capital having been kept a secret until the afternoon of the 12th, there was no possibility of making greater preparations, and it must be confessed that the inception of the new Delhi was decidedly modest. This, however, is no great matter. What is of more importance is that its progress should be in accordance with the aspirations expressed with no uncertain voice by the King. "It is my desire," said His Majesty, "that the planning and designing of the public buildings to be erected should be considered with the greatest deliberation and care, so that the new creation may be in every way worthy of this ancient and beautiful city." Here is an opportunity indeed for a great architect of original genius and ideas, not only to give India a capital worthy of herself, but to obliterate the reproaches to British architecture which at present stand unabashed in Calcutta and Bombay.

From the avenue Their Majesties drove to the polo-ground, where a force of over twenty-seven hundred Indian Police had been drawn up for the King-Emperor's inspection. Considerably more than half of them were from the Panjab, about one-fifth from the United Provinces, and the remainder small contingents from all the other provinces of India, all of whom had been on duty at the Durbar. Having ridden up and down the line the King dismounted, and the men filing past received each a medal from his hand; after which His Majesty expressed to the Inspector-General, Sir E. Lee-French, his satisfaction at the arrangements made and the work done by the police during the past week. The compliment was well deserved, for, though on every occasion when His Majesty drove out at Delhi the way was lined with troops, the strain upon the police was very heavy and was admirably met. No one who had not seen it would credit how immense were the mass and variety of vehicles, and the rush of traffic with which they had to contend, and the patience and good temper with which they handled the native crowds. Privileged motors by the score were dashing along the roads at all hours, imperiously demanding passage; and the way was always cleared somehow, without bustle and without bullying. A word, however, must be added in praise of the additional police, both mounted and afoot, which was drawn from the British regiments of cavalry and infantry. Any one might have thought that they had passed an apprenticeship in the Metropolitan Police under Sir Edward Henry, and I know of no higher praise that could be given them. As to the work done by British

Dec. 15.

Dec. 15. officers of the Indian police force, I saw with my own eyes during the religious processions on the 13th a young fellow, who could not have been more than twenty-three, gently manœuvring a mass of from two to three thousand Sikhs into their right places, single-handed, without putting his horse into a trot, without a harsh word, without so much as a violent gesture.

In the afternoon Their Majesties drove to the polo-ground to witness point-to-point races and a military tournament. The Indian cavalry may be called the creators of our military tournaments, and their feats of horsemanship, fully equal to those of many circus-riders, in leaping on and off a galloping horse, picking up objects from the ground without quitting a horse's back, and such like, are too well known to need description here. But when the whole, or at any rate the greater part, of a regiment of Sikhs charges forward together, every man galloping at the top of his speed to pick up his tent-peg—this is not an ordinary spectacle. For the rest, the British Seventeenth Lancers, as usual faultlessly turned out, performed a musical ride with great skill. Possibly indeed many of the spectators did not appreciate that skill, nor realise how much more difficult it is to make two equine quadrupeds waltz together than two human bipeds. Finally, a battery of Horse-Artillery in line charged a mud-wall three feet high ; and the whole of the six teams, with their guns, jumped it simultaneously without mishap

THE MAHARAJA OF BIKANER.   SIR PRATAP SINGH.

To face page 185.

to drivers or horses. When one reflects that the slightest mismanagement of any one of the eighteen pairs of horses would have thrown down a part, if not the whole of the team, this stands out as a great feat of driving. Dec. 16.

The last day was now come, and it began early for the King-Emperor. At half-past nine His Majesty received a number of civil and military officials who had been concerned with the arrangements for the Durbar, and distributed among them medals in honour of the occasion. At a quarter-past eleven the Ruling Chiefs came to the reception-tent to take leave of His Majesty, and among the last of them were the Maharana of Udaipur, Ruling Chief-in-Waiting, and the chiefs and distinguished Indian soldiers who are aide-de-camps to the King-Emperor. These were the Maharaja Sindia of Gwalior, the Maharaja of Bikaner, the Nawab of Rampur, Sir Pratap Singh of Jodhpur, and Colonels Sir Muhammad Aslam Khan and Nawab Sir Muhammad Abdullah Khan; though some of them, as shall be seen, were again in waiting on the King at Calcutta. This farewell was a mere formality, as recorded in the dry official manner for readers of the newspapers, but a very different matter for those who took part in it. All felt that a great occasion, without a parallel in the history of India, was come and gone; few could count upon seeing the King again; and the great majority knew that they would look upon his face no more.

Dec. 16. He had received every one of them, not only in public as their suzerain, but in private as their friend; and they had realised the true secret of His Majesty's coming, namely that he cared very much for them and for India.

Therefore they parted from him in sorrow. There were few who were not profoundly moved, while some could hardly restrain their tears; and the King himself was not less troubled than they. Many harsh criticisms had been passed in England upon his resolution to visit India; but the fervent welcome accorded to him by all classes from the Ruling Chiefs to the humblest peasant had proved to him that he had done well. It is small wonder that he was grieved at taking leave of such friends.

At noon Their Majesties drove in procession to the Selimgarh station. The last farewells were spoken; the last salutes were fired; the train steamed away, and the first great meeting of the King-Emperor with his subjects of all India was over. To say that its success exceeded the most sanguine expectations is to say little. Englishmen with the longest experience of the country stood amazed at the enthusiasm manifested by the inhabitants assembled at Delhi; and the phrase constantly recurred "Such a thing has never been seen, no nor even dreamed of, in India before." And what was it that brought forth these extraordinary results? It was not the mere organisation of pageants. Great praise is due to the Committee of Management for its labours; but they would be the last to claim that all their arrangements had, from a spectacular point of view, been faultless. Yet even if all the setting had been perfect, it would have availed nothing without the precious stone in its midst. It was the King and not the King's clothes or the King's surroundings that so profoundly impressed India. The inhabitants, it must be repeated, believe in no vague abstraction called a Government; they believe in the one ruler whom God has set over them; and when he comes among them they fall down and worship. Nor, if the matter be considered, is this surprising. In the ordinary routine of life one man is better than another; but in the presence of the King all men are so immeasurably below him as to be merged together on the same footing. The King is the King. All others are his subjects; as such they are equal; and in the King's presence the humblest peasant feels himself on the same level with the Viceroy. In the King's absence, indeed, the Viceroy is above all, but only as the King's vicegerent; and it is solely in virtue of the powers deputed to him by his Sovereign that he may enjoy respect and command obedience. In the presence of the King the Viceroy is nothing; and no number of guards, salutes and escorts will make him anything in the eyes of the people. If he effaces himself and walks humbly before his Sovereign, he will be honoured; and the greater and truer his humility the higher will

Dec. 16

Dec. 16. be his honour and his influence among those who are placed under his rule. For he can then say to any who offer him disrespect, "If I bow to the ground before the King, you owe the like homage and obedience to me as his vicegerent." If on the other hand any Viceroy should aspire to take rank with his Sovereign in that Sovereign's presence and put himself forward as of equal importance, so much the worse for him. He would be set down not only as ill-mannered, but as a foolish man who knows not that all subjects alike sink into insignificance before the King. This is the reason why His Majesty's visit to India filled even the poorest classes with a mysterious joy—a joy which was mightily increased when King George showed himself to be in true sympathy with all his subjects. The lowest peasant feels that he has a part in this Sovereign Lord, which no man can take from him, and his heart is uplifted as to something given of Heaven.

XI

At the Selimgarh station the King and Queen took different routes, the first to Nipal, and the second to Agra. It will be convenient first to follow the movements of His Majesty. Travelling by special train the King reached Arrah at ten o'clock on the morning of Sunday the 17th of December; where he stopped for two hours and

THE KING-EMPEROR. THE MAHARAJA OF NIPAL.

THE ROYAL PARTY IN NIPAL.

To face page 130.

a half in order to attend Divine Service. Before starting again he went to visit the billiard-room which was the scene of the famous defence against the mutineers in 1857.[1] Two Indians who had taken part in the defence were present, the one a bowed and shrivelled old man over one hundred years old ; the other younger in years, having been at the time a boy, who stole out of the compound and gave information to the relieving force concerning the beleaguered garrison. To both of them the King said a few words, ordering also a present to be given to them of a certain sum for every year that they had lived. Returning to the train before one o'clock the King on arrival at Bankipore embarked at Digha Ghat and steamed for three or four miles down the Ganges, the vessel hugging the bank on the side of Patna city, which was lined with crowds of cheering inhabitants. Here there was leisure to think of the fatal errors of the Agent at Calcutta, which led to the massacre at Patna in 1763, the desperate fighting of the victims before they finally succumbed, the escape of the sergeant who bore a charmed life, and the vengeance taken for the massacre by Major Adams. Dec. 17

Soon after ten on the morning of the 18th the train arrived at Bikna Thori, on the borders of British India and Nipal. Here the Hereditary

[1] The story of the defence of Arrah has been written once for all by Sir George Trevelyan, to whose book any readers who do not know it should turn without delay. I have no intention of spoiling their enjoyment, nor of marring a noble narrative by attempting to abridge it.

Dec. 17. Prime Minister and actual ruler of Nipal, Sir Chandra Sham Sher Jang Bahadur Rana, G.C.B., was awaiting His Majesty with his three sons, his military commander-in-chief, the British Resident, Colonel Manners Smith, V.C., and one or two more. Having presented the members of his suite to the Maharaja,[1] the King-Emperor, followed by the rest of the party, motored by a road, specially cut through the jungle for some thirteen miles, to a spot where elephants were awaiting him.

The ground here was flat and undulating, being in fact the lower slopes of the lower hills of the Himalayas, the main range of which, rising to a height of twenty-five thousand feet, could be seen in all its majesty of unbroken snow, apparently twenty miles, but really seven times that distance, away to the northward. Below this great wall of white the lower hills loomed gaunt and blue, and below them again the blue melted into the green of the nearer thicket and forest. For many months the Maharaja had been making preparations for the King's visit, clearing the ground for camps, cutting roads for miles through the jungle, and keeping careful watch upon the game. In all he had six hundred and forty-five elephants ready for the sport, the need of which number

[1] The Duke of Teck, Lord Durham, Lord Stamfordham, Lord Annaly, Lord C. Fitzmaurice, Sir E. Henry, Sir H. Smith-Dorrien, Sir Derek Keppel, Sir Colin Keppel, Sir C. Cust, Sir Havelock Charles, Capt. G. Faussett, Major Wigram, Sir R. Grimston, Col. Watson, Capt. Hogg, Mr. Jacomb Hood.

will be more readily understood when the methods of proceeding are explained. Dec. 17.

Over night, or in the afternoon bullocks are tied up in likely places for a tiger, generally at the edge of thick jungle; and in the morning the shikaris (or gamekeepers as we should call them) go round to see if any of these have been killed. A tiger does not necessarily kill his victim because he is in want of food, for he will often do so from sheer wantonness; but having done so he generally, though not always, drags it a little way into the thick jungle, devours enough to satisfy himself if he is hungry, or simply leaves it and lies down not far away to sleep. In the morning the shikaris come in with reports of the "kills," upon which about a hundred and fifty "pad" elephants, that is to say elephants not intended to carry guns, proceed to the appointed place. These include many of the female elephants, with their young ones roped to them to train them up in the right way. The whole, having been formed into line a mile or more from the "kill,' advance through the jungle, and, as they approach nearer to it, the flanks of the line move forward from right and left and meet beyond it, thus forming a ring of perhaps half a mile in diameter. All of the elephants in the ring then advance towards the centre, closing in gradually until they almost touch each other, by which time the diameter of the circle is reduced to two or three hundred yards. At this point the "howdah-elephants,"

Dec. 17. which carry guns or privileged spectators, enter the ring at intervals which leave eight or twelve pad-elephants between each of them. It is necessary to keep the guns pretty close together, otherwise an incautious or erratic shot might slay his neighbour on the other side of the circle.

Such a ring was already formed when the King arrived. A ride of a mile and a half through the jungle on pad-elephants brought the whole party to the howdah-elephants, to which they transferred themselves, His Majesty being accompanied by the Maharaja, and took their places in the ring. Four or five staunch pad-elephants then went inside the ring, tramping through the grass to move the tiger; and here it must be explained that the grass and reeds are incredibly high, often rising not merely above the backs of the elephants but over the very tops of the howdahs. In such an undergrowth, if the term may legitimately be employed, a tiger or a rhinoceros looks like a rabbit among rushes, visible only in open patches and disappearing very rapidly. Very soon a tiger dashed out with a roar, leaped over a nullah (watercourse), and disappeared, but presently charged back straight upon the King, who fired and wounded him badly. Again he disappeared, but a second tiger came out, rose in the air to leap the nullah, and fell stone-dead, in sight of every one except the King, who had killed him with a snap-shot

A CLOSE SHOT BY THE KING.

To face page 193.

through the neck as if he had been a rabbit. Dec. 18. The howdah-elephants then advanced, the wounded tiger was presently found and despatched by His Majesty; and a move was then made in motors to another ring, nineteen miles away; the Duke of Teck, Sir Charles Cust and Sir Horace Smith-Dorrien going in a different direction in search of another tiger.

After luncheon the howdah-elephants entered the new ring, His Majesty announcing that Lord Durham and Lord Annaly should have first shot. The tiger presently charged. Lord Annaly fired and hit him; but the animal went on until, as it was turning back into the long grass, Lord Durham stopped its progress for ever. The elephants then formed line to beat for rhinoceros, and soon a very fine one broke away at great speed, offering a difficult shot to the King, who fired without apparent effect, for the huge creature disappeared into impassable jungle, and was seen no more. The line continued to advance, and by chance the King happened upon two more rhinoceros, killed the first dead with one barrel, and with his second wounded the other, which was followed, and in due time despatched by His Majesty. Yet another was wounded by Lord Durham and Lord Annaly, and led his pursuers a long chase, being quite invisible in the tall grass; and it was not until many shots had been fired into the moving reeds that he was at last killed.

By half-past five the camp, being close at

Dec. 19. hand, was reached, a most beautiful spot from which the jungle had been cleared on the bank of the Rapti river, with a noble view of the great wall of the Himalayas to northward. Here the Maharaja had erected a spacious wooden hut with six rooms, replete with every comfort, for the King, and tents close by for the suite, the whole being lit by electric light. This camp offered a very pleasant contrast to that at Delhi which, so far as the suite was concerned, was incomparably the worst in every respect that we encountered in India. The nights were cold, and the dew after sunset so heavy that it was hopeless to think of reaching the mess-tent dry-shod without waterproof overshoes, which, however, the King's Indian staff had been careful to provide. In the mornings there was always thick fog until ten o'clock or rather later, when it cleared off, giving place to a very hot sun. Reports of the "kills" during the preceding night could not therefore come in until that time, nor could a start be made for the day's shooting.

On the 19th no news of tiger came in until half an hour after noon, when His Majesty, the Duke of Teck, Lord Durham and Lord Annaly set off at once on pad-elephants, travelling at good speed, and therefore with considerable shaking and discomfort, to the spot where the ring was formed. A tiger was soon found, but wisely kept himself under cover, charging continuously from side to side in the long grass, until at last he fell to the King's rifle. After luncheon a line was formed to beat homeward, but nothing was seen. The remainder of the suite went out in several different parties, among whom Sir Charles Cust got a tiger, and Sir Colin Keppel and Sir Horace Smith-Dorrien each a rhinoceros. Dec. 20.

News came in earlier on the 20th, and three parties started out, two after tiger and one after rhinoceros. In the first His Majesty was the only gun, though several were with him as spectators; and the ring being close at hand was reached before eleven o'clock. In the first ring the King shot a tigress; after which a second ring was formed close by. Here there was another tiger, but also a cow-rhinoceros and calf, which charged straight at the ring and broke it at once, for no elephant will face the charge of a rhinoceros. The tiger probably slipped out at the same time, for no more was seen of him. After luncheon yet another ring was reached in which four tigers were enclosed; and here the sight was a wonderful one. The imprisoned tigers charged the line of elephants at various points; and everywhere the mahouts scared them back by throwing sticks at them and by frantic shouts, which the elephants swelled by loud trumpetings and screams. One succeeded in breaking the ring, but some elephants were quickly passed round him and again he was hemmed in; another actually made a spring at an elephant, mauling its trunk with his claws; but for the most part

Dec. 20. the elephants plucked branches of trees, stripped them of leaves and small twigs, and holding them horizontally under their trunks, kept brandishing them to avert any such assault. Ultimately every one of the four tigers fell to the King's rifle. A line was then formed to move homeward, when a solitary bull rhinoceros suddenly appeared before His Majesty, and though only wounded by his first shot, was eventually killed by him. Five tigers, a rhinoceros and a hog-deer were the King's bag for the day; to which Captain Godfrey Faussett and Sir Colin Keppel added each one tiger; Captain Godfrey Faussett and Sir Horace Smith-Dorrien each a bear; and the Duke of Teck a rhinoceros.

By great good fortune this party witnessed a very singular scene. A tiger, slightly wounded by Sir Colin Keppel, took refuge in thick grass, where he came upon a she-bear and cub. Furious at being disturbed the enraged mother at once fell upon the tiger, standing up to her full height and striking at him savagely with her fore-paws. The tiger, whose temper had been ruffled by his wound, was in no mood to endure such aggression tamely; and the two settled down to a regular fight with savage grunting and snarling, until the bear made off in one direction and the tiger in another, both of them to meet their end by a rifle bullet. But perhaps the most exciting experience was that of Major Wigram, whose pad-elephant, while on the way home, was pursued by a rhinoceros.

THE KING, AND THE SPOIL OF HIS RIFLE.

To face page 193.

The elephant of course ran madly away through the jungle, and the Major was obliged to lie down at full length on his back, clinging with all his strength to the pad, with the second mahout on top of him. After a burst of half a mile the rhinoceros fortunately abandoned the chase of Major Wigram, and transferred his attentions to another pad-elephant, which he hunted for four miles before at last allowing it to go in peace. The mahouts, however, had the enjoyment of this latter pursuit to themselves. Dec. 21.

On the 21st the King reached the first ring, not far from home, before noon, and found in it four tigers and a Himalyan bear—the last named a very rare visitor in the low country—all of which he killed, one tiger and the bear right and left, each with a single bullet. This ended his day's sport, for a second ring in the afternoon proved to be blank. On this day Captain Faussett and Lord Charles Fitzmaurice went out in another direction after rhinoceros; and the former underwent the uncomfortable experience which had befallen Major Wigram on the 20th, his elephant being hunted for some distance by a fine bull rhinoceros, which he eventually killed.

On the 22nd Sir Charles Cust and Captain Faussett accompanied the King with rifles, several other gentlemen going as spectators. The first ring, being near home, was reached before noon, and three tigers were found to be within it. Two at once dashed out towards the

Dec. 23. King, who killed with his first barrel but missed with his second. The second tiger, however, again charged towards him and was killed; and the third met with the same fate at a single shot. A line was then formed to beat for rhinoceros, and after a long time one was reported to be on the left of the line. All the elephants therefore started in that direction at once, and in ten minutes the whole were scattered about the dense jungle in hopeless confusion. From the midst of them there suddenly emerged a fine bull rhinoceros. He received a bullet from Sir Charles Cust, blundered on past the King who had an awkward shot at him, but missed, and finally charged three pad-elephants close to Captain Faussett, who killed him just as he had passed them. On this day Lord Durham, Lord Charles Fitzmaurice, Sir Derek Keppel, Sir Colin Keppel and Sir Henry McMahon killed between them seven tigers and a Himalayan bear, making a total bag of ten tigers, a bear and a rhinoceros; a wonderful day's sport.

On the 24th, being Sunday, the King and suite attended Divine Service, which was conducted by the Rev. J. Godber, chaplain to the Bishop of Calcutta. In the evening His Majesty with the whole of his suite moved to a new camp at Kasra, a duplicate of the former camp at Sakhi Bar and about eight miles from it. Early on the 25th all again attended Divine Service; and towards noon the whole party went with the King to the jungle about three

A GOOD BAG IN NIPAL.

To face page 198.

miles away, where a ring had been formed. Dec. 25.
With hardly any delay a very fine tiger came charging through the grass, and was killed stone dead by the King with a shot through the heart. He measured 9 feet 6 inches in length. Another ring had been formed two miles away, but His Majesty made this over to the Duke of Teck and Lord Durham, preferring to beat for rhinoceros. After a time a cow with a well-grown calf was found, which made off, but being fired at and missed by the King, turned back at once and charged at the top of her speed. A second bullet from His Majesty's rifle laid her stone dead with a shot through the chest; and every effort was then made to capture the calf by forming a ring about him. But the gallant little fellow rushed straight at the circle of elephants, broke through it and disappeared. The ladies and Colonel Manners Smith's three little girls came out to luncheon by the King's invitation; and when the meal was over, another line of elephants was formed, when the King again killed a rhinoceros dead with a single shot. Meanwhile the Duke of Teck's party had found four tigers, and had enjoyed some excitement with them, no fewer than three of the animals having jumped on to the elephants' trunks, and one having actually climbed up within striking distance of the mahout. They then hid themselves in thick grass, growling continually, while the mahouts shouted and the elephants trumpeted all round

Dec. 26-27. them, afraid to come nearer. Ultimately they were dislodged by three or four bullets, and the party returned with three tigers and a rhinoceros, making four tigers, three rhinoceros and a hog-deer (shot by the King) for the day. In the evening, being Christmas night, the whole of the suite dined with His Majesty.

The sport of the previous days by this time had begun to tell on the quantity of game still afoot. The reports of the morning of the 26th set forth that though sixty bullocks had been tethered in the jungle on the previous night, one only had been killed. The King appointed that the Duke of Teck, Lord Durham and Lord Annaly should draw lots for the single tiger, and the lot fell upon Lord Durham, who duly killed him. His Majesty himself, with Sir Charles Cust, Sir Henry McMahon and Lord Charles Fitzmaurice beat for rhinoceros with a line of elephants. One only was found, which was killed by the King; and the afternoon was absolutely blank. There was therefore little surprise, when on the 27th there came news that not a single bullock had been killed. However the King started forth at noon on an elephant to a place where a tiger had been tracked; and a ring was formed, but no tiger was within. After luncheon therefore the party was divided; and a line of elephants was formed in which His Majesty, Sir Henry McMahon and Colonel Watson carried rifles. Presently the King noticed the grass moving before him; a tiger dashed out, and the flank elephants were quickly thrown round to form a ring. The tigress, however, for such she was, was one of those who would not be pent in. Charging straight at the ring, she broke through it not far from the King, who missed her with his first barrel, but rolled her over stone dead outside the ring with his second, making the twentieth tiger that he had shot since his arrival in Nipal. Dec. 28.

On the 28th there was again news of a tiger, and the King started at a little before noon for his last day's sport. A ring had been formed, but it was some time before the tiger broke, crossing straight in front of the King and the Duke of Teck. Both fired simultaneously, and the beast fell dead with two bullets in the neck. After luncheon a move was made by motor to another ring twelve miles distant, where the King killed his twenty-first tiger, and fired his last shot in India. The total bag for the ten days was thirty-nine tigers, eighteen rhinoceros, of which the King killed eight, and four bears, of which the King killed one. An unexpected addition was made to the tale of the killed by the motor mail-cart while on its way from the camp to Biknathori on the night of the 27th, when it ran over a full-grown panther, smashing the lamps and the glass shield and apparently breaking the unlucky animal's back, for he could only with difficulty struggle again into the jungle by the help of his fore-paws. Were it not that the next rains will infallibly wash away all

Dec. 28. the roads made by the Maharaja, motorists in search of new emotions might do worse than take their vehicles to Nipal.

In the evening His Majesty took leave of the Maharaja, who had housed him and his suite with such admirable comfort and provided him with such excellent sport. On Christmas Eve the King had pinned on his breast the Grand Cross of the Victorian Order and a golden Coronation medal; but the Maharaja's gifts to His Majesty were not so easily carried away, for they included a young elephant, a young rhinoceros, bears, panthers, snow panthers, a Tibetan jackass (very wild and very active with his heels), a pair of Tibetan mastiffs (both rather savage), bara singh deer, sambhur deer, hog deer, cheetul, jackals, and others of the same order, mongeese and other smaller quadrupeds, with peacocks, jungle fowl, pheasants, partridges, and all manner of lovely birds, besides beautiful products of native art in various kinds. But no such remembrances will be necessary to recall to memory the most courteous and hospitable of hosts, from whom His Majesty, and not less the whole of his suite, parted with deep gratitude and very sincere regret.

At six o'clock in the evening the Royal train steamed away to the sound of a salute of one hundred and one guns, and of cheering from a great crowd of natives, many of whom ran alongside the train for so long as they could keep up with it. At every station where the train stopped throughout the night there was a crowd of natives shouting in their own tongue "Victory to the King," and on the following day, the 29th, at every crossing and every station, whether the train stopped or not, they were assembled in thousands to greet him with the same cry. At Muzaffarpur the throng broke through the barriers and swarmed round both sides of the train, trying only to touch the feet of His Majesty, as he stood visible to all on the platform of his saloon-car with his suite about him. Arriving at Paleza Ghat on the Ganges in the afternoon, the King and his party embarked on a steamer, and went down the river towards the city of Patna, again hugging the bank of the river for five miles amid the uproarious enthusiasm of a great multitude of people. Then landing at Digha Ghat he entered the train, and twenty minutes later met the Queen at Bankipore. It is now time to follow Her Majesty's movements during the days when the King was in Nipal. Dec. 29

XII

Leaving the Selimgarh station at Delhi with a suite of eight persons,[1] the Queen travelled by train to Agra, arriving at the cantonment station at five o'clock. Here Her Majesty was received

[1] Prince George of Battenberg, Duchess of Devonshire, Lord and Lady Shaftesbury, Miss Baring, Maj.-Gen. Sir S. Beatson, Lt.-Col. Bird (Indian Medical Service), Major Hill, Major Money, Mr. Fortescue.

Dec. 16. by Mr. Reynolds, Commissioner for the District, and drove to the Agra Circuit House, which had been made ready for her, with a camp pitched about it for the suite. After the rush and turmoil of Delhi the change to this quiet and beautiful camp was very pleasant. The ground about the Circuit House has been laid out as a park ; and standing by the entrance one could see to the left, two miles distant across the valley of the Jumna, the noble red-sandstone fort of Agra, and to one's right front the swelling dome and slender minarets of the Taj Mahal gleaming white above a bank of dark foliage a few hundred yards away. In spite of the exhausting week at Delhi, a most busy morning, and four hours of a very dusty railway journey, the Queen went almost immediately to the Taj to revisit it before the light should fail. One after another the suite drifted away in the same direction, to watch the scarlet of the sunset blazing over the fort of Agra and on the face of the Jumna, and blushing faintly on the silent marble of the Taj, till the last light died away, and dome and minarets again loomed white against a sky of cold steel blue.

Our new camp, having been formed under the superintendence of the King's Indian staff, contrasted very favourably with our late quarters at Delhi. The tents were pitched at a proper distance from each other, they were comfortably warmed, and they were clean. All other arrangements for messing and so forth were equally good, and immeasurably superior to the corresponding arrangements at Delhi; while Colonel Bannerman, the political officer who was in charge of the Queen's tour, speedily installed himself among the suite as the most attentive and courteous of hosts, and a very welcome companion. To all intent, between journeys and functions, this was the first quiet night that we had enjoyed since we left the *Medina*; and the Queen, who needed rest more than any of us, took advantage of it. The suite, for their part, found very agreeable guests in the officers of the Royal Irish and of the Thirteenth Rajputs, which regiments furnished the guards of the camp. Dec. 17

On the morning of the next day, Sunday the 17th of December, the Queen, attended by her suite, drove to St. George's Church for Divine Service, the sermon being preached by Dr. Westcott, Bishop of Lucknow and son of the late Bishop of Durham. The church, which was built by the East India Company in 1828, has, like all of its kind, no architectural pretensions, but as usual carries on the walls many sad memorials of young lives cut short. "Died of exposure during the Indian Mutiny" is a curt phrase which sums up a long and dreary account of human misery, and reminds one that the casualties of a campaign do not end at the conclusion of peace. "Fell in action" are words that stir the heart; but "Died of cholera," "Died of fever," leave behind a dull sense of pain, as we reflect on the frightful toll of British lives which has been levied during the last century

Dec. 17. and a half by India. Her Majesty had wished to go to church as quietly as possible, but the Thirteenth Hussars, who had escorted the Royal procession from the station on the previous day, begged permission to have the honour of furnishing a full escort. We had remarked the regiment at Delhi; but even so we were not quite prepared for what we saw on that Sunday. All the officers in the suite agreed that the escort was the most perfect that they had ever seen, so admirably were the distances and the dressing preserved. This may seem to be a small matter, but such details count for much in the discipline of a regiment; for those that are careful in small matters are unlikely to be careless in great. Moreover, it is a real pleasure in this imperfect world to see anything faultlessly done.

In the afternoon the Queen, still attended by her suite, motored to the fort of Agra, where Mr. Sanderson of the Archæological Department guided her over the huge palaces of Akbar, Jahangir and Shah Jahan. Excellent work has been done here in clearing away modern excrescences and excavating the foundations of ruined buildings. The palaces are too well known to need description by me; but one or two points respecting the Mohammedan architects may be noted. First, they thoroughly realised—what has too often been forgotten in England—that, if a court is to look beautiful, the buildings around it must be low; and hence

their courts wear a peculiar grace of spaciousness. Dec. 17
Secondly, their construction was often very slovenly; Akbar's palace, for instance, having a very loose core of brick, held together by a great deal of soft mortar, and very thinly faced with slabs of red sandstone. The walls of Delhi fort are another example of this, being simply rubble with a thin stone face. Thirdly, they delighted in architectural puzzles. They seldom if ever built a true arch, so that the structure of arch-shaped apertures often presents some mystery; but this pales beside the problem presented by a ceiling of flat marble slabs. According to all the rules of gravity this ought to fall on the floor, being to all appearance an inverted pavement; but it does not; and although no doubt there are many ways of performing the trick, it would be interesting to know how in this instance it is accomplished.

From thence the Queen proceeded a short distance farther to the tomb of Etmad-ud-dowlah, a very marvellous example of fretted marble-work, beautiful in detail but lacking the imposing simplicity of earlier and ruder Mohammedan tombs. There was still time for another visit to the Taj after our return; but indeed being so near at hand, we wandered into its silent garden at all unoccupied hours, the most constant visitor and admirer of all being the Queen. In the evening Her Majesty gave a small dinner-party, in which the Bishop of Lucknow, the Commissioner and Mrs. Reynolds, and a few more were included.

Dec. 18. On the morning of the 18th the Queen with her suite started early in motors to the deserted palace of Akbar at Fatehpur Sikri, some twenty miles distant. It is easy to understand why it was deserted, but difficult to comprehend why even an Oriental despot should have set down a gigantic palace in so barren and waterless a region. Mr. Sanderson again acted as guide to the Queen, to the great good fortune of those who were lucky enough to be with Her Majesty; and the hours passed rapidly as we wandered through the deserted courts and chambers or stood in the hall of audience with its marvellously carved superstructure, where the greatest of the Mogul Emperors received the petitions of suitors and meted out justice to high and low. The buildings are interesting, too, as including an effort at a feature which the Mohammedan architects as a rule neglected, a great flight of steps. What they understood best was gateways, but steps for some reason were beyond them. The stairways in the buildings of the Mogul period are always bad, so high, steep and narrow indeed, even in the zenanas, that one wonders how the little ladies of the harem can have climbed up them. Even the different levels of the platforms of the Taj are connected by stepping-stones and not by steps. At Fatehpur Sikri, however, below the magnificent gateway is an attempt at a flight of steps, which, if executed, as it might have been, on a great scale and carried down the side of the height, on which the palace stands, to the plain, would have been one of the most magnificent architectural objects in the world. Dec. 19.

On the morning of the 19th, after a last visit to the Taj, the Queen left Agra by train for Jaipur, where she arrived in the evening. At the station she was met by the Maharaja, who laid his sword at her feet with the chivalrous courtesy of the East; and from thence she drove some two miles to the Residency through a host of the Maharaja's armed retainers. Very picturesque was the spectacle that they presented, in colours of every variety and shade—red, orange, dark green, pea-green, sage-green. Here there was a long row of stately mace-bearers; hard by a troop of gorgeous spearmen on Arab horses; beyond them imposing ranks of matchlockmen. Here again were companies of fifty or sixty camels, some carrying wild-looking warriors with lances, others heavy swivel-guns, which must have been most dangerous in the field, yet others a few kettle-drummers of inexhaustible thumping power; there stood a noble array of forty elephants with their faces coloured in fantastic patterns, and gorgeous housings of gold and silver on their backs; here an assembly of half-naked Nagas with gigantic quivering swords; there a train of great grey bullocks harnessed to gorgeous litters, to humbler carriages or to quaintly painted guns, their sleek hides often hidden by pea-green housings and their horns by pea-green cases, but their great

Dec. 19. soft eyes looking kindly upon the world. And the drummers drummed, and the pipers piped, and the horses pranced, and the patient elephants saluted, and the Nagas leaped, and the spearmen, flintlockmen and matchlockmen brandished or presented arms; and so through a blaze of colour and every description of gleaming weapon Her Majesty drove to the Residency. It was a true Oriental welcome, where a host displays all that he has as a courtly intimation that it is at the disposal of his guest. Arrived at the Residency the Queen was received by the Resident, Colonel Showers; and the suite had just time before dark to learn the ways of a very comfortable camp, pitched in the garden. The day ended with a small dinner-party given by Her Majesty.

On the morning of the 20th the Maharaja had motors waiting at the door; and the Queen with her suite drove to the deserted town of Amber, which lies in a deep cleft of the hills, seven miles from Jaipur. Here Her Majesty mounted an elephant and, followed by her suite likewise on elephants, went up the steep ascent to the palace built by Raja Man Singh, the favourite of the Emperor Akbar, in 1592. Amber has been described by Mr. Kipling, and therefore needs no description from me. In bygone ages it was a stronghold of the aboriginal Meenas who were dispossessed, through highly questionable methods, by a family of Rajputs at the end of the tenth century of our era; and with the Rajputs it has remained ever since. A huge deserted city set with deserted temples and crowned by a deserted palace, none of them of any great architectural interest, is a sufficiently bleak and melancholy object, even when repeopled by such an imagination as Mr. Kipling's. But there is eloquent testimony to the troubled past of India in the choice of such a site for a city as a gap in the barrenest hills of a barren country, approachable only through narrow and dangerous defiles and defended by ring within ring of walls and towers and circular bastions. The fortifications crumble without, and the houses clustered upon the steep hillsides crumble within. The men who dwelt in them must have lived in fear and trembling. One may still see in the palace a hall supported by columns which at their core are of carved sandstone, but have been cased in stucco. The Emperor Jahangir, hearing that there were pillars at Amber which vied with the glories of Agra and Delhi, in high wrath sent commissioners to overthrow them. The Raja, however, had been warned; and when the commissioners arrived they found nothing more ambitious than stucco, with which he had prudently veiled the perilous glory of the sandstone. No doubt he was wise in his generation; but in so strong a place as Amber one would have preferred him to defy the Emperor and stand a siege. Dec. 20.

In the evening the Queen gave a second small dinner-party, at the close of which the Maharaja's Naga warriors danced a war-dance.

Dec. 21. The characteristics of all war-dances are the same—much brandishing of weapons, much leaping in the air, and remarkably little clothing—so that it is not worth while to describe this one at greater length. One is inclined to agree with Corporal Trim that one push of the bayonet is worth the whole of it.

On the morning of the next day the Queen took leave of the Maharaja and started with her suite for Ajmer, which was reached early in the afternoon. At the station she was received by the Resident, Sir Elliot Colvin, and from thence drove straight to Mayo College, the place of education favoured by all ruling Princes for their sons, and therefore called the Eton of India. After inspecting the college buildings under the guidance of the Principal, Mr. Waddington, Her Majesty proceeded to the cricket pavilion, on the sloping front of which were banked up the whole of the two hundred students, making the most beautiful group of colour which we saw in India. All wore native dress—a cassock of rich material and delicate colour buttoned from neck to waist, and with long skirts from the waist to the heel, and a turban of stronger and more decided tint. The Queen requested that every one of them might be presented to her individually; and accordingly they filed past her, each bowing gracefully over his hands pressed palm to palm before him, and returning to his place. The Queen then obtained for them an extra week's holiday, the grant of which they received in silence, bowing almost to their knees. One could not help contrasting their behaviour both on this occasion and when presented to the Queen with the awkward self-consciousness of English boys in parallel circumstances. The elder students then withdrew, and presently reappeared mounted on polo-ponies, on which, while the Queen drank tea with the Principal, they went through such sports as tent-pegging by sections, jumping by sections, and a "bending race." Finally, when the light began to fail Her Majesty drove to the quarters prepared for her at the Residency. Dec. 21.

This building, beautifully situated on the top of a steep eminence, overlooks the lake of Ajmer, along one side of which lies the town with a stern fortified height rising behind it; while on the other is a narrow stretch of plain bounded by a wall of rugged rocky hills. The situation and surroundings of the town suggest a home of romance, and such a home Ajmer undoubtedly was. The foundation of the citadel by the royal race of Chauhan Rajputs is lost in extreme antiquity, but it seems certain that as early as A.D. 712 these Princes were the most determined opponents of Mohammedan invasion. Three hundred years later the mighty Mahmoud of Ghazni fell back, foiled and wounded from before Ajmer; and it was not until 1556 that it was finally occupied by Akbar, upon whom, as also upon both of his two immediate successors, it exerted an irresistible fascination. Here it was

Dec. 21. that Jahangir received Sir Thomas Roe, the ambassador of King James the First of Britain, in 1615, and here it was that the same Emperor and his son Shah Jahan spent their happiest days with their adored wives Nur Mahal and Mumtaz Mahal. Possibly it was the place last recalled to memory by the dying Shah Jahan, as he looked with dim eyes from his palace at Agra to the Taj, and knew that the time was come at last for him to rejoin his beloved under the white dome where they still sleep side by side in peace.

The hill on which the Residency stands is so steep that only a few tents could be pitched near the house; and the main most comfortable camp was situated on the plain at its foot. The Queen gave a small dinner-party in the evening; and after dinner every one sought the terrace of the Residency to see the illuminations of the lake, the fort and the city. The art of illumination is nowhere so perfectly understood as in India, where it is not confined to hard straight lines of glaring electric light on public buildings, but follows the beautiful curves of lake and hill, fortress and bastion, in myriads of tiny flames fed by oil only. The cost is trifling, for little earthenware bowls, wicks and oil are all alike cheap: and hundreds of natives can be found, for the reward of a few pence, to arrange them by natural instinct in perfect order.

On the morning of the 22nd the Queen with her suite drove in motors through a pass in the ring of hills to Pushkar, a village about nine miles Dec. 22. distant, where there is a tank which is of peculiar sanctity to the Hindus and therefore the resort of many pilgrims. Part of the road was extremely steep, and the country, as commonly in Rajputana, is miserably barren and inhospitable; but as usual on every progress of the Queen during this tour, the people swarmed up from no one knew whence to see her go by. Pushkar itself, a picturesque village of a single long narrow street, was alive with spectators, the women being clustered like flies on the roofs, where their deep red clothing made a delightful mass of rich colour. The tank itself is about five hundred yards in diameter, and surrounded on all sides by the houses of Rajput and Maratha chiefs, with steps down to the water. At the end of the village is a temple, to which the Queen ascended by many steps to wild music of pipe and tabor, and left, after the precedent of all distinguished visitors before her, a present of fifteen hundred rupees. As usual on such occasions the ministers of the temple were ready with garlands which they hung round the necks of all their visitors. At a *ghat* (landing-stage) hard by the inhabitants presented the Queen with an address, and there was more hanging of garlands. In curious contrast to the festal appearance of the village, fakirs, smeared with ashes, sat here and there about the shrines, with limbs hideously deformed and atrophied by sitting for months and even years in the same

Dec. 22. natural or distorted posture. One of them, who sat motionless but for the twitching of his fingers as he told his beads, had a singularly beautiful face, and would have seemed from his closed eyes and grey-stained features to be dead indeed to the world, had not close observation revealed that, when not conscious of being watched, he opened his eyes and took a lively interest in things mundane.

In the afternoon Her Majesty, with her suite in attendance, again drove out; and the Cadet Corps of Mayo College asked and obtained permission to furnish her escort. A very fine appearance they made in the white tunics and sky-blue turbans of the Noble Guard; and if there was more cantering and less trotting than an orthodox riding-master might have approved, the Queen at any rate found no fault with the characteristic eagerness of young men mounted on young horses. The objects of Her Majesty's visit were a Mohammedan mosque and a Hindu temple of peculiar holiness, named respectively the Dargah and Adhai-din-ka-Jhoara, the former of little architectural interest, but the latter possessing a fine Hindu screen and hall of pillars. As usual the adornment was in detail most beautiful, but the general effect, to an eye trained in the Hellenic school, was marred by the impression of excessive decoration. It is impossible, however, to visit any Hindu or Mohammedan building of any architectural pretension without lamenting that our Roman and Gothic scripts fall so far behind the Arabic and Persian, or indeed almost any Oriental character, in grace and variety. Bands and panels filled with texts possess in the East a decorative value such as we cannot approach in the West. Dec. 23

On the morning of the 23rd the Queen and her suite left Ajmer on a journey of about one hundred miles by motor to Bundi. Her Majesty stopped on the way to visit the sites of projected memorials to King Edward VII. and Sir Curzon Wyllie, and to receive the valedictory salutations of the students of Mayo College, who were drawn up at the entrance to the grounds. She also caused speed to be reduced when passing by the orphan school of the Scotch mission at Nasirabad, so that the children might see her. A drearier country it would be difficult to traverse—mile upon mile of stony desert dotted with thorns, or from time to time varied by a patch of uncomely and unprofitable jungle. Here and there only was a patch of cultivation. The sole excitement was the overhauling of motors which had broken down, and the only amusement the multitude of conflicting opinions as to the best method of restoring their suspended animation. After three hours we reached an oasis—Deoli—where Her Majesty was received at the Agency by the Agent, Major Peacock, and a halt was made for luncheon. The Deoli Regiment has its quarters here, and Colonel Waller and his officers had most kindly arranged for shooting a large

Dec. 23. tank[1] or mere, about eleven miles farther on the road, in case any of the Queen's suite should care for the sport. Two of them were very ready for it, and were well rewarded. The evening was delightfully warm and nearly cloudless, and the sun went down slowly and reluctantly in a blaze of scarlet and orange, which was reflected on the still surface of the mere—a sheet of water perhaps three miles in circumference, dotted with tiny islands, overhung in places with low-roofed temples, and fringed with a margin of green, doubly refreshing to the eye after some days of travel through the desert of Rajputana. And in the air was every description of water-bird, cranes and storks and coots and endless varieties of duck. When they came within range, they taxed one's best skill to bring them down, and, when they did not, it was an equal pleasure to watch them and the beautiful scene around. After about two hours, darkness drove us reluctantly back to our motors, with a bag of close upon one hundred and fifty duck, widgeon and teal to five guns; and we were fain to take leave of our most hospitable hosts and resume our journey.

The Maharao Raja of Bundi, true to the

[1] It is curious that the word tank should be invariably used in India where in England we should employ the words, pond, mere or even lake. Derived through the French *estang*, *étang* from the Latin *stagnum*, the word tank (or, in its earlier form, stank) is known to me best through old deeds, where it generally signifies the reservoir of water for turning a water-mill. On the other hand, the word creek universally used in America and the Australasian Colonies to signify a stream or river, is never heard in India, and rarely, if ever, in this sense in England.

courtesy of his race, had meanwhile come forward to the marches of his territory to escort Her Majesty to her camp. We belated ones of the shooting-party, however, had the rare experience of traversing the city of Bundi after dark. We entered a narrow defile between high rocky hills, and plunged into a labyrinth of narrow, tortuous streets, through which it seemed hopeless to attempt to make one's way. Again and again, not knowing the road, we found ourselves in what appeared to be a blind alley, from which sometimes, though not always, a narrow lane turning at the sharpest of angles led us into a fresh puzzle of the same kind. But these delays were welcome, for the sight was extraordinary. The whole city was lit up in honour of the occasion, and was swarming with people, whose brilliant sashes and turbans of orange and yellow and red, passing continuously from deep shadow into glaring light, against the background of their white robes, presented marvellous effects of colour. At length we passed through the city and reached our tents, which were arranged in three sides of a square on a carefully prepared lawn of grass, making the prettiest and most comfortable camp that we encountered in the whole of the tour. Even Her Majesty was for once lodged in a tent, and was well content to be so in such a camp. Dec. 2

On the morning of the 24th the Maharao Raja came with carriages to escort the Queen to his palace, and Her Majesty accordingly drove

Dec. 24. off with him followed by her suite. The palace, a huge white building, stands on the side of a very steep hill within a fortified enceinte, with two outer lines of fortification above, and the town crouching below it. The entrance is reached by a very steep paved ramp, from three to four hundred yards long, at the head of which one turns at right angles in to the gateway. The scene here was one which an artist might have despaired of setting on canvas. The Maharao Raja had provided palanquins to carry the whole party up the ascent; and the bearers, some in scarlet robes and yellow turbans, mingled with guards in rich dark green or in yellow, were scattered about at the foot of the ramp; the gorgeous silver palanquin, which was to be occupied by the Queen, blazing like fire in the midst of them. Hard by stood the leading nobles of Bundi, a group of some twenty or thirty splendid figures with beards brushed fiercely away from the face, but all, whether the beards were grey or white, bearing the unmistakable mark of high lineage and ancient race. The Maharao Raja was dressed in a black gown with an orange turban, and a broad orange shawl of different shade round the waist. Most of the nobles wore the same colours over a white linen gown with bell-shaped skirts; but a few added new and different touches of colour. One was in sky blue with three shades of yellow—from sulphur to orange—in turban and shawl; another had a gown of deep chocolate brown,

THE MAHARAO. THE QUEEN-EMPRESS.

IN THE PALACE OF BUNDI.

To face page 220.

relieved by brilliant green round head and waist; and a third, whose hair was white, wore dove-colour and crimson. All looked well; it seems to be impossible for them to err in the choice and blending of colours. Then the palanquin-bearers took up their burdens, and the whole party—royal, noble and simple—streamed in irregular procession up the ramp under the lofty weather-worn white walls of the inner enceinte, with the sun blazing down upon them—a sight such as a man does not see twice in a lifetime. Dec. 24.

Over the gateway, as usual, pipers and drummers made strenuous music as Her Majesty entered; and within the courtyard we came upon the lower walls of the main building, towering up to a gigantic height and looking all the higher for being somewhat narrow. The palace, which was built in 1644, shows no great variation from the usual Hindu architecture of the period, though to me, personally, it was more pleasing than most, being chaste and subdued in decoration. A detailed description would be tedious, and it can only be said that under the guidance of the Maharao Raja, Her Majesty and her suite roamed with perfect contentment over the palace for an hour and a half. Above all, they admired the armoury, a beautiful little hall, supported by columns which (a rare thing in India) were ornamented on the capital only and were perfectly plain in the shaft, so that for once they looked stout enough to carry the roof. From the very summit the view of city

Dec. 24. and lake below was magnificent, while in the foreground the grace of the cupolas and of the inner courts of the ladies' apartments was delightful. Altogether I think that of all the sights seen in the Queen's tour in Rajputana, the palace of Bundi was the most enjoyable, and in some respects the most interesting.

From the palace the Maharao escorted the Queen to a very beautiful garden, which is the place of cremation of the dead of the reigning family, and contains domed pavilions which are the cenotaphs erected to their memory. Simple and unpretentious, yet lacking neither richness nor dignity in due measure, this Valhalla has a pathos and a charm that is all its own. The garden has no ostentatious gloom of cypresses, but cheerful spreading trees and broad spaces of sunlight and shade in which the domes stand white and silent, telling that this is a resting-place of the dead, indeed, but of the happy dead.

A visit to the Maharao Raja's hunting-box through three miles of jungle brought the morning and a too short visit to Bundi to a close. After luncheon His Highness came to take his leave of the Queen; and Her Majesty, followed by the suite, started by motor for Kotah, under thirty miles away. Here again the Maharao of Kotah came forth to escort Her Majesty when she entered his borders, with artillery to fire a salute, musicians, elephants and a host of armed retainers. Very welcome

THE QUEEN. THE MAHARAO.

IN THE PALACE OF BUNDI.

To face page 222.

was the sight of the Chambal, flowing broad Dec. 25.
and deep, for we had wandered for days through arid country over endless dry watercourses, but without a glimpse of a running stream. Here, too, memory called up a thought of the remnants of Monson's army of 1804, weary, dispirited and demoralised, dragging themselves painfully away from the city where the Raja dared not offer them asylum. Her Majesty proceeded to the Agency, where she was received by the Political Agent, Colonel Berkeley, while the rest of us found quarters in a camp, as usual most comfortable, in the grounds. In the evening Her Majesty, her suite, and the few Europeans at Kotah attended Divine Service in a tent.

Christmas Day opened with Divine Service in the same tent; and in the afternoon the Maharao provided two launches for a trip up the Chambal, himself accompanying Her Majesty in one, and leaving three rifles with the men of the party, as he had arranged to beat the jungles on the banks. Her Majesty returned in time for tea, having seen four bears making away; and the second launch was following hers when the villagers shouted that they could see a leopard. The banks of the Chambal rise in sheer cliffs of sandstone to a height of about forty feet above the water; and on a ledge just below the summit we caught sight of the leopard from the launch, while he at the same moment caught sight of us and crouched down. It was curious to watch him. The animal was

Dec. 26. halting between two opinions, having one eye upon us, and the other upon a bullock fifty yards away, which had been tied up for his delectation and towards which he was making his way. For half an hour he remained motionless, until some beaters crossed the river from the other bank and moved him, when he bounded quietly along a ledge of the cliff like a cat on a garden wall. A lively fusillade greeted him from the launch, and he fell down the face of the cliff as if dead, but recovered himself and continued his flight along a lower ledge, where he crept into a deep cleft and disappeared, no doubt to die. On this evening, being Christmas night, Her Majesty asked the whole of her suite to dine with her, even as the King at the same moment was entertaining the whole of his suite in Nipal. As the party broke up, we came upon the Maharao on his way to inspect the sentries and turn out the guard of the Kotah Regiment at the Agency, a duty which His Highness fulfilled punctually on every night of the Queen's stay.

On the morning of the 26th the Queen drove with her suite to the Maharao's palace, the Maharao in person commanding the escort of Her Majesty's carriage, and afterwards conducting her over the building. Perhaps the most remarkable thing to be seen in it was the collection of arms and armour, which included some wonderfully beautiful specimens of native workmanship. Indeed it may be questioned whether Indian art ever exhibits itself to greater advantage than in the decoration of weapons, whether it be applied to the handle of a sword or to the barrel of a matchlock. After luncheon the Queen and her party, under the Maharao's guidance, went to the tank of Abhera, at a short distance from the city, where a dozen alligators, one of them very large, came swimming up from a distance at the call of the keeper to be fed. Great efforts were made to induce them to put their heads on the landing steps in search of food, in order that their portraits might be taken by photograph, but they were too shy to make the venture. An endeavour to hold them in the necessary position by a rude wooden hook was equally unsuccessful. They swallowed the bait greedily, but speedily disgorged it on feeling the strain of the line. They therefore forfeited such chances of immortality as the camera can confer. Dec. 26.

In the evening the Queen gave a small dinner-party; and at night the city, the banks and the islands of the Chambal were illuminated with very beautiful effect. The Indians have a real genius for seizing the finest lines of a contour for illumination, and for making the most of the effect by breaking those lines at intervals with little structures of bamboo which, at a short distance, present the appearance of tiny towers of flame. While the Queen was still watching and admiring, there arose a sound of much trumpeting on the other side of the house;

Dec. 27. and there were seen six or eight elephants and as many horses, gorgeously caparisoned, while the verandah was literally covered with the most costly and beautiful of Indian and Persian fabrics, mingled with a few caskets of priceless jewels. This was the ceremony of the *Pesh Kash*, signifying that the Maharao laid all of his most precious possessions at the feet of Queen Mary for her acceptance. Her Majesty accordingly inspected the costly gift, and then, as is customary, remitted it, fully appreciating that this compliment is the highest and most sincere that an Indian Prince can tender to his suzerain.

On the 27th the Maharao, being very anxious to show the Queen a wild tiger in the jungle, arranged to beat the Bundi jungle some eight miles from Kotah, and conveyed Her Majesty and the suite thither in motors, providing rifles for such of the gentlemen as had not brought them from England. Arrived at the jungle Her Majesty with her ladies and Lord Shaftesbury were stationed on a broad platform constructed at some height up a tree. Other guns were likewise installed in trees to right and left; and it was I think the inward wish of every one that the tiger might pass close to the Queen and fall, if not to Lord Shaftesbury's rifle, then to that of Prince George of Battenberg, who was as keen as only a midshipman ashore can be. The beaters, quite half of them native soldiers in khaki uniform, then started to drive the jungle towards the guns with wild shouts and screams, mingled with terrific aspersions upon the tiger's ancestry and upon the virtue of his female relations. All the most nervous inhabitants of the jungle at once hurried forward, a crowd of pea-hens the foremost, then the young cocks and finally the old cocks, the most cunning of which lay fast just in sight of the guns, watching for an opportunity to fly back. Last of all came the tiger, slowly slinking forward; but such is the perversity of the feline nature that instead of passing near the Queen, he made straight for the two guns next to the right of Her Majesty, who happened to be the one a man of letters and the other a man of drugs. The former had drawn by lot the right of first shot, but so intensely interested was he in watching the creature's movements that he quite forgot the rifle in his hand, and waiting far too long, he let slip his chance of an easy shot, and only sent an erratic bullet crashing through the bushes when it was too late. Dec. 27.

However, it was thought that the tiger would not have gone far, and the Maharao determined to drive the jungle back in the hope of recovering him. The new beat therefore began, and with diabolic persistence everything again made for the same two guns—first a sambhur, then a pig, both of which were allowed to go by, and lastly the tiger, this time galloping fast. Happily he came in full view of the Queen, but unfortunately not of Lord Shaftesbury, who had more ground to

Dec. 27. command than one gun could watch; and hence it was that for the second time he passed nearest to the two erudite guns on the right flank. This time it was the man of drugs who fired. Tiger-shooting was no novelty to him; but the shot was a difficult one, and the animal galloped off unhurt. The Maharao, however, tried yet another beat over the same ground; and the beaters, being now reinforced by drums, bugles and abundance of blank cartridge, raised din enough to make any self-respecting animal seek new lodgings at once in a quieter neighbourhood. Nothing, however, came forward but a black bear, which was killed by Lord Shaftesbury. Her Majesty therefore had at least the satisfaction of seeing the picturesque assembly of men and elephants which gathers together on such occasions for the removal of the corpse; and so ended a very amusing day, unfortunately the last of Her Majesty's tour.

The morning of the 28th was taken up in preparations for departure; and with keen regret we had to take leave not only of the generous host who had done so much for the amusement and pleasure of Her Majesty and her suite, but of Colonel Bannerman, who was in charge of all the arrangements for the tour. At noon the Queen entered the Royal train; the Maharao, with the princely courtesy which had marked his every action, attending Her Majesty to the last minute; and our rambles about Rajputana had come to an end. Everything concerning it had been easy and pleasant from beginning to close. The evenings and nights had grown steadily warmer at every change of station, while the days were so gloriously fine and cloudless as to make us very sympathetic with sun-worship. The air of Rajputana is incredibly bracing; it is, in fact, rather too like champagne, for it sometimes causes headache in the morning. The people are both friendly and courteous, while their tall figures and the daring colours which they wear make them a perpetual delight to the eye. At every progress of the Queen they came in swarms to greet her; even on the railway there were crowds at every station, whether it were a stopping-place or not, and not a man allowed the Royal train to pass without a salute. As to the Rajput nobles and their chiefs, Her Majesty's hosts, they were delighted beyond measure at the opportunity of displaying their loyalty and devotion to the King-Emperor and the Queen-Empress; and that with no fulsome ostentation of self-abasement, but with the chivalry that comes naturally to a proud and ancient race. Dec. 28.

Arriving at five o'clock at Guna the Queen found the Thirty-eighth Central India Horse drawn up by the station to receive her, and alighted to see them pass in review before her, and to drink tea with the officers. The two regiments of Central India Horse were formed in 1859 and 1860 to suppress the brigandage to which the defeated mutineers had resorted after

Dec. 29. the British victories at Delhi and Lucknow. They are not what is called parade-regiments, and I have seen many that marched past better than the Thirty-eighth ; but a finer body of men it would be hard to find, and their appearance showed them to be what they actually are, ready for work in the field at the shortest notice. After the review Her Majesty resumed her journey, always through great crowds of people, and rejoining the King on the evening of the 29th at Bankipore, travelled from thence to Calcutta in company with His Majesty.

XIII

Calcutta was reached at noon of the 30th. Their Majesties were received at the station by the Governor-General and Lady Hardinge ; and after the presentation of the officials of the railway and the inspection of the guard of honour, they embarked on the steamship *Howrah* to cross the river Hugli. At the moment of embarkation a salute of one hundred and one guns was fired by H.M.S. *Highflyer*, whose men lined decks and gave three cheers for Their Majesties as they passed. All the ships in the river were dressed with bunting, and the bridge of boats was packed from end to end with a dense crowd of spectators. Upon landing at Prinsep's Ghat a procession was formed to an amphitheatre containing some two thousand spectators, where a dais and thrones

THE PROCESSION INTO CALCUTTA—THE QUEEN-EMPRESS IN HER CARRIAGE.

To face page 231.

had been erected under a canopy. Here Their Majesties took their seats; and the Lieutenant-Governor then presented first the members of his Executive Council, next the Indian Princes of Bengal, and lastly, in groups, the members of the principal municipal and administrative bodies. This done, an address of welcome was read from the Corporation, to which the King read a cordial reply; and Their Majesties then entered a carriage drawn by six horses for their State entry into the city; the escort being composed of the Viceroy's bodyguard, two regiments of regular cavalry, a battery of Horse Artillery and a body of Volunteer Light Horse. Dec. 30.

The greater part of the route was lined with stands, and for some distance it ran alongside the Maidan, which is the Hyde Park, on a greater scale, of Calcutta. The crowd of spectators was enormous. For days the country people around had been pouring into the city. There was ample space for them to stand in the Maidan, and they were ranked to an amazing depth in this open space, where, the ground being a dead flat, it is to be feared that tens of thousands could see nothing. Whole lengths of plaster balustrade were thrown down by the press, but there was no disorder; and, whether they could see or not, all the people were enthusiastic to a degree which astonished every English resident. The Bengali is a man who rarely smiles, unless at jests which perhaps he would do better to receive with gravity; but he proved by grave

Dec. 30. salutations and loud acclaim that he shared the deep feeling of reverence, manifested alike at Delhi and on the journey in Nipal, for the person of the King-Emperor.

On arrival at Government House the King and Queen were received by the Viceroy and Lady Hardinge; a great number of other officials, civil and military, being also in attendance, some of whom were presented to Their Majesties. Government House was, pardonably enough, too small to hold Their Majesties, Lord Hardinge's guests and the whole of the King's suite; so a great many of us found ourselves again under canvas, very comfortably lodged in the garden within a stone's throw of the house. The only drawback was that we were within a stone's throw also of the public street and of some very noisy trams; but that was in the circumstances inevitable, being due entirely to the persons, long since forgotten, who blundered in the planning of Government House grounds a century ago. It is satisfactory to think—or at any rate to hope—that the Governor-General will be more worthily housed in the new capital than he is at present in Calcutta. In the afternoon Their Majesties, attended by the Viceroy and Lady Hardinge, visited the Zoological Gardens, which it may be remarked are exceedingly good and attractive in Calcutta; and so the first day in the capital came to an end.

On Sunday the 31st the King and Queen attended Divine Service in the cathedral, where the Bishop of Calcutta preached the sermon, and in the afternoon the Queen visited the Botanical Gardens under the guidance of Major Gage, the superintendent. Monday, the 1st of January 1912, was also comparatively a quiet day, the only functions being Their Majesties' visit to the polo-ground in the afternoon to witness a match between the Thirteenth Hussars and the Scouts, and a State dinner to nearly one hundred guests at Government House. The festival of the Mohurram being in progress, the streets were densely crowded. On Tuesday the 2nd there was the usual "Proclamation Parade" to commemorate the assumption of the title of Empress of India by Queen Victoria, which took place in the presence of Their Majesties; but this, being an affair of fewer than ten thousand men, seemed small after the fifty thousand at Delhi. Curiously enough, however, the excellences and defects of Delhi were exactly reproduced. The Volunteers, both cavalry and infantry, made a very creditable display; but the gallop past of the regular cavalry and horse artillery was too headlong, with the usual result that there was a lagging gun in the battery and great appearance of raggedness among the cavalry. The Sixteenth Lancers, a Hindu regiment, was perhaps that which acquitted itself best. In the afternoon the King and Queen were present at a garden party, to which the Viceroy had invited some two thousand guests; and in the evening His Majesty held a levee at Govern- Jan. 1-2.

Jan. 3. ment House, at which there was a very large attendance.

On the 3rd the King drove to the polo-ground to witness the final match of the Calcutta Coronation Polo Tournament between the Tenth Hussars and the Scouts, and at the conclusion handed the cup, which was his gift, to the Scouts who were the winning team. In the afternoon Their Majesties drove to the Calcutta Races, the fourth race being for a cup presented by the King-Emperor, which was won by Mr. J. C. Galstaun's horse, Brogue, and placed in the owner's hands by His Majesty. In the evening after dinner Their Majesties witnessed a torchlight tattoo in the Maidan from a pavilion erected near the southern entrance to Government House.

First, the Sixteenth Cavalry executed a musical ride, carrying torches at the end of their lances, and ended a very good performance by a wild charge down to the Royal pavilion, where they halted sharply, saluted and retired. Next men of the Black Watch danced a sword-dance, and men of the Twenty-seventh Punjabis some description of war-dance round a huge fire. The infantry, about two thousand strong, then advanced, all dressed in white, and after a number of intricate manœuvres, both at the quick step and at the double, formed battalion before the Royal pavilion, and saluted. Their movements were executed principally in single file, which is the right formation for a tattoo, so that they covered the plain with winding fiery lines;

while the illumination of the trees, as usual in admirable taste, made a fine background of fixed beacons. Altogether this tattoo was extremely well managed and a very beautiful sight. Even the fireworks, with which the display ended, could not outshine it. But perhaps the most remarkable spectacle of all was the crowd. Natives of India love nothing better than illuminations and fireworks, and they were present literally in hundreds of thousands. A great length of stands had been erected along the Maidan for spectators who had paid sufficient sums for a seat; but the greater part of the space, so far as I could see, was silently appropriated by the populace before the ticket-holders arrived. The roads of approach were more hopelessly blocked than any that I have ever seen even in London on the greatest occasions; and the police—perhaps they could hardly be blamed—completely lost control of the traffic, at any rate for some time. Yet the crowd was most orderly, civil and good-tempered, and there was no trouble of any kind, though many carriages were unable to come near the ground at all, and many that did reach it can hardly have been released before dawn. Jan. 3.

On the morning of the 4th the King-Emperor drove in a motor to the site of the Victoria Memorial Building, and later proceeded to the Calcutta Museum, where the treasures designed for exhibition in the Memorial Hall are temporarily displayed. The Queen-Empress also

Jan. 4-5. visited the Museum in the course of the morning, under the guidance of Mr. Percy Brown, and was particularly interested in the exquisite drawings by native artists, and in the portraits of the so-called "Patna School," who were native artists under the influence of English miniaturists. In the afternoon Their Majesties went to a horse-show and jumping competition at the Tollygunge Club, at the close of which the Queen distributed the prizes to the successful competitors, one of whom was the Commander-in-Chief. In the evening, after the King had held an investiture, Their Majesties held a court in the Throne-room at Government House.

On the 5th the King and Queen went down the Hugli to visit the jute factories of Sir David Yule, who had been knighted on the previous day; and, enlightened by his explanations, inspected with the greatest interest everything that was to be seen of this important Indian industry. In the afternoon Their Majesties drove to the Maidan to witness a pageant which had been organised for the occasion. On arriving at the pavilion set apart for them they were received by the Lieutenant-Governor of Bengal, the Nawab of Murshidabad, the Maharajadhiraja of Burdwan and other members of the committee; and then followed an interesting ceremony. The Maharaja of Gidhour handed a purse of one hundred and one gold mohurs to the Nawab, who presented it as *Pesh Kash* to His Majesty from the people of Bengal, Orissa and Behar, Eastern Bengal and

Assam. The Nawab was of course attired in rich native dress, and wore on his right arm an enormous flat engraved emerald, more than an inch square—an historic jewel and talisman which attracted many covetous female eyes. Jan. 5.

The pageant itself came next, and consisted of two processions, first the Nawroz or New Year's Day procession of Murshidabad, and secondly the Dasehara. The festival of Nawroz itself goes back to very remote times in Persia; but the processions were first instituted by Akbar, the contemporary of Queen Elizabeth, and adopted by the Nawabs of Murshidabad in the time of our Queen Anne, since which date they have been regularly kept up. The Dasehara traces its origin far back to the mythological traditions of the Hindus, having been established to commemorate the final triumph of Rama the King of Oudh, in whom the god Vishnu for the good of men took incarnate shape, over Ravana, the King of an island, now submerged, in the south of India. Both processions in the Maidan strictly followed former precedents, and the equipment of "properties," if the term may be permitted, was furnished by the generosity of some of the greatest of the Ruling Chiefs. The pageant displayed a train of elephants, camels and horses, all in sumptuous housings and trappings, interspersed with small parties of men armed with every description of weapon; and in the case of the Dasehara a special feature was furnished by two gorgeous gilded cars, drawn by

Jan. 5. elephants, the one containing court poets and literary men, and the other personations of the Indian King and his courtiers. Otherwise the pageant was simply a defile of much the same interesting and picturesque figures as the Maharaja of Jaipur had stationed along the road for the reception of the Queen, and depended not a little for its effect upon schemes of colour.

As such it was certainly successful. Elephants are so staid and wise that it is always a pleasure to see them in numbers; and their stately carriage makes them worthy bearers of huge cloths that are one sheet of gold thread and of howdahs that gleam with the precious metals. Camels also, if well groomed and of good breed, can wear fine raiment with dignity, though no camel can share in the doings of man without evincing, at any rate outwardly, intense and unconquerable boredom. Arab stallions can also carry off the splendour of sumptuous trappings; and dancing horses, especially when they dance past for a hundred yards on their hind legs, are at least a surprise. Scatter these broadcast among troops of horsemen and of footmen, each troop in flowing robes of green and blue, or red and yellow, no two being of the same shade; let the whole file past in not very regular order; and there, roughly speaking, is the pageant. If there be a criticism which might justly be passed upon it, it is that the clothes of the actors were rather too new, and in many cases suggested aniline dyes.

As an interlude there was a war-dance of Paiks, a relic of ancient warriors of Orissa, whose duties are now practically those of Palace-guards to the native princes of that province. Half of them were stained grey with ashes and dressed in scanty garments of blue, and the other half stained with yellow and arrayed in pink, so that the contrast of colour should be complete. Lastly, it must be mentioned that the entire pageant went forward to the accompaniment of music by living Indian composers, arranged for performers whose instruments had been carefully copied from ancient models—a new and interesting experiment upon which only a well-trained musician could pronounce an opinion. To the inexpert ear the music seemed to bear very strong traces of European influence. Perhaps the most striking moment of the whole display came after all the actors had defiled past the King, when, having formed an irregular line a thousand yards in length across the Maidan, they made a general advance in review order, to use a military phrase, towards Their Majesties. Jan. 5.

So much must be said for the pageant itself, but an even more wonderful scene was to follow. An immense crowd had assembled to witness the show, the great bulk of which was gathered in a huge semicircle behind the stage, so to speak, and in face of Their Majesties and of the stands erected for privileged spectators. At the close of the entertainment the King and Queen entered their carriage and drove very slowly along the

Jan. 5. whole length of this great ring and within a couple of yards of it, so that all could see them. It was a happy inspiration. The people—and these really were the people—received them with deep reverence and joyful acclaim; the men bowed to the ground, and the women uttered the peculiar guttural sound which is reserved for the religious service of the temple only. There was nothing to restrain them, or prevent them from swarming over the carriage, but they made no attempt to do so, well content to have looked upon the face of their King. Only when the Royal procession had at last moved off did they break loose, and then with one impulse they flew across the open sward to the King's pavilion, pierced through the guard of soldiers as if it had been made of paper, and, catching up the earth which had been trodden by the King's feet, pressed it in lowly homage to their brows. To our cold Western notions such an action may seem to be extravagant; but the multitude which shouted "Life and Victory to Charles Augustus, crowned by God, the peace-giving Emperor," round the basilica of St. Peter on Christmas Day of the year 800, would have understood it. The Bengalis in the past have been a patient but never a combatant people. They did not struggle desperately like the Rajputs, and fall back into the desert sooner than yield their independence. They remained upon their rich lands, and bowed their heads in submission to each succeeding wave of conquest;

AN INDIAN GREETING TO THEIR MAJESTIES.

To face page 240.

and the testimony to the keenness of their prolonged suffering is their adoration of the peace-giving Emperor, through whose authority the poor man may sow in full confidence that he will also reap. It may be that in the West also coming years will see political differences decided by the primitive method of force, and a weary people prostrating themselves before some soldier, as did the French before Napoleon in 1799, because he has restored order and enabled inoffensive citizens once more to do their daily work in quietness. Jan. 5-6.

During the drive home the people again burst the barriers and swarmed all round the Royal carriage with an enthusiasm such as not only had never been seen, but had never even been dreamed of. The evening of the 5th closed with a ball at Government House, to which a select number of guests were invited by the Viceroy and Lady Hardinge to meet Their Majesties. At half-past eight on the morning of the 6th the King was on his horse, riding out to visit the camps of the troops. In the forenoon His Majesty received a deputation from the University of Calcutta, while the Queen visited a number of philanthropic institutes and hospitals. Their Majesties could not even make their way to Pollygunge steeplechase in the afternoon without taking two hospitals on their way. In the evening the King and Queen honoured the Governor-General and Lady Hardinge with their presence at a dinner-party, after which they

Jan. 7-8. ascended to the roof to see the illumination of Calcutta, a most wonderful and beautiful sight; for, as I have said before, the humblest native of India seems instinctively to possess the secret of artistic illumination; and these were the finest ever known in Calcutta. It is a pity that those who are responsible for such decorations in London do not pay the East a visit in order to learn their business. The crowds in the street were gigantic; and it was curious to see the tall Pathan sentries watching the endless flow of sleek, white-robed, bare-headed Bengalis with a hungry look, as of a captive fox that eyes chickens playing just beyond the length of his chain.

On Sunday morning Their Majesties were present at Divine Service in the Cathedral, and in the afternoon went down by river to Barrackpur, attended by the Viceroy and Lady Hardinge and a number of their suite, to enjoy a few hours of peace in the beautiful gardens. On the morning of the 8th half of the suite left for Bombay betimes; at half-past ten the principal officials assembled at Government House to take leave of Their Majesties; and a few minutes later the King and Queen drove away with the like escort as upon their arrival to Prinsep's Ghat. The people had assembled in vast crowds to see them pass, and received them with unexampled enthusiasm. At the Ghat representatives of the principal local bodies and associations were gathered together to meet them, and an address was presented by the Legislative Council of Bengal, to which the King read a reply. Their Majesties then crossed the river in the steamship *Howrah*, under a salute from the British warships, to the station; and here the King-Emperor bade farewell to the three Indian Princes of his personal staff, the Maharajas of Gwalior and Bikanir, and Sir Pratap Singh. The parting was a very melancholy one, for the Maharaja Scindia, an honoured friend of the King, could not repress his tears, and the gallant veteran Sir Pratap could only stammer out that he was growing an old man before he broke down completely. At noon the Royal train steamed away under a final salute of one hundred and one guns from the ramparts of Fort William. Jan. 8.

At noon on the 10th Their Majesties arrived at the Victoria Terminus, Bombay, where they were received by the Governor-General, who had preceded them, and drove in procession at a slow pace to the Apollo Bandar. The demonstration as they passed through the streets showed the impression that they had made during their visit, for the Indians threw off all reserve, shouting and waving with unrestrained enthusiasm. Upon arrival at the appointed place the King and Queen alighted opposite the amphitheatre, which was once again crowded with spectators, and a procession was formed to the pavilion at the edge of the landing-steps. Here Their Majesties took their seats upon their thrones, and the Vice-President of the Legislative

Jan. 10. Council of Bombay presented a happily-worded address of farewell. The King then read his reply slowly and clearly, as is his wont ; and it is worth while to reproduce here the concluding sentences : "It is a matter of intense satisfaction to me to realise how all classes and creeds have joined together in true-hearted welcome which has been so universally accorded us. Is it not possible that the same unity and concord may for the future govern the daily relations of their public and private lives? The attainment of this would indeed be a happy outcome of our visit to India. To you, the representatives of Bombay, who have greeted us so warmly on our arrival and departure, I deliver this our loving message of farewell to the Indian Empire."

Here the King's voice broke, and for some seconds he was unable to speak further. Then collecting himself, he read on : "May the Almighty ever assist me and my successors to promote its welfare and to secure to it the blessings of prosperity and peace."

The members of the Legislative Council were then presented to Their Majesties, next several of the leading officials, civil and military, and lastly the Indian Chiefs, conspicuous among whom were the Maharaja of Kolhapur, the Begum of Bhopal and the Maharao of Bundi. With many of these high personages Their Majesties shook hands on taking leave, and with none more warmly than with the Begum and the Maharao, the courtly host of the Queen at Bundi. All farewells had been said, and all present were expecting the King and Queen to enter their launch, when, by a sudden impulse, Their Majesties walked forward quite alone towards the amphitheatre. The King was in the plain white uniform of the Army in the tropics, the Queen was dressed in a dress of cream-colour shot with gold; there were not even the Indian attendants by them with umbrella and shade, and they stood at the edge of the sunlight, two white figures on the red carpet, the King with his hand to his helmet and the Queen as quietly bowing, to pay their farewell greeting to the last assembly of their Indian subjects. The movement was so evidently unpremeditated, so simple and so natural, that for a moment the two or three thousand spectators hardly realised what was going forward; and then they leaped to their feet with one accord, not a few with the tears streaming down their cheeks, and answered the salute of the King and Queen with a storm of cheers. Slowly and reluctantly Their Majesties turned round, walked back to the launch that was awaiting them, and embarked. The Viceroy followed them, remaining to luncheon on the *Medina*, a meal to which the King had invited a large party of guests, including the Governor of Bengal and Lady Clarke, and the Aga Khan. After luncheon His Majesty presented Delhi Coronation medals to a number of officers and men of the Royal Navy, first, however, investing the Maharao of Bundi with the Grand Cross of

Jan. 10.

Jan. 10. the Victorian Order. Then followed more farewells, never very pleasant things, and doubly unhappy when they involve parting from such unselfish friends as the officers of the King's Indian staff had been to all of us. How great and endless were the labours, anxieties and worries of Brigadier Sir Rollo Grimston, Major Stockley, Major Money, Captain Hogg, Captain Amir Ahmad, and their coadjutors during the Royal visit, only they can know; but I may at least bear grateful testimony to their inexhaustible courtesy, patience and good temper. Last of all the Viceroy took leave of Their Majesties; and at six o'clock in the evening the great white ship and her four escorting cruisers spun round, so to speak, on their heels, and steamed away in single line ahead.

XIV

Of the homeward voyage there is little to be said. We had beautiful calm warm weather until we reached Port Sudan on the 17th, where, as Lord Kitchener had warned us, the temperature suddenly cooled. The *Medina* came alongside the wharf early, and immediately the foreshore was crowded with people. Pipers and drummers presently set to work at their instruments with frantic energy, and in a very few minutes black warriors with long woolly locks were bounding about like long slips of india-

ARABS ALONGSIDE AT PORT SUDAN.

To face page 246.

rubber, with terrific brandishing of sword and spear. At eight o'clock Their Majesties disembarked, and were received by Lord Kitchener, Sir Reginald and Lady Wingate, Sir Rudolph Slatin Pasha and other gentlemen. An address of welcome was read, and answered by the King; and then a number of Sheikhs in red robes embroidered with gold were presented to His Majesty, who gave them decorations and gifts. It was strange to see them. Many of them had fought against us; one had been reader of the Koran to the Khalifa; another had been the right-hand man of Osman Digna. There they were, all peaceful and friendly, wearing dresses of honour given by the Government of the Soudan, and excessively proud of them. Jan. 17.

After half an hour the King and Queen returned on board for breakfast; and at about ten started with their suite by train for Sinkat, a name well known in 1884 and 1885 as the centre of Osman Digna's operations. The journey occupied close upon five hours, the climb being long and steep from the sea to the lofty plateau of Sinkat. Shortly before two o'clock a great crowd of men and camels, between two and three thousand according to one account, were seen alongside the railway, and presently the train stopped at a small station, opposite to which was a line of troops of all arms, chiefly Soudanese, drawn up on parade. Here Their Majesties alighted, and taking their place in a tent, saw the troops march past, very

Jan. 17. steadily and well, cavalry, camel corps, artillery and infantry, to the music of Soudanese military bands, which played native march-tunes with a magnificent swagger of drummers. The cavalry and camels then trotted past, and the infantry came by again at the double, one of them—a newly raised corps of wild Arabs—with a lightness and spring delightful to see. We heard without surprise that they were astonishing marchers. Then the camel-men marched past in irregular array, tribe by tribe, with their chiefs at the head, and returned again at a more rapid pace. The programme promised us a gallop past of these wild levies; but not above half a dozen galloped, and only one camel whirled by at the top of his speed. It was interesting to see the British soldiers of the Nineteenth Yorkshire Regiment quite as much at home upon their camels as any of the Arabs. Then there was a war-dance of Dinkas, a wild jet-black tribe from the south of Fashoda, the performers wearing a little clothing for this occasion only; there was a sham fight of other tribesmen, who threw stones at each other with great accuracy and parried them very skilfully with their shields; and there was yet another dance of woolly heads such as we had seen in the morning. Altogether it was a very remarkable scene, and it became the more so when we learned that many of the tribes had, not many years before, fought desperately against us; that some had travelled hundreds of miles to see the King; and that the

ARAB TRIBES AT SINKAT.

To face page 248.

greater part had never seen nor hardly heard of each other before. However, having met upon this occasion, they decided that it would be well to meet again; and so they have arranged to assemble every year at Khartoum upon the 17th of January to celebrate King George's Day. Jan. 17.

At the close of the review Their Majesties motored into Sinkat to see the wells, their equerries, for the first time in the history of the British monarchy, attending them on camels; and at four o'clock Their Majesties re-entered the train for Port Sudan, the tribesmen running and galloping by hundreds alongside the train until it distanced even the fleetest horses and camels. Upon our journey we had the advantage of travelling with some of the leading officials of the Soudan, governors of districts and so forth, all without exception military men, though many were holding civil office. Few people realise that the Soudan means roughly one million of square miles, and that under this little knot of Englishmen it is making very remarkable progress. I am afraid that I could not help contrasting the modest and manly simplicity of these gentlemen with the very different demeanour of civil officials in other parts of the Empire. The truth is that, as I have already hinted, the British officer in command of native troops has this great advantage over the civilian, that he is in constant touch with the native mind through the medium of his

Jan. 20-24. native officers and men, and thus learns how to handle the inhabitants with tact and ease.

Soon after dusk the *Medina* resumed her journey, Lord Kitchener by the King's invitation taking a passage on board as far as Port Said, which was reached on the 20th. Here once again His Highness the Khedive came on board to greet the King, and the ceremonies of His Majesty's first visit in November were in great measure repeated. Two of the cruising squadron, which had been detached at Aden to coal, rejoined us, and five hundred tons of coal were put on board the *Medina* herself in an hour. At noon on Sunday the 21st we sailed again, and on the 24th at ten o'clock in the morning entered Malta Harbour. Five French ships, the *Danton*, *Justice*, *Vérité*, *Carabinier* and *Lansquenet* were lying in the harbour, under the flags of Admiral Boué de Lapeyrère and Rear-Admiral Moreau; and the roar of salutes from them as well as from the British ships of the Mediterranean squadron,[1] as the *Medina* entered into that narrow, echoing inlet was deafening. Unfortunately, after picking up her mooring the *Medina's* hawser parted, and she was obliged to go astern, with the result that the cable of a mooring aft became entangled

[1] *Exmouth*, flagship of Admiral Sir E. Poe, Capt. Stuart Nicholson; *Duncan*, flagship of Rear-Ad. Jerram, Capt. F. L. Field; *Triumph*, Capt. Waymouth; *Swiftsure*, Capt. Tower; *Cornwallis*, Capt. Anstruther; *Russell*, Capt. R. H. Anstruther; *Bacchante*, flagship of Rear-Ad. Sir Douglas Gamble, Capt. Tyrwhitt; *Hampshire*, Capt. Hunter; *Lancaster*, Capt. Tothill; *Barham*, Capt. Cotton; *Medea*, Commander Keane; *Hussar*, Commander Diggle.

round the shaft of her starboard screw. Divers were at once sent down to cut the cable away; and meanwhile the Governor, Sir Leslie Rundle, and several naval officers came on board to wait upon the King and Queen. Jan. 24.

Shortly before noon Their Majesties landed and went to the Governor's palace, where the leading civil and ecclesiastical dignitaries were presented to them; after which they witnessed a defile of the troops of the garrison. For the first time since the island has been in British hands an armed force of French bluejackets was landed—sturdy active men, who marched past the King with the light jaunty step for which the French are famous. A British naval brigade numbering over twenty-five hundred from the *Duncan*, *Triumph*, *Exmouth*, *Hampshire* and *Bacchante*, had also been disembarked, and these went past with a swing which left the soldiers far behind. In due time followed the Old Fourteenth West Yorks, to the music of *Ça ira*, which they have played ever since their colonel at Famars in 1793 bade them beat the French Republicans "to their own d——d tune"; the Forty-eighth Northamptons, a very fine battalion, the Ninetieth Scottish Rifles, and the Argyll and Sutherland Highlanders. But a defile past in column of fours is an over-lengthy process.

Their Majesties lunched at the palace with the Governor, the King subsequently visiting Admiral Boué de Lapeyrère on the *Danton*. In the evening Their Majesties dined with Admiral

Jan. 25. Sir Edmund and Lady Poe at their house in Valetta, after which they attended a gala performance at the Opera.

On the 25th the Queen went to St. John's Cathedral to see the celebrated Flemish tapestries, made after designs of Rubens, which were given to it by the Grand Master in 1707. The Archbishop and all the principal ecclesiastical dignitaries were present to receive Her Majesty, and Canon Alfredo Mifsud, Librarian of the Public Library, acted as guide and interpreter. The Canon's great historical knowledge and enthusiasm for the romance of the Knights of Malta made the visit of no ordinary interest; and he pointed out with quiet humour to one of the suite the effigy, on the roof, of his ancestor, an English knight who had been beheaded in the sixteenth century by one of His Majesty's ancestors on the throne of England. In the afternoon the Queen was present, together with the King, at a gymkhana at Messa; and in the evening Their Majesties dined with the Governor at the palace, and held a levee afterwards. The palace at Malta, I may remark, is incomparably the finest and most interesting Government House in the British dominions, as is perhaps natural, seeing that it was built in the sixteenth century for the Grand Master of the Knights of Malta.

On the 26th the *Medina* was brought early in the morning into dry dock, where the slight damage done on the 24th was made good in a few hours, enabling the ship to return to her moorings before dark. The King this morning visited the three flagships *Exmouth*, *Duncan* and *Bacchante*, proceeding afterwards in company with the Queen to the Naval Hospital, which Their Majesties inspected very thoroughly. Early in the forenoon the Queen also made a dash into the country to see a subterranean temple known as the Hypogæum, which was accidentally discovered a year or two ago. Seemingly unique of its kind, both in design and decoration, and reckoned to be at least three thousand years old, this Hypogæum is of extraordinary interest; nor did Her Majesty leave it until, under the guidance of Professor Zamit, she had explored every corner, and heard all that was to be told concerning it. Then in the afternoon the King and Queen motored out some nine miles to the Governor's summer residence at Verdala, returning in time to drink tea at the mess of the Royal Artillery and Engineers in another palace at Valetta. The people assembled in thousands to see them pass, and received them with an enthusiastic welcome; in fact it was not easy for the motors to make their way through the press in the villages. This unfortunately left the Queen little time for the pastime which she enjoys most keenly. The Museum at Malta contains very much that is of the greatest interest; the Library possesses some beautiful illuminated manuscripts and some remarkably fine old bindings; and the walls of the main guard are covered with Jan. 26.

Jan. 27-29. perhaps the most striking collection of military caricatures, painted by generations of British officers, that is to be found in the Empire. Her Majesty contrived to see at least something of all three of these institutions, lamenting greatly that there was no time to go through them more thoroughly. Malta at large, in fact, offers a great field, both to historian and antiquarian ; and its old fortifications, apart from their stupendous magnitude and remarkable comeliness, contain the graves of more than one modern hero, the greatest of whom are Thomas Maitland, once famous as King Tom of the Ionian Islands, and gentle old Sir Ralph Abercromby.

On the 27th the *Medina* sailed from Malta, and on the 28th ran into cold, rough, unpleasant weather. On the evening of the 29th the King received the sad news of the death of the Duke of Fife at Khartoum. Few had realised that, at the height of the festivities at Delhi, Their Majesties had been kept for some hours in anxious suspense as to the fate of the Princess Royal, the Duke, and the two Princesses their daughters, after the wreck of the steamer *Delhi* on the 13th of December. Not indeed until the morning of the 15th had the King at last received a reassuring telegram from the Princess Royal to say that, after passing through great peril, she and all of her family were safe. But it now appeared too evidently that shock and exposure had left a fatal mark upon the Duke of Fife ; and the mournful intelligence came

with the greater bitterness to the King, inasmuch Jan. 30.
as it was impossible for him to go to the Princess Royal, upon whom this sorrow had come when she was far away from home and from all relations and friends. At ten o'clock on the morning of the 30th the *Medina* went alongside the dockyard quay at Gibraltar, in dismally wet and windy weather. The *Venerable*, Captain Chapman, and *Cumberland*, Captain Boyle, were lying in harbour, the latter filled with naval cadets. The Governor, Sir Archibald Hunter, the captains of the two cruisers above mentioned, Sir Reginald Lister from Tangier, Sir Maurice de Bunsen from Madrid and other high officers presently came on board to wait upon the King; but in consequence of the sad news of the previous day most of the arrangements had to be cancelled. At two o'clock in the afternoon the King received addresses from the inhabitants of Gibraltar, the Roman Catholic priests, the Jews and the Moorish mission, the last named to the number of eight or ten attending in their graceful white robes. They read their address in their native tongue, an interpreter being present to translate it and to render into Moorish His Majesty's reply. In the afternoon Their Majesties went ashore and inspected first the Colonial Hospital, and next the huge tanks recently made to store water for the fortress, afterwards drinking tea with the Governor and returning to the ship to dine quietly on board.

Early on the morning of the 31st three

Jan. 31. Spanish men-of-war were seen steaming over from Algeçiras, forming the escort of the Infante Don Carlos of Spain, who was come to bid the King welcome in the name of His Most Catholic Majesty. This was said, probably with truth, to be the first time since 1704 that a Spanish Prince and a Spanish man-of war had come to Gibraltar except with hostile intent; and there was no want of salutes to do honour to the occasion. His Royal Highness presently came on board with his suite, attended further by the Admiral of the Spanish squadron and his staff. The King a little later returned the visit on board the Spanish flagship *Cataluña*, whereupon the saluting was renewed; and it may be said that first and last the guns were not silent until nearly three o'clock in the afternoon, when the Spanish squadron returned to Algeçiras.

Meanwhile, after paying the return visit, the King went ashore with the Queen to the Alameda, which I suppose may be described as the Hyde Park of Gibraltar. His Majesty having promised to present new colours to the first battalion of the South Staffordshire Regiment, better known, perhaps, as the old Thirty-eighth, the whole of the garrison was drawn up on this small space, the Thirty-eighth being formed up in line opposite to the saluting point, and the remainder massed on both flanks. The parade was an extremely pretty one, and the occasion was worthy of it; for the Thirty-eighth, albeit a corps of which newspapers, and as a natural consequence the public, knows nothing, has one of the most remarkable records of service to be found in the Army. The regiment has been in existence two hundred and ten years, of which it has spent one hundred and sixty abroad, fifty-eight of them consecutively in the West Indies, and has missed very few campaigns during the last century and a half. "North America, Central America, South America," said His Majesty in his address to them, "North Africa and South Africa, Northern Europe and Southern Europe, the plains of India and the mountains of India—nothing has come amiss to you; and you have served in all these countries with honour." One could not help reflecting that if this regiment wore the kilt the whole British Empire would ring with its fame. However, it matters not. They can uphold their great name without the help of newspapers, these sturdy, solid, old English battalions of the Line. Jan. 31.

The ceremony of presentation over, the garrison marched past the King. Owing to the straitness of the space, the troops could not be passed from one end of the ground to the other without some extremely clever manœuvring of the old-fashioned kind, which gave one some idea of what must have happened when Wellington formed his lines of battle. Moreover, as they all started for the march down a considerable decline, they swung past with such a stride as I have rarely witnessed. There was a large crowd to see this parade, and the

Jan. 31. inhabitants did not fail to give the King an enthusiastic welcome; but it was very hard upon all in Gibraltar that, after twice making every preparation for the reception and entertainment of Their Majesties, Fate should have interfered on both occasions at the last moment to disappoint them. In the afternoon Their Majesties drove round Gibraltar, and after visiting the Naval and Military Hospitals, drank tea with Admiral and Mrs. Pelham, who together with the Governor and Lady Hunter and Bishop Corfe were Their Majesties' guests at dinner in the evening.

At six P.M. on the 31st of January the *Medina* steamed away from Gibraltar for Spithead. A melancholy reminder of the loss that had befallen the King came before us next morning as we sighted the masts and funnel of the ill-fated steamer *Delhi*; but it was pleasant to hear the deep sympathy with which every naval officer, past and present, from the highest downwards, spoke of her most unlucky commander. At night we became aware that the southerly wind, under which we had started, had shifted to south-westward and was freshening rapidly. By the morning of the 2nd it was blowing a full gale, and in fact we were repeating our experience of the outward voyage in the Atlantic, only with the wind more or less abaft instead of straight ahead. We made good way, therefore, in spite of a heavy sea, though nearly every ship that we passed was comfortably lying to; and the casualties from sea-sickness were considerably fewer than in November. Nevertheless, it was so long since we had experienced any bad weather that few, if any of us, had taken any precautions against it. The result was that on the first night we were roused by a succession of crashes, and jumped out of bed to find the floors of our cabins a chaos of loose articles, which were rolling joyously to and fro. Fortunately we were all too much occupied in securing them, and in maintaining our equilibrium meanwhile, to listen to each other's language, which, I fancy, must have amused the sentries in the passages considerably. Feb. 1-3

On the afternoon of the 3rd we entered the Channel, by which time the wind had shifted to the north-east, blowing bitterly cold with occasional savage snowstorms—by no means a pleasant thing for the Admiral in a water-way crowded with traffic. In the night these storms became so blinding that it was impossible to see a hundred yards ahead, and Sir Colin signalled the squadron to reduce speed from sixteen to eight knots. Wild whooping of the siren proclaimed this fact to us more fortunate mortals as we lay snug and warm in our beds; but the Admiral and his officers on the bridge spent a very comfortless and anxious night. Fortunately the squalls diminished in severity, and before daylight the *Medina* and her escort were anchored at Spithead.

On the morning of Sunday the 4th of

Feb. 4. February therefore, we woke to see, through falling snow, the Home Fleet of battleships on one side, and the shore of England on the other. There was no mistaking the fact that we were at home and not in India, for it was freezing at sea, and there were eighteen degrees of frost ashore, with a bitter wind to make matters more pleasant. The *Medina*, being intended for voyages in hot latitudes, was not well-equipped for such a visitation; and after seeking in vain for some warm spot outside the engine-room, we were fain to huddle on greatcoats, and live generally as if we were making a cold journey by railway. As soon as Divine Service was over Their Majesties entered upon a task, which few excepting themselves would have thought of undertaking, that of giving to every soul in the ship with their own hands a memento of the voyage to India in the *Medina*; the more highly privileged being summoned to the King's cabin, while the ship's company, marines and servants filed past the King and Queen in the saloon. Then came the last dinner, at which Lord Durham asked permission to propose in a few words the health of Their Majesties, and to offer them the congratulations of the suite upon the splendid success of their visit to India; and the King with equal brevity but much feeling replied. There were few, I think, among the suite who did not regret the breaking up of a party in which it may truly be said that not an unpleasant word had passed from the beginning

THE RETURN TO LONDON.

to end of the journey. It still remained for us to take leave of our friends in the wardroom, to which we repaired as soon as Their Majesties had retired. Our stay there was protracted until late; and the evening in such good company was of the cheerfulest. Feb. 5.

Early next morning Queen Alexandra, the Prince of Wales and Princess Victoria, who had slept on the Royal yacht on the previous night, came on board; and soon after ten the Royal train started in bitter cold for London. As it whirled past Arundel Castle the Duke of Norfolk with stately courtesy dipped his flag, which was flying on the tower—the last flag of many hundreds to salute the King on his progress to India and back. On arriving at Victoria the Ministers and other officials were present to receive Their Majesties.

Their Majesties and the Prince of Wales then drove in procession to Buckingham Palace by way of Victoria Street, Whitehall and the Mall, followed by the suite in six carriages; and, in spite of a savage north-east wind, large and enthusiastic crowds were assembled in the streets to welcome them. At the Palace the suite took leave of the King and Queen, assembling again for the last time on the morrow at St. Paul's Cathedral, whither Their Majesties drove in procession to attend a special service of thanksgiving to God for His mercies vouchsafed to them. The noble chorale, *Nun danket alle Gott*, sung by the massed choirs and a vast congregation, brought to a worthy close the episode of the King's visit to India.

RESULTS OF THE VISIT

XV

Will the results of the visit be permanent and lasting for good? That is a question which many have asked and are still asking. Beyond all doubt a great wave of emotion swept over India during the King's progress, and found vent in such outward manifestations of loyalty as astonished both Indians and Europeans. But has the wave spent its force in these demonstrations, or is it itself but the visible forerunner of a great tide, "too full for sound or foam," which will bear India steadily on her course of peace and contentment? If we are to believe the utterances, transparently genuine and sincere, of thoughtful Indian writers, the good effects of the King's visit will not be transient, but enduring. Of course we cannot look for all evil to vanish and for the golden age to return forthwith. We cannot expect all difficulties to be smoothed away, and future, or even present, mistakes to recur no more. Endeavour as we may, neither we nor the people of India can hope to escape from the decrees of Fate or from the consequences of our own faults. The task which men set themselves, who strive to live together in peace, is beset by many and great dangers; and by reason of our frailty we cannot always stand upright. We seem to have found our footing and to be walking cautiously indeed, but stably; when some gust of passion, or prejudice, or intolerance, or it may be of sheer folly only, sweeps down upon us, and in a moment we are overthrown. How long and painful is the effort of recovery, and how deep the humiliation through which it is at last accomplished, is written large for those who will read in the pages of history.

To occasional falls and failures, then, both English and Indian, being human, must look forward; yet not without cheerfulness and good courage. Very full of hope and comfort is the message sent by the Princes and people of India to the Prime Minister upon the day of the King's return to England:—

"The Princes and people of India desire to take the opportunity afforded by the conclusion of the Royal visit, to convey to the great English nation an expression of their cordial good-will and fellowship; also an assurance of their warm attachment to the world-wide Empire of which they form a part, and with which their destinies are now indissolubly linked. Their Imperial Majesties' visit to India, so happily conceived and successfully completed, has produced a profound and ineffaceable impression throughout the country.

"Their Imperial Majesties, by their gracious demeanour, their unfailing sympathy, and their deep solicitude for the welfare of all classes, have drawn closer the bonds that unite England and India, and have deepened and intensified the traditional feeling of loyalty and devotion to the

Throne and person of the Sovereign, which has always characterised the Indian people.

"Conscious of the many blessings which India has derived from the connection with England, the Princes and people rejoiced to tender in person their loyal and loving homage to their Imperial Majesties. They are confident that the great and historic event marks the beginning of a new era, ensuring greater happiness, prosperity and progress to the people of India under the aegis of the Crown."

The British press, with few exceptions, failed altogether to appreciate the profound interest and significance of this message. Never before has any body of men attempted to speak with one voice on behalf of an united and one-minded India ; and never before has it been possible that such an attempt should be made. Yet here the one voice cries aloud, resonant, sincere and spontaneous, finding utterance for many peoples, nations and languages in the Imperial tongue. I say the Imperial and not the English tongue, because no Englishman was concerned with this message. It sprang straight from the hearts of the Indian Princes and peoples, and sped on its way untouched by any British pen, untaught by any British inspiration.

And the language of the message has found both anticipation and echo among thoughtful contributors to the Indian periodical press. "We are on the threshold of a new era," says a writer in the Indian magazine *East and West*, "with the

King's message of hope still ringing in our ears; and we shall strive for greater unity in our endeavours for the common good, and tread the path of progress with a larger hope in our hearts and a firmer faith in our destiny." In other words, India is proud of her place in the British Empire; and to prove herself worthy of it she will try to quench old internal animosities, and to co-operate heartily with England in working out her future. And England on her side, who has long worked honestly according to her lights *for* India, will try to work more and more *with* India. For a long time she must lead, and India will be content to allow her to lead, provided that she will also learn. What is needed in both parties is sympathy and patience. It is patience, as the great Marlborough said, "which conquers all things"—patience, not faith in education, nor in representative institutions, nor in heroic phrases, nor even in heroic measures. Englishmen are too fond of proclaiming that Parliamentary institutions have made them a great nation; whereas it is really because they are a great nation, very peculiarly situated, that they have been able for two hundred years to make of Parliamentary institutions a comparatively successful form of government. When India, after long and patient search and many inevitable errors, has found for herself a path of true progress, which she can follow with faith and with hope, then she may, if she will, make trial of representative institutions; but let her not suppose that by snatching at them prematurely she will abridge that search or diminish the number of those errors. Rather let both England and India remember that though for countless centuries men have put forth their petty remedies for the evils of this world, there is one reform and one only that has ever availed them—the inward and spiritual reform which bids every man seek first to abate the evil that is in himself. So shall we strive, not in vain, for greater unity in our endeavours for the common good.

APPENDIX A

November 11, 1912.

THE ASSEMBLAGE AT VICTORIA.

Prince and Princess Christian of Schleswig-Holstein, with Princess Marie Louise of Schleswig-Holstein, Princess Louise (Duchess of Argyll) and the Duke of Argyll, Princess Beatrice (Princess Henry of Battenberg), with Prince Alexander, Prince Leopold, and Prince Maurice of Battenberg, the Duchess of Albany, the Grand Duke Michael Michaïlovitch of Russia, the Duchess of Teck, the Countess Feodora Gleichen, the Lady Valda Machell, and the Duke of Fife took leave of Their Majesties at Victoria Station.

The following Members of the Government in the Cabinet were present :—

The Rt. Hon. H. H. Asquith, M.P. (Prime Minister and First Lord of the Treasury) and Mrs. Asquith, the Viscount Morley of Blackburn (Lord President of the Council), the Earl Carrington (Lord Privy Seal) and the Countess Carrington, the Viscount Haldane (Secretary of State for War), the Rt. Hon. R. McKenna, M.P. (Secretary of State for the Home Department) and Mrs. McKenna, and the Rt. Hon. Sir Edward Grey, Bt., M.P. (Secretary of State for Foreign Affairs).

Members of the Corps Diplomatique :—

Their Excellencies the German Ambassador (Count Paul Wolff-Metternich), the Russian Ambassador (Count Benckendorff), the Austro-Hungarian Ambassador (Count Mensdorff-Pouilly-Dietrichstein), the United States Ambassador and Mrs. Whitelaw Reid, the Spanish Ambassador (Señor Don Wenceslao de Villa Urrutia), the Turkish Ambassador (His Highness Tewfik Pasha), the Italian Ambassador and the Marchesa Imperiali, the Swiss Minister (Monsieur Gaston Carlin), the Belgian Minister and the Countess de Lalaing, the Swedish Minister and the Countess Wrangel, the Danish Minister (Monsieur Constantine Brun), the Uruguayan Minister (Señor Don Federico R. Vidiella), the Colombian Minister and Madame Perez Triana, the Norwegian Minister and Madame Vogt, the Liberian Minister (Mr. J. P. Crommelin), the Argentine Minister and Madame de Dominguez, the Chilian Minister and Madame Edwards, the Siamese Minister (Phya Akharaj Vardthara), the Persian Minister (Mirza Mehdi Khan Mushir-ul-Mulk), the Mexican Minister (Señor Don Miguel de Beistegui), the Portuguese Minister (Senhor M. Teixeira Gomes), the Haytian Minister-Resident and Madame Heraux, and the Peruvian Chargé d'Affaires and Madame de Lembcke, the Bolivian Chargé d'Affaires and Madame Saurez, the Servian Chargé d'Affaires and Madame Grouitch, the Netherlands Chargé d'Affaires and Madame van der Goes, the Japanese Chargé d'Affaires and Mrs. Yamaza, and the Roumanian Chargé d'Affaires (Prince Antoine Bibesco).

There were also present :—

The Archbishop of Canterbury, the Marchioness of Salisbury, the Marchioness of Crewe, the Marquis de Soveral, the Viscount Esher, the Lord Strathcona and Mount Royal (High Commissioner for the Dominion of Canada) and the Lady Strathcona and Mount Royal, the Rt. Hon. Sir George Reid (High Commissioner for the Commonwealth of Australia), the Rt. Hon. Sir Thomas Crosby (Lord Mayor of London) and the Lady Mayoress, Field-Marshal Sir W. G. Nicholson (Chief of the Imperial General Staff and First Military Member of the Army Council), the Hon. Sir Richard Solomon (High Commissioner for the Union of South Africa), Lieut.-General Sir A. Paget (General Officer Commanding in Chief, Eastern Command), the Hon. Sir William Hall-Jones (High Commissioner for the Dominion of New Zealand), Major-General Sir A. E. Codrington (General Officer Commanding the London District), and Major Sir Frederick Wodehouse (Acting Commissioner of Police).

ARRIVAL AT PORTSMOUTH.

Their Majesties were received on arrival at Portsmouth by—

The Duke of Wellington (Acting Lord Lieutenant of the County of Hampshire), the Rt. Hon. Winston Spencer-Churchill, M.P. (First Lord of the Admiralty), Admiral of the Fleet Sir Arthur K. Wilson (First Lord Commissioner of the Admiralty), Admiral the Lord Charles Beresford (M.P. for Portsmouth), the Mayor of Portsmouth, and by Admiral Sir Arthur Moore (Commander-in-Chief at Portsmouth), General Sir C. W. H. Douglas (General Officer Commanding in Chief, Southern Command), Rear-Admiral A. G. Tate (Superintendent of Portsmouth Dockyard), Rear-Admiral Sir Colin Keppel, and Major-General W. E. Blewitt (General Officer Commanding Southern Coast Defences), and the respective Staffs.

THEIR MAJESTIES' LUNCHEON-PARTY.

Their Majesties' luncheon party on board H.M.S. *Medina* included :— Queen Alexandra, the Queen of Norway, the Prince of Wales, the Princess Mary, the Princess Victoria, Prince Arthur of Connaught, the Duke of Teck, the Duke of Devonshire, the Duke of Wellington, the Hon. Lady Keppel, the Rt. Hon. Winston Spencer-Churchill, M.P., Mrs. Winston Spencer-Churchill, the Rt. Rev. Bishop Corfe, D.D., Sir Walter Lawrence, Bt., Admiral of the Fleet Sir Arthur K. Wilson, Admiral the Lord Charles Beresford, Sir Thomas Sutherland, Admiral Sir Arthur Moore, General Sir C. W. H. Douglas, Sir Richmond Ritchie,

APPENDIX A

Rear-Admiral A. G. Tate, Major-General W. E. Blewitt, Lieut.-Colonel Sir Charles Frederick, the Hon. Charlotte Knollys, Colonel Sir Arthur Davidson, the Hon. John Ward and the Suite in attendance upon the King and Queen.

November 15.

GIBRALTAR.

This morning Their Majesties received the Governor (General Sir A. Hunter), the Governor of Algeçiras, the Governor of Cadiz, the Captain of the Spanish cruiser *Reina Regente*, the Captain of the Portuguese cruiser *Adamaster*, Vice-Admiral Sir John Jellicoe, Vice-Admiral Commanding the Atlantic Fleet, and the Captains of the ships of the Atlantic Fleet, and Rear-Admiral Frederick Pelham, Admiral-Superintendent and in charge of all Naval Establishment at Gibraltar.

November 20.

PORT SAID.

The following, with the Duke of Teck and the Ladies and Gentlemen in Attendance, had the honour of dining with Their Majesties :—Field-Marshal the Viscount Kitchener, Lieut.-General Sir F. Reginald Wingate, Major-General Sir John Maxwell, and Captain Michael Culme-Seymour, R.N., H.M.S. *Argyll*.

November 21.

PORT SAID.

The King this morning received a visit from His Highness the Khedive and also from his Imperial Highness Prince Zia-ed-Din, who had been deputed by the Sultan to greet Their Majesties and to deliver to the King a letter from His Imperial Majesty.

His Highness the Khedive was attended by His Excellency Said Zoulificar Pasha (Grand Master of Ceremonies) and His Excellency Lewa Ramzi Tahir Pasha, Chief A.D.C.

His Imperial Highness Prince Zia-ed-Din was attended by His Excellency Djenani Bey, Grand Master of Ceremonies of His Imperial Majesty the Sultan, Colagarhi Ahmed Bey, A.D.C., and Murtaza Bey, Private Secretary.

His Majesty then received a visit from His Highness Prince Mohamed Ali.

After the Khedive's visit the following had the honour of being presented to the King by Field-Marshal the Viscount Kitchener :—His Highness Kiamel Pasha, ex-Grand Vizier ; His Excellency Mohateed Said Pasha, President of the Council of Ministers ; His Excellency Hussein Rushdi Pasha, Minister of Foreign Affairs ; Sir Paul Harvey, British Adviser for

Finance; Mr. Ronald Graham, British Adviser for Interior; and the French Minister, Monsieur De France, who presented Monsieur Ribot (Secretary), Monsieur Charles Roux, Director of the Suez Canal; and the three principal Officials of the Suez Canal, Count De Serionne (Agent Supérieur), Monsieur Perier (Ingénieur en Chef), Monsieur Coullant (Chef du Transit).

Field-Marshal the Viscount Kitchener also presented Mahomed Mahmud Bey, Governor of the Suez Canal; and Mr. E. C. Blech, British Consul-General at Port Said.

Later His Majesty visited His Highness the Khedive on board His Highness's yacht *Mahroussa*, attended by Field-Marshal the Viscount Kitchener, the Duke of Teck, the Marquis of Crewe, Commander Sir Charles Cust, Bt., R.N., and Captain B. Godfrey-Faussett, R.N.

At the conclusion of the visit His Majesty landed and inspected the Guards of Honour of the 1st Batt. Scots Guards, under the Command of Major Carpenter Garnier, and of the 3rd Batt. Egyptian Army, under the Command of Captain Ali Effendi Fahmi.

The King and Queen gave a luncheon-party on board the *Medina* in honour of the Khedive and Prince Zia-ed-Din. Prince Mohamed Ali was present, and the following had the honour of being invited:—His Highness Kiamel Pasha, His Excellency Mohamed Said Pasha, His Excellency Djenani Bey, Monsieur De France, Field-Marshal the Viscount Kitchener, His Excellency Hussein Rushdi Pasha, Major-General Sir John Maxwell, Sir Paul Harvey, Lieut.-General Sir Reginald Wingate, Mr. Ronald Graham, His Excellency Said Zoulificar Pasha, His Excellency Lewa Ramzi Tahir Pasha, Mohamed Mahmud Bey, Monsieur Charles Roux, Mr. E. C. Blech, and Mr. R. H. Greg (Diplomatic Secretary to Field-Marshal the Viscount Kitchener).

This evening Field-Marshal the Viscount Kitchener, Major-General Sir John Maxwell, Lieut.-General Sir R. Wingate, El Lewa Watson Pasha, Rear-Admiral Sir Douglas Gamble (H.M.S. *Bacchante*), Captain Tyrwhitt, R.N. (H.M.S. *Bacchante*), Captain Tothill, R.N. (H.M.S. *Lancaster*), and Captain Moubray, R.N. (H.M.S. *Suffolk*), were included in Their Majesties' dinner-party.

December 2.

BOMBAY.

Walking Procession from the Landing Pavilion to the Dais.

Staff of Governor of Bombay.
Staff of Governor-General.
King-Emperor's Indian Staff.

The Hon. J. Fortescue.	Sir R. H. Charles.	Mr. F. H. Lucas.
Capt. B. Godfrey-Faussett.	Comr. Sir C. Cust.	Hon. Sir D. Keppel.

Sir J. Dunlop-Smith.	Rear-Admiral Sir C. Keppel.
Sir Edward Henry.	Lieut.-Gen. Sir H. Smith-Dorrien.
The Lord Stamfordham.	The Lord-in-Waiting.

APPENDIX A

The Lord Chamberlain to the Queen-Empress.	The Lord High Steward.
THE QUEEN-EMPRESS.	**THE KING-EMPEROR.**

The Governor of Bombay.		The Governor-General.
The Duke of Teck.	Mistress of the Robes.	The Marquis of Crewe.
The Hon. V. Baring.	Lady Clarke.	The Countess of Shaftesbury.
The Military Secretary.		Major-Gen. Sir S. Beatson.
Major Clive Wigram.		Major the Lord C. Fitzmaurice.

THE PROCESSION THROUGH THE CITY.

First Carriage.

THE KING-EMPEROR. THE QUEEN-EMPRESS.

Second Carriage.—The Governor-General, The Marquis of Crewe.

Third Carriage.—The Mistress of the Robes, the Duke of Teck, the Lord-in-Waiting, the Lord Chamberlain to the Queen.

Fourth Carriage.—The Governor of Bombay, Lady Clarke, the Lord Stamfordham, Lieut.-General Sir Horace Smith-Dorrien.

Fifth Carriage.—The Countess of Shaftesbury, the Lord High Steward, Sir Edward Henry, Rear-Admiral Sir Colin Keppel.

Sixth Carriage.—The Hon. Venetia Baring, Lieut.-Colonel Sir James Dunlop-Smith, Commander Sir Charles Cust, the Hon. Sir Derek Keppel.

Seventh Carriage.—Captain B. Godfrey-Faussett, R.N., Sir Richard Havelock Charles, Mr. F. H. Lucas, the Hon. John Fortescue.

The following Equerries were in attendance on horseback :—Major-General Sir Stuart Beatson, Major the Lord Charles Fitzmaurice, Major Clive Wigram.

The route of the procession was by Apollo Bandar Road, Esplanade Road, Hornby Road, Cruickshank Road, Kalbadevie Road, Parel Road, Sandhurst Road to Sandhurst Bridge, Queen's Road, Church Gate Street, Mayo Road, and thence to the Apollo Bandar. The Escort was furnished by the Y Battery Royal Horse Artillery, 7th Dragoon Guards, 26th Cavalry, the Bombay Light Horse, and the Governor's Bodyguard.

The King-Emperor and the Queen-Empress gave a dinner-party on board the *Medina* at night, to which the following had the honour of being invited :—The Governor-General, the Military Secretary to the Governor-General, the Commander-in-Chief of His Majesty's Forces in the East Indies and Lady Slade, the Hon. Mr. M. B. Chaubal, the Hon. Sir Narayen G. Chandavarkar and Lady Chandavarkar, the Hon. Mr. Justice D. D. Davar, the Hon. Mr. Justice J. J. Heaton and Mrs. Heaton, the Hon. Mr. Justice N. C. Macleod and Mrs. Macleod, the Hon. Sir Sassoon J. David, the Hon. Sir Vithaldas Thakersey, the Hon. Mr. C. H. Armstrong and Mrs. Armstrong, the Hon. Mr. W. H. Lucas, the General Officer Commanding the 6th (Poona) Division and Mrs. Anderson, the Roman Catholic

Archbishop, the Consul-General for Portugal, Mr. Ratan Tata and Mrs. Tata, and Colonel R. W. L. Dunlop and the Captains of H.M.S. *Argyll*, H.M.S. *Cochrane*, H.M.S. *Natal*, and H.M.S. *Defence*.

December 3.

BOMBAY.

Their Majesties guests at dinner on board H.M.S. *Medina* included the following:—The Governor of Bombay and Lady Clarke, the Hon. Sir Basil Scott, the Lord Bishop of Bombay, the Hon. Mr. W. T. Morison, the Hon. Mr. R. A. Lamb and Mrs. Lamb, the Aga Khan, the Hon. Mr. Justice L. P. Russell and Mrs. Russell, the Hon. Mr. Justice S. L. Batchelor and Mrs. Batchelor, the General Officer Commanding the Bombay Brigade, the Hon. Sir Henry Procter, the Director Royal Indian Marine and Mrs. Lumsden, Sir Jamsetji Jeejeebhoy, Mr. C. A. Kincaid and Mrs. Kincaid, Mr. P. R. Cadell, Mr. Shapurji Burjorji Broacha. The Captain of H.M.S. *Fox* and the Captain of H.M.S. *Highflyer* had the honour of dining with the King-Emperor and Queen-Empress on board H.M.S. *Medina* this evening. Lady Jeejeebhoy had the honour of being invited, but was unavoidably prevented from obeying Their Imperial Majesties' commands.

December 4.

BOMBAY.

A Guard of Honour of the 127th Baluchis was mounted at the Apollo Bandar.

PROCESSION TO THE CHILDREN'S FÊTE.

First Carriage.

THE KING-EMPEROR. THE QUEEN-EMPRESS.

Second Carriage.—The Mistress of the Robes, The Marquis of Crewe, the Lord Chamberlain to the Queen-Empress, the Lord-in-Waiting.

Third Carriage.—The Countess of Shaftesbury, the Duke of Teck, Lieut.-General Sir H. Smith-Dorrien, Rear-Admiral Sir Colin Keppel.

Fourth Carriage.—The Hon. Venetia Baring, the Lord High Steward, Lieut.-Colonel Sir J. Dunlop-Smith, Captain B. Godfrey-Faussett, R.N.

An escort was furnished by the 7th Dragoon Guards and the 20th Cavalry.

The route was by the Mayo Road and Esplanade Road.

Guards of Honour of the Bombay Volunteer Rifles and Cadets for the same Corps were mounted at the entrance and within the arena.

December 5.

BOMBAY.

This afternoon the King-Emperor and the Queen-Empress, attended by the members of their Household, visited the Caves of Elephanta.

APPENDIX A

At 10 P.M. Their Imperial Majesties, attended by the Mistress of the Robes, the Marquis of Crewe, the Duke of Teck, the Lord High Steward, and Rear-Admiral Sir Colin Keppel, left H.M.S. *Medina*. The remainder of the Suite, having previously landed at 2.25, were in attendance at the Apollo Bandar, where a Guard of Honour of the 104th Wellesley's Rifles was mounted.

The King-Emperor and the Queen-Empress then drove to the Victoria Terminus Station, a procession being formed in the following order :—

First Carriage.

THE KING-EMPEROR. THE QUEEN-EMPRESS.

Second Carriage.—The Mistress of the Robes, the Marquis of Crewe, Brigadier-General R. E. Grimston and Commander Sir Charles Cust.

Third Carriage.—The Countess of Shaftesbury, the Duke of Teck, the Lord Chamberlain to the Queen-Empress, and Lord Stamfordham.

Fourth Carriage.—The Hon. Venetia Baring, the Lord High Steward, and Rear-Admiral Sir Colin Keppel. Major Clive Wigram (Equerry-in-Waiting), and Major L. O. Graeme and Captain B. S. Grissell (Extra Aides-de-Camp) were in attendance on horseback.

An Escort was furnished by the 7th Dragoon Guards and the 26th Cavalry.

On arrival at the station Their Imperial Majesties were received by the Governor of Bombay, Lady Clarke, the Chief Justice, the Bishop of Bombay, the Members of the Executive Council, the General Officer Commanding the Bombay Brigade with the Brigade Staff, the Inspector-General of Police, the Municipal Commissioner, the Commissioner of Police, the Executive Engineer to the Presidency, the Under-Secretary to the Government (Political Department), and the Deputy Inspector-General of Police (Southern Range). A Guard of Honour of the 96th Berar Infantry was mounted on the platform, and was inspected by His Imperial Majesty.

At 10.45 P.M. the Royal train left for Delhi.

December 7.

DELHI.

Their Imperial Majesties alighted at Selimgarh Station at 10 A.M. Guard of Honour at the station : Royal Berkshire Regiment. Guard of Honour before the Reception-Tent : 16th Rajputs.

THE ROYAL PROCESSION MOUNTED.

Captain Raban.		Captain H. Hill.
Capt. L. F. Ashburner.	Capt. R. E. T. Hogg.	Major the Hon. W. G. S. Cadogan.
Major H. R Stockley.	Hon. Col. Hafiz Muhammad Abdullah Khan.	Major E. D. Money.

APPENDIX A

Hon. Col. Sir Muhammad Aslam Khan.	Col. Viscount Hardinge.	Col. F. Goodwin.
Col. H. E. Stanton.	Br.-Gen. H. D'U. Keary.	Br.-Gen. C. J. Melliss.
Br.-Gen. Birdwood.	Capt. B. G. Godfrey-Faussett.	H.H. Prince George of Battenberg.
The Hon. Sir Derek Keppel.	Br.-Gen. R. E. Grimston.	Commander Sir C. Cust.
Sir Edward Henry.	Gen. Sir E. Barrow.	Lt.-Gen. Sir H. Smith-Dorrien.
Sir Henry McMahon.	The Lord-in-Waiting.	Lord Stamfordham.
H.H. The Maharaja of Bikaner.		H.H. The Maharaja of Gwalior.

Bodyguard.

Household Cavalry Orderlies.

H.E. The Commander-in-Chief.	H.H. The Duke of Teck.
Major C. Wigram.	Major Lord C. Fitzmaurice.

THE KING-EMPEROR.

	O.C. Escort.
The Marquis of Crewe.	H.E. The Governor-General.

THE QUEEN-EMPRESS
(in a carriage with the Duchess of Devonshire and the Earl of Durham).

The O.C. Bodyguard riding on the right of the carriage; Major-Gen. Sir Pratap Singh on the left.

Lt.-Col. Watson, Major-Gen. Sir Stuart Beatson (on horseback).

Second Carriage.—Lady Hardinge, the Earl of Shaftesbury, and A.D.C.-in-Waiting.

Third Carriage.—The Countess of Shaftesbury, the Hon. Venetia Baring, Mr. J. H. Du Boulay.

Fourth Carriage.—Mr. F. H. Lucas, Sir James Dunlop-Smith, Rear-Admiral Sir Colin Keppel.

Fifth Carriage.—Lieut.-Colonel Bird, the Hon. J. Fortescue, Sir R. Havelock Charles.

The route of the procession was by—

Delhi Gate of the Fort.
Khas Road.
Round the Jumma Musjid.
Esplanade Road.
Chandni Chowk.
Fattehpur Bazar.
Queen's Road.
Dufferin Bridge.
Mori Gate.
Boulevard Road.

APPENDIX A

Rajpur Road.
Chouburja Road.
Through the pavilion on the ridge.

A Guard of Honour of the Royal Navy, Royal Marines, the Royal Fusiliers, and the 130th Baluchis, was mounted in front of the Royal Tents in the King-Emperor's Camp.

In the afternoon the King-Emperor held a reception of the Ruling Chiefs in the Reception-Tent. Their Highnesses were conducted to the Audience Chamber, and were in turn received in audience by His Imperial Majesty.

The following had the honour of being received :—The Nizam of Hyderabad, the Gaekwar of Baroda, the Maharaja of Mysore, the Maharana of Udaipur, the Maharaja of Jaipur, the Maharaja of Jodhpur, the Maharao Raja of Bundi, the Maharaja of Bikaner, the Maharao of Kota, the Maharaja of Kishengarh, the Maharaja of Bharatpur, the Maharawal of Jaisalmer, the Maharaja of Alwar, the Maharaj Rana of Dholpur, the Maharao of Sarohi, the Maharawal of Dungarpur, the Maharaja of Kollahpur, the Rao of Kutch, the Maharaja of Idar, the Mir of Khairpur.

During the ceremony a Guard of Honour of the Royal Berkshire Regiment and the 16th Rajputs was mounted in front of the Reception-Tent.

December 8.

DELHI.

This morning the King-Emperor held a reception of the Ruling Chiefs.

Their Highnesses were conducted to the Audience Chamber, and were received in turn by His Imperial Majesty.

The following had the honour of being received :—The Maharaja of Travancore, the Raja of Cochin, the Maharaja of Jammu and Kashmir, the Maharaja of Gwalior, the Maharaja of Indore, the Begum of Bhopal, the Maharaja of Rewa, the Maharaja of Orchha, the Raja of Dhar, the Raja of Dewas (senior branch), the Raja of Dewas (junior branch), the Maharaja of Patiala, the Nawab of Bahawalpur, the Raja of Nabha, the Maharaja of Bhutan, the Maharaja of Sikkim, the Khan of Kalat.

A Guard of Honour of the King's Royal Rifle Corps and the King's Own Sappers and Miners was mounted in front of the Reception-Tent during the ceremony.

PROCESSION TO THE SITE OF THE KING EDWARD MEMORIAL.

First Carriage.

THEIR IMPERIAL MAJESTIES.

Second Carriage.—The Duchess of Devonshire, the Marquis of Crewe, the Lord Chamberlain to the Queen-Empress, the Lord-in-Waiting.

Third Carriage.—The Countess of Shaftesbury, the Duke of Teck, the Lord Stamfordham, Sir John Hewett.

Fourth Carriage.—The Hon. Venetia Baring, the Lord High Steward, Sir H. Smith-Dorrien, Sir Edward Henry.

Fifth Carriage.—The Commander-in-Chief, General Sir Edward Barrow, Sir Stuart Beatson, Colonel J. Dunlop-Smith.

An Escort was furnished by the 10th (Prince of Wales's Own Royal) Hussars and the 11th King Edward's Own Lancers.

The route was by the Alipur Road, Kashmir Gate and Elgin Road, and was lined throughout by troops.

Guards of Honour of the Royal Navy, Royal Marine Artillery, the Gordon Highlanders, and the 2nd Batt. 2nd King Edward's Own Gurkha Rifles, were mounted within the enclosure, and detachments of the following regiments (of which the late King-Emperor was Colonel-in-Chief) with standards and colours were grouped around the base of the memorial:—10th Royal Hussars, Royal Regiment of Artillery, King's Own Royal Lancashire Regiment, Norfolk Regiment, Gordon Highlanders, 6th King Edward's Own Cavalry, 11th King Edward's Own Lancers, 102nd King Edward's Own Grenadiers, 2nd King Edward's Own Gurkha Rifles, the 33rd Queen's Own Light Cavalry, the Queen's Own Corps of Guides, the 2nd Queen's Own Sappers and Miners, 2nd Queen's Own Rajput Light Infantry.

PROCESSION TO THE SHAMIANA.

Governor-General's Staff.

Sir Hafiz Mohamed.		Sir Aslam Khan.
Major Wigram.		Major the Lord C. Fitzmaurice.
Capt. Godfrey-Faussett.	Sir D. Keppel.	Commander Sir C. Cust.
Sir J. Dunlop-Smith.	Gen. Sir Edmund Barrow.	Sir H. Smith-Dorrien.
Sir Edward Henry.		The Lord-in-Waiting.
Sir J. Hewett.		The Lord Stamfordham.
The Lord Chamberlain to the Queen-Empress.		The Lord High Steward.
THE QUEEN-EMPRESS.		THE KING-EMPEROR.
The Marquis of Crewe.		The Governor-General.
The Duchess of Devonshire.		The Duke of Teck.
The Hon. Venetia Baring.		The Countess of Shaftesbury.
Hon. Col. H.H. the Maharaja Sir Pratap Singh.	H.H. the Maharana of Udaipur.	H.H. the Maharaja Scindia of Gwalior.
H.H. the Maharaja of Bikaner.		Hon. Col. H.H. the Nawab of Rampur.
Brigadier-General R. E. Grimston.		H.E. the Commander-in-Chief.

On returning to the Camp His Imperial Majesty inspected the Guards of Honour of the King's Royal Rifle Corps and King George's Own Sappers and Miners, which were mounted in front of the Royal Tents.

THEIR MAJESTIES' DINNER-PARTY.

The Governor-General and Lady Hardinge, Sir Arthur Lawley and Lady Lawley, the Earl and Countess of Sefton, Lord Alington, the Jam

Saheb of Nawanagar, the Raja Saheb of Dhrangadra, the Raja of Rajpipla, the Nawab of Radhanpur, the Thakur Saheb and Thakurani of Gondal, the Nawab of Jangira, Sir Mohamed Ali Muhammed Khan of Mahmudabad, the Hon. Mr. M. Mazarul Haque, the Hon. Maung Bah Too and Mrs. Bah Too, the Hon. Mr. M. B. Dadabhoy and Mrs. Dadabhoy, the Hon. Mr. G. M. Chitnavis, the Hon. Sir Vithaldas Damodar Thackersey, the Hon. Mr. G. K. Gokhale, the Hon. Mr. Mohammad Ali Jinnah, the Hon. Nawab Abdul Majid, the Hon. Mr. F. C. Gates and Mrs. Gates, the Hon. Mr. F. A. ff. Phillips and Mrs. Phillips, the Hon. Sir Sassoon David, the Hon. Sir Trevredyn Wynne, the Hon. Mr. J. S. Meston and Mrs. Meston, the Hon. Mr. J. B. Brunyate and Mrs. Brunyate, the Hon. Mr. C. Stewart-Wilson and Mrs. Stewart-Wilson, the Hon. Rao Bahadur R. N. Mudholkar, the Hon. Mr. B. Robertson and Mrs. Robertson, the Hon. Mr. L. C. Porter, the Hon. Major-General M. H. S. Grover and Mrs. Grover, the Hon. Mr. C. H. Armstrong and Mrs. Armstrong, the Hon. Mr. Ghulam Muhammad Khan, walad Khan Bahadur Wali Muhammad Bhurgri, the Hon. Mr. W. H. Vincent and Mrs. Vincent, the Right Rev. Eyre Chatterton, D.D. (Bishop of Nagpur), and Mrs. Chatterton, the Right Rev. R. S. Fyffe (Bishop of Rangoon), the Right Rev. G. H. Wescott (Bishop of Lucknow), Mr. W. H. Wood and Mrs. Wood, Mr. S. Finney, C.I.E., and Mrs. Finney, Mr. G. W. Shaw, the Hon. Mr. Justice H. S. Hartnoll and Mrs. Hartnoll, the Hon. Mr. Justice E. W. Ormond and Mrs. Ormond, Mr. W. W. Drew and Mrs. Drew, Sir John Benton and Lady Benton, Surgeon-General F. W. Trevor and Mrs. Trevor, Major-General B. T. Mahon, Major-General Sir A. A. Barrett and Lady Barrett, Mr. Claude Hill and Mrs. Hill, the Hon. Mr. D. C. Baillie, the Hon. Mr. G. A. Tweedy, Colonel P. Z. Cox and Mrs. Cox, the Raj of Chhota Udaipur, the Raja of Baria, the Raja Saheb of Wankaner, the Nawab of Cochin, the Thakur Saheb of Limbri, the Thakur Saheb of Rajkot, Brigadier-General W. E. Peyton, D.S.O., and Mrs. Peyton, Brigadier-General H. V. Cox and Mrs. Cox, Lieut.-Colonel F. A. Maxwell and Mrs. Maxwell, the Aides-de-Camp-in-Waiting to His Excellency the Governor-General, the ladies and gentlemen of Their Imperial Majesties' Household in attendance—the Duke of Teck, the Marquis of Crewe, the Lord High Steward, the Mistress of the Robes, the Earl of Shaftesbury, the Countess of Shaftesbury, the Lord-in-Waiting, Lord Stamfordham, the Hon. Venetia Baring, Lieutenant-General Sir H. L. Smith-Dorrien, Sir E. R. Henry, Prince George of Battenberg, the Hon. J. W. Fortescue, Commander Sir Charles Cust, and Rear-Admiral Sir Colin Keppel (Equerries-in-Waiting).

December 9.

DELHI.

The King-Emperor this morning held a further reception of the Ruling Chiefs, when the following had the honour of being received in turn by His Imperial Majesty in the Audience Chamber :—

Bombay Chiefs.—The Nawab of Palanpur, the Jam of Navanagar, the Maharaja of Bhavanagar, the Raj Saheb of Dhrangadra, the Raja of

Rajpipla, the Nawab of Cambey, the Nawab of Radhanpur, the Thakur Saheb of Gondal, the Nawab of Janpira, the Sultan of Lahej, the Sultan of Sherer and Mokalla, the Fadhli Sultan, the Raja of Dharampur, the Raja of Bansda, the Raja of Chhota Udepur, the Maharawal of Bariya, the Nawab of Sachin, the Rao Saheb of Wankaner, the Thakur Saheb of Palitana, the Thakur Saheb of Limbdi (Limri), the Thakur Saheb of Rajkot, the Chief of Bhor, the Chief of Mudhol.

Rajputana.—The Maharaja Rana of Jhalawar.

Central India.—The Maharaja of Samthar, the Nawab of Jaora, the Raja of Rutlam, the Maharaja of Panna, the Maharaja of Charkhari, the Maharaja of Bijawar, the Maharaja of Chhatarpur, the Raja of Sitamau, the Raja of Sailana, the Raja of Rajgarh, the Raja of Narsinghgarh, the Rana of Barwani, the Raja of Alirajpur.

Bengal.—The Maharaja of Cooch Behar, the Raja of Karond.

United Provinces.—The Nawab of Rampur, the Maharaja of Benares, the Raja of Tehr (Garhwal).

Panjab.—The Raja of Jhind, the Raja of Kapurthala, the Raja of Mandi, the Raja of Sirmur (Nahan), the Raja of Bilaspur (Kohlra), the Nawab of Kotla, the Raja of Faridkot, the Raja of Chamba, the Raja of Suket, the Nawab of Loharu.

Madras.—The Raja of Pudukota.

Eastern Bengal and Assam.—The Raja of Hill Tippera, the Raja of Manipur.

Burma.—The Sawbwa of Kengtung, the Sawbwa of Yanghur, the Sawbwa of Hsipaw.

Baluchistan.—The Jam of Las Bela.

After the reception the King-Emperor inspected the Guards of Honour of the 1st Batt. Northumberland Fusiliers and the 1st Batt. King George's Own Gurkha Rifles, which were mounted in front of the Reception-Tent.

PROCESSION TO THE POLO-GROUND.

First Carriage.

THE KING-EMPEROR. THE QUEEN-EMPRESS.

Second Carriage.—The Duke of Teck, the Duchess of Devonshire, Captain G. Godfrey-Faussett.

Third Carriage.—The Marquis of Crewe, the Lord High Steward, Major the Lord C. Fitzmaurice.

The Escort was furnished by the 13th Hussars and 3rd Skinner's Horse.

December 10.

DELHI.

PROCESSION TO THE CHURCH PARADE GROUND.

First Carriage.

THE KING-EMPEROR. THE QUEEN-EMPRESS.

Second Carriage.—The Duchess of Devonshire, the Lord High Steward, the Marquis of Crewe, and Lord Shaftesbury.

Third Carriage.—The Duke of Teck, the Countess of Shaftesbury, the Lord-in-Waiting, and Lord Stamfordham.

Major Lord C. Fitzmaurice and Major Clive Wigram were in attendance on horseback.

The Escort was furnished by the 6th Inniskilling Dragoons and the 9th Hodson's Horse. The route of the procession, which was by the Kingsway and the Military Road, was lined throughout by British and Indian Infantry and the Imperial Service Troops.

The return route was by the Military Road, Parade Road, and Prince's Road.

December 11.

DELHI.

Mounted Procession to Parade Ground for Presentation of Colours.

First Division of Escort.

Orderly. Orderly.

Orderly with Royal Standard.

THE KING-EMPEROR.

The Duke of Teck. The Gov.-General.

Major C. Wigram. Sir Charles Fitzmaurice.

The Maharaja of Bikaner. The Nawab of Rampur. Maj.-Gen. Sir Pratap Singh. The Maharaja of Gwalior.

Gen. Sir E. Barrow. Lord Annaly. The Commander-in-Chief.

Maj.-Gen. Sir S. Beatson. Lt.-Gen. Sir H. Smith-Dorrien. Lord Stamfordham.

Colonel Maxwell. Br.-Gen. Grimston.

Royal Groom. Royal Groom.

THE QUEEN-EMPRESS

(in a carriage with the Mistress of the Robes and the Lord High Steward).

Captain Hill. Lt.-Colonel Watson.

LADY HARDINGE

(in a carriage with the Marquis of Crewe and Capt. P. Burn).

Second Division of Escort.

The Escort was furnished by the 13th Hussars and 36th Jacob's Horse.

Guards of Honour at the King-Emperor's Camp were furnished by the 2nd Batt. King's Royal Rifle Corps and 2nd Batt. King Edward's Own Gurkha Rifles.

APPENDIX A

December 12.

DELHI.

Programme of the Ceremonies to be observed on the Occasion of the Coronation Durbar, December 12, 1911.

The Members of the Household, including the Minister in Attendance, will leave the King-Emperor's Camp at 10.45 A.M. and will proceed by the Kingsway to the Durbar Amphitheatre, where they will be conducted to their places.

2. Their Excellencies the Governor-General and Lady Hardinge will leave the King-Emperor's Camp at 11.10 A.M. with an escort of one regiment of British Cavalry and one regiment of Indian Cavalry.

On approaching the Amphitheatre, their carriage will pass to the right along the front of the Spectators' Mound, turn down the Centre Road and proceed to the left by the Circular Road to the Durbar Shamiana, where they will be received by the Governor-General's Staff and conducted to their seats.

On arrival in the Amphitheatre they will be received with salutes by the troops massed in the arena and by the Guards of Honour. All present will rise and remain standing until Their Excellencies have alighted and taken their seats.

3. Their Imperial Majesties the King-Emperor and Queen-Empress will drive from the Camp at 11.30 A.M. attended by two equerries-in-waiting on horseback and with an escort of one regiment of British Cavalry (10th Hussars), a Battery of Royal Horse Artillery, the Bodyguard, the Imperial Cadet Corps, and one regiment of Indian Cavalry (18th Lancers).

The cortège will proceed to the Durbar Shamiana by the route described above.

The Imperial Cadet Corps and the Bodyguard will remain in the procession throughout, but the remainder of the escort will leave the procession as it is about to enter the Circular Road to pass in front of the Amphitheatre and will form up outside the arena.

4. As Their Imperial Majesties enter the Amphitheatre a salute[1] of 101 guns will be fired, and when they reach the Durbar Shamiana the Royal Standard will be hoisted, a Royal Salute will be given by the Guards of Honour and all the troops present, and the Massed Bands will play the National Anthem.

Their Imperial Majesties will be received by His Excellency the Governor-General as they alight from their carriage, and conducted to their Thrones.

All present will rise as Their Imperial Majesties enter the arena and will remain standing until they have taken their seats.

---

[1] The salute will be timed so as to terminate as Their Imperial Majesties enter the Durbar Shamiana.

5. On the conclusion of the salute the Master of the Ceremonies will obtain the KING-EMPEROR's command to open the Durbar.

The opening of the Durbar will be signalised by a flourish of trumpets and roll of drums from the Massed Bands in the arena.

The KING-EMPEROR has announced his gracious intention of then addressing the assemblage.

6. After this, the Governor-General, the High Officials and the Ruling Chiefs will do Homage in the following order :—

(1) His Excellency the Governor-General.

(2) His Excellency the Commander-in-Chief and the Ordinary Members of the Governor-General's Executive Council.

(3) The Ruling Chiefs in political relations with the Government of India, and the Agents to the Governor-General and Residents,[1] in the following territorial order, *i.e.*—

Hyderabad.
Baroda.
Mysore.
Kashmir.
Rajputana.
Central India.
Baluchistan.
Sikkim and Bhutan.

(4) The Chief Justice and Puisne Judges of the High Court, Bengal.
(5) The Governor-General's Legislative Council.
(6) His Excellency the Governor of Madras.
(7) The Governor's Executive Council.
(8) Ruling Chiefs in political relations with the Government of Madras.
(9) Provincial Representatives of Madras.
(10) His Excellency the Governor of Bombay.
(11) The Governor's Executive Council.
(12) Ruling Chiefs in political relations with the Government of Bombay.
(13) Provincial Representatives of Bombay.
(14) His Honour the Lieutenant-Governor of Bengal.
(15) The Lieutenant-Governor's Executive Council.
(16) Ruling Chiefs of Bengal.
(17) Provincial Representatives of Bengal.
(18) His Honour the Lieutenant-Governor of the United Provinces.
(19) Ruling Chiefs of the United Provinces.
(20) Provincial Representatives of the United Provinces.
(21) His Honour the Lieutenant-Governor of the Panjab.
(22) Ruling Chiefs of the Panjab.
(23) Provincial Representatives of the Panjab.
(24) His Honour the Lieutenant-Governor of Burma.
(25) Ruling Chiefs of Burma.
(26) Provincial Representatives of Burma.
(27) His Honour the Lieutenant-Governor of Eastern Bengal and Assam.
(28) Ruling Chiefs of Eastern Bengal and Assam.

---

[1] The Agents to the Governor-General and Residents will each precede their Chiefs and remain until the last of these has done Homage.

(29) Provincial Representatives of Eastern Bengal and Assam.
(30) The Hon. the Chief Commissioner of the Central Provinces.
(31) Representatives of the Central Provinces.
(32) Representatives of Baluchistan.
(33) The Hon. the Chief Commissioner of the North-West Frontier Province.
(34) Representatives of the North-West Frontier Province.

7. At the conclusion of the ceremony, the KING-EMPEROR and QUEEN-EMPRESS will move in procession from the Durbar Shamiana to the Royal Pavilion.

They will advance hand-in-hand, their robes being held by Pages and the golden umbrellas held over their heads.

Then will follow Their Excellencies the Governor-General and Lady Hardinge, the Minister in Attendance, His Highness the Duke of Teck, the Duchess of Devonshire, and at a suitable interval the remainder of the suite in attendance.

All will rise as the KING-EMPEROR and QUEEN-EMPRESS leave the Thrones in the Durbar Shamiana and will remain standing until THEIR IMPERIAL MAJESTIES are seated in the Royal Pavilion.

Their Excellencies the Governor-General and Lady Hardinge, the Minister in Attendance and His Highness the Duke of Teck with the Duchess of Devonshire, the Countess of Shaftesbury and the Hon. Venetia Baring will stand on the second tier of the Royal Pavilion ; His Excellency and Lady Hardinge on the right and the others above named on the left of the Thrones, round which the Pages will be grouped.

The Staffs will stand on the next lower platform.

8. The Bands within the arena will then sound a summons to the Heralds.

The Heralds with the Trumpeters, who will be posted outside, will reply with a flourish of trumpets and will ride up to the Amphitheatre. They will halt at the entrance to the Centre Road beyond the Spectators' Mound and sound another flourish of trumpets. They will then ride to the front of the Royal Pavilion, form up and sound a third flourish.

The Herald will then be commanded to read in English the Royal Proclamation announcing the Solemnity of HIS IMPERIAL MAJESTY'S Coronation in London on the 22nd June 1911, after which it will be read in Urdu by the Assistant Herald.

When the Proclamation has thus been read, the Trumpeters will sound another flourish.

As this flourish concludes, the Massed Bands will play the National Anthem, and the Guards of Honour and troops massed in the arena will present arms. All the spectators will rise from their seats and remain standing while the National Anthem is being played. On its completion a salute of 101 guns by salvos of batteries will be fired, and the troops outside the arena will fire a *feu de joie*.

9. When the Royal Salute has been fired, the Herald and Trumpeters will sound a prolonged flourish, after which His Excellency the Governor-General will make such announcement as HIS IMPERIAL MAJESTY may command.

The Herald and Trumpeters will then sound another flourish, and the Herald, raising his helmet, will call for three cheers first for the KING-EMPEROR and then for the QUEEN-EMPRESS, which will be joined in by all the spectators and the troops inside the Amphitheatre. As soon as these cheers have subsided, the General Officer Commanding the Troops outside the arena will similarly call for cheers from them.

10. THEIR IMPERIAL MAJESTIES will then return to the Durbar Shamiana in procession [1] as before, and, when they are again seated, the Trumpeters will sound another flourish, after which the Herald and Trumpeters will retire from the arena.

The Master of the Ceremonies will next request the KING-EMPEROR'S permission to close the Durbar, whereupon the Massed Bands will play the National Anthem, which will be sung by the whole assembly.

11. THEIR IMPERIAL MAJESTIES will then depart in the same manner and with the same ceremonies as when they came. All present will remain standing until they have left the arena.

The procession will pass to the Centre Road by the Circular Road on the opposite side of the Durbar Shamiana to that by which it arrived, and, when it reaches the end of the Centre Road, will turn to the left and proceed below the Spectators' Mound to the Prince's Road and thence by that route to the King-Emperor's Camp.

The first gun of the salute will be fired as the procession leaves the arena by the Prince's Road.

After the departure of the Royal cortège, Their Excellencies the Governor-General and Lady Hardinge will leave the Durbar in the same way and with the same honours as on their arrival, the spectators rising as they enter their carriage.

After the Governor-General, the members of the Royal Household will depart.

High Officials and Ruling Chiefs will then be conducted to their carriages.

All others are requested to remain in their places until the above have left, and they will then leave in the same manner as on arrival.

Full dress [2] will be worn. Gentlemen not entitled to wear uniform will appear in Court or Morning Dress.

Collar Day.

A. H. MCMAHON.

DURBAR PROCESSION FROM THE SHAMIANA TO THE PAVILION.

Lord Chamberlain to the Queen-Empress.	Lord High Steward.
THE QUEEN-EMPRESS.	THE KING-EMPEROR.
Pages.—The Thakur Saheb of Palitana, Rajkumar Ramchandra Singh of Sailana,	*Pages.*—The Maharaja of Bharatpur, Maharaja Kumar Himmat Singh of Idar, Ver

[1] The Massed Bands will play a March during the procession.

[2] With trousers and not knee-breeches.

Maharaja Kunwar Gulab Singh of Rewa, Maharaja Mandhata Singh of Sailana.

Singh (grandson of the Maharaja of Orchha), the Maharaja of Jodhpur, Maharaja Kunwar Sadul Singh of Bikaner, Sahibzada Muhammad Wahid-uz-Zafar Khan of Bhopal.

ATTENDANTS.

Lady Hardinge.		The Governor-General.
The Duke of Teck.	The Duchess of Devonshire.	The Marquis of Crewe.
The Hon. Venetia Baring.		The Countess of Shaftesbury.
Sir Pratap Singh.	Maharana of Udaipur.	Maharaja of Gwalior.
The Maharaja of Bikaner.		The Nawab of Rampur.
Sir John Hewett.	The Lord Annaly.	The Lord Stamfordham.
Sir Edward Henry.	Sir H. McMahon.	Lt.-Gen. Sir H. Smith-Dorrien.

Lt.-Col. Sir J. Dunlop-Smith.	Sir C. Keppel.	Sir Stuart Beatson.	Br.-Gen. Grimston.
Major Lord C. Fitzmaurice.	Hon. Sir D. Keppel.	Commander Sir C. Cust.	Capt. B. G. Godfrey-Faussett.
Lt.-Col. H. D. Watson.	H.H. Prince George of Battenberg.	Major Wigram.	Sir R. H. Charles.
Col. Lord Harris.	Br.-Gen. H. D'U. Keary.	Br.-Gen. Birdwood.	Br.-Gen. C. J. Melliss.
Br.-Gen. Mercer.	Col. Goodwin.	Col. Viscount Hardinge.	Col. Stanton.
Major Stockley.	Hon. Col. Nawab Sir Hafiz Mohamad Abdullah Khan.	Hon. Col. Nawab Sir Mohamad Aslam Khan.	Major Money.
Lt.-Col. Bird.	Hon. J. Fortescue.	Mr. Lucas.	Captain Hogg.
Captain Raban.	Capt. Ashburner.	Major Cadogan.	Captain Hill.

Governor-General's Staff (8).

Gentlemen-at-Arms.

Royal Archer.

The King-Emperor and Queen-Empress gave a State banquet this evening, to which the following had the honour of being invited :—The Governor-General of India and the Lady Hardinge of Penshurst, the Governor of Bombay and Lady Clarke, the Governor of Madras and Lady Carmichael, the Lieutenant-Governor of the Panjab and Lady Dane, the Governor of Ceylon and Lady McCallum, the Governor of the Straits Settlements and Lady Young.

The Nizam of Hyderabad, the Gaekwar of Baroda, the Maharaja of Kolhapur, the Commander-in-Chief in India and Lady Creagh, Sir John Hewett (President Coronation Durbar Committee) and Lady Hewett, the

APPENDIX A

Lieutenant-Governor of Burma and Lady Adamson, the Lieutenant-Governor of Eastern Bengal and Assam and Lady Bayley, the Lieutenant-Governor of the United Provinces, the Lieutenant-Governor of Bengal and Mrs. Duke, the Chief Justice of Bengal and Lady Jenkins, Sir Guy Fleetwood Wilson (Ordinary Member of the Council of His Excellency the Governor-General), Mr. J. L. Jenkins (Ordinary Member of the Council of the Governor-General) and Mrs. Jenkins.

Mr. R. W. Carlyle (Ordinary Member of the Council of the Governor-General) and Mrs. Carlyle, Mr. S. H. Butler (Ordinary Member of the Council of the Governor-General) and Mrs. Butler, Mr. Syed Ali Imam (Ordinary Member of the Council of the Governor-General), Mr. W. H. Clark (Ordinary Member of the Council of the Governor-General) and Mrs. Clark, the Roman Catholic Archbishop of Simla.

The Earl and the Countess of Mar and Kellie, Lord Charles Montagu, Admiral the Hon. Sir H. and Lady Meux, Major-General the Maharaja of Gwalior (Hon. A.D.C. to the King-Emperor), the Maharaja of Indore, Major-General the Maharaja Sir Pratap Singh Bahadur, Regent of Jodhpur (Hon. A.D.C. to the King-Emperor), Colonel the Maharaja of Bikaner (Hon. A.D.C. to the King-Emperor), the Maharaja of Patiala, the Maharaja of Bhutan, the Raja of Behar, the Raja of Dewas (senior branch), the Raja of Dewas (junior branch), the Maharaja of Keshangarh, the Maharaja of Alwar, the Maharaja of Sikkim, the Maharaja Rana of Dholpur, the Maharawal of Dungarpur, the Maharaja of Idar, Colonel the Nawab of Rampur (Hon. A.D.C. to the King-Emperor), the Nawab of Jaora, the Raja of Hill Tippera, the Aga Khan.

The Commander-in-Chief of His Majesty's Naval Forces in the East Indies and Lady Slade, Lieut.-Colonel Sir Henry McMahon (Master of Ceremonies) and Lady McMahon, Sir Charles Arnold White (Chief Justice of the High Court of Judicature at Madras) and Lady White, Sir Basil Scott (Chief Justice of the High Court of Judicature at Bombay), Mr. H. G. Richards (Chief Justice of the High Court of Judicature for the North-Western Provinces) and Mrs. Richards, the Bishop of Madras and Mrs. Whitehead, the Bishop of Bombay, Sir Murray Hammick (Ordinary Member of Council, Madras) and Lady Hammick, Mr. M. B. Chaubal (Ordinary Member of Council, Bombay), Mr. W. T. Morison (Ordinary Member of Council, Bombay), Mr. R. A. Lamb (Ordinary Member of Council, Bombay) and Mrs. Lamb.

Mr. Krishnaswami Aiyer (Ordinary Member of Council, Madras), the General Officer Commanding the Southern Army and Lady Barrow, the Chief of the General Staff and the Hon. Lady Haig, the General Officer Commanding the Northern Army and Lady Willcocks, the Agent to the Governor-General in Rajputana and Mrs. Colvin, the Resident in Kashmir and Mrs. Fraser, the Chief Commissioner of the Central Provinces and Mrs. Craddock, the Chief Commissioner of the North-West Frontier Provinces, the Resident in Mysore and Mrs. Daly, Mr. F. A. Slacke (Member of the Executive Council of the Lieutenant-Governor of Bengal) and Mrs. Slacke, Rai Kisori Lall Goswami Bahadur (Member of the Executive Council of His Honour the Lieutenant-Governor of Bengal), the Agent to the Governor-General of Baluchistan and Mrs. Ramsay, the Agent to the Governor-General in Central India and Mrs. O'Dwyer, the

Resident in Hyderabad and Mrs. Pinhey, Mr. R. F. Greer (Member of the Executive Council of the Lieutenant-Governor of Bengal) and Mrs. Greer.

Justice Sir G. H. Knox (Puisne Judge of the High Court of Judicature for the North-Western Provinces) and Lady Knox, Mr. Justice P. C. Banerjee (Puisne Judge of the High Court of Judicature for the North-Western Provinces), Justice Sir Ralph Benson (Puisne Judge of the High Court of Judicature at Madras) and Lady Benson, Justice Sir Richard Harington, Bart. (Puisne Judge of the High Court of Judicature at Fort William, in Bengal) and Mrs. Harington, Mr. Justice C. N. W. Brett (Puisne Judge of the High Court of Judicature at Fort William, in Bengal) and Mrs. Brett, Mr. Justice H. L. Stephen (Puisne Judge of the High Court of Judicature at Fort William, in Bengal) and Mrs. Stephen, Mr. Justice J. E. P. Wallis (Puisne Judge of the High Court of Judicature at Madras) and Mrs. Wallis, Mr. Justice C. Sankaran Nair (Puisne Judge of the High Court of Judicature at Madras) and Mrs. Sankaran Nair, Mr. Justice H. D. Griffin (Puisne Judge of the High Court of Judicature for the North-Western Provinces) and Mrs. Griffin, Mr. Justice Abdur Rahim (Puisne Judge of the High Court of Judicature at Madras), Sir Charles Fox (Chief Justice of the Chief Court of Burma) and Lady Fox, Sir Arthur Reid (Chief Judge of the Chief Court, Panjab) and Lady Reid, the Lieutenant-General Commanding the 1st (Peshawar) Division and Lady Nixon, Lieut.-General Sir A. R. Martin (commanding the 2nd (Rawalpindi) Division), the Lieutenant-General Commanding the 7th (Meerut) Division and Lady Lake, the Lieutenant-General Commanding the 3rd (Lahore) Division and Lady Pearson, Lieut.-General Sir J. B. Moon (commanding the 9th (Secunderabad) Division), the Lieutenant-General Commanding the 4th (Quetta) Division and Mrs. Sclater, the Bishop of Lahore, Mr. J. B. Wood (additional Secretary to the Government of India in the Foreign Department) and Mrs. Wood, Brigadier-General R. E. Grimston (Military Secretary to the King-Emperor), Mr. H. V. Cobb (Resident at Baroda), Major F. W. Wodehouse (Political Agent, Kolhapur), Mr. C. A. Bell (Political Officer, Sikkim), the Private Secretary to the Governor-General and Mrs. Du Boulay, Captain the Hon. E. Hardinge (Aide-de-Camp-in-Waiting to the Governor-General).

Ladies and gentlemen of the Household in attendance :—The Duke of Teck (Silver Stick and personal A.D.C. to the King-Emperor), the Marquis of Crewe (Minister in Attendance), the Earl of Durham (Lord High Steward), the Duchess of Devonshire (Mistress of the Robes), the Earl of Shaftesbury (Lord-in-Waiting), the Lord Annaly (Lord in-Waiting), the Lord Stamfordham (Private Secretary to the King-Emperor), the Hon. Venetia Baring (Maid of Honour), Lieut.-General Sir H. L. Smith-Dorrien (Aide-de-Camp), General Sir E. R. Henry (Extra Equerry to the King-Emperor), Major-General Sir S. B. Beatson (Private Secretary to the Queen-Empress), Rear-Admiral Sir C. R. Keppel (Extra Equerry to the King-Emperor), Lieut.-Colonel Sir J. R. Dunlop-Smith (Political A.D.C. to the Secretary of State), Commander Sir C. L. Cust, Bart. (Equerry-in-Waiting to the King-Emperor), Lieut.-Colonel the Hon. Sir D. W. G. Keppel (Master of the Household), Captain B. G. Godfrey-Faussett (Equerry to the King-Emperor), Lord Charles G. F. P. Fitzmaurice (Equerry to the King-Emperor), Major Clive Wigram (Assistant Private

Secretary and Equerry to the King-Emperor), Prince George of Battenberg, Lieut.-Colonel Sir R. Havelock Charles (Sergeant-Surgeon to the King-Emperor), Mr. F. H. Lucas (Private Secretary to the Secretary of State for India), the Hon. J. W. Fortescue (Official Historian to the King-Emperor), Mr. Jacomb Hood (Official Artist to the King-Emperor).

The Nawab of Tonck also had the honour of being invited, but was unavoidably prevented from obeying His Majesty's commands.

December 13.

DELHI.

The King-Emperor left camp by motor at 8 A.M. this morning, attended by the Duke of Teck, the Commander-in-Chief, the Lord Annaly, General Sir E. Barrow, Lieut.-General Sir H. L. Smith-Dorrien, Brigadier-General R. E. Grimston, Major Lord C. Fitzmaurice, Major Clive Wigram.

On arrival at the camp of the Naval Contingent, His Imperial Majesty mounted his charger and rode through the camps of the Naval Contingent, the 19th Infantry Brigade, the 20th Infantry Brigade, the 21st Infantry Brigade, the 9th Brigade, the 8th Brigade, the 7th Infantry Brigade, the 1st Composite Infantry Brigade.

His Imperial Majesty returned to camp by motor by the Kingsway.

PROCESSION TO THE SHAMIANA.

Presentation of Volunteer Officers, Indian Officers, and Officers of the Imperial Service Troops.

Brigadier-General Grimston.		Two Equerries-in-Waiting.	
	THE KING-EMPEROR.		
The Duke of Teck.	The Commander-in-Chief.	The Governor-General.	The Marquis of Crewe.
Nawab of Rampur.	Maharaja Sir Pratap Singh.	Maharaja of Gwalior.	Maharaja of Bikaner.
Sir E. Henry.	Gen. Sir E. Barrow.	Lord Stamfordham.	Lt.-Gen. Sir H. Smith-Dorrien.
Lord Harris.	The Hon. D. Keppel.		Br.-Gen. Birdwood.
Col. Goodwin.	Br.-Gen. Melliss.	Br.-Gen. Keary.	Col. Viscount Hardinge.
Col. Stanton.	Nawab Sir Hafiz Muhammad Abdulla Khan.	Col. Sir Aslam Khan.	Br.-Gen. Mercer.
	Governor-General's Staff.		

The Volunteer officers first had the honour of being presented to the King-Emperor. The Indian officers and Imperial Service officers then had the honour of being presented.

The Governor-General's Bodyguard, the Governor's Bodyguard (Madras), the Governor's Bodyguard (Bombay), the Escort to the Lieutenant-Governor of Burma.

3rd Skinner's Horse, 8th Cavalry, 9th Hodson's Horse, 11th Lancers, 30th Lancers, 36th Horse.

31st Mountain Battery, 32nd Mountain Battery, 1st Sappers and Miners, 2nd Sappers and Miners, 25th and 26th Railway Companies' Sappers and Miners, 31st, 32nd and 33rd Delhi Signal Companies.

16th Rajputs, 18th Infantry, 25th Panjabis, 23rd Pioneers, 28th Panjabis, 33rd Panjabis, 34th Pioneers, 36th Sikhs, 1-39th Garhwal Rifles, 2-39th Garhwal Rifles, 41st Dogras, 45th Sikhs, 47th Sikhs, 48th Pioneers, 53rd Sikhs, 57th Rifles, 74th Panjabis.

90th Panjabis, 107th Pioneers, 116th Maharattas, 126th Pioneers, 130th Baluchis, 1-1st Gurkha Rifles, 2-1st Gurkha Rifles, 2-2nd Gurkha Rifles, 1-3rd Gurkha Rifles, 2-3rd Gurkha Rifles, 2-4th Gurkha Rifles, 2-9th Gurkha Rifles, 2-10th Gurkha Rifles.

1st Lancers, 6th Cavalry, 26th Cavalry, 38th Horse, 39th Horse, 104th Rifles, 61st Pioneers, 102nd Grenadiers, 1-2nd Gurkha Rifles, 33rd Cavalry, the Corps of Guides, 2nd Infantry, Malay States Guides, 14th Lancers, 3rd Sappers and Miners, 31st Lancers, 2nd Lancers, 12th Cavalry, 7th Rajputs, 60th Panjabis.

Indian Aides-de-Camp to the Governor-General, the Commander-in Chief, the General Officer Commanding Northern Army, the General Officer Commanding Southern Army.

Medical Department, Transport units.

Imperial Service Troops.—Alwar Lancers, Bhavnagar Lancers, Bhopal Lancers, Gwalior Lancers, Hyderabad Lancers, Jodhpur Lancers, Kashmir Lancers, Mysore Lancers, Navanagar Lancers, Patiala Lancers, Rampur Lancers, Kashmir Artillery, Faridkote Sappers, Malar Kotla Sappers, Sirmur Sappers, Tehri Garhwal Sappers, Bhawalpur Camel Corps, Bikaner Camel Corps, Khairpur Camel Corps, Alwar Infantry, Bharatpur Infantry, Bikaner Infantry, Gwalior Infantry, Jind Infantry, Kapurthala Infantry, Kashmir Infantry, Nabha Infantry, Patiala Infantry, Rampur Infantry, Gwalior Transport Corps, Indore Transport Corps, Jaipur Transport Corps.

At the conclusion of the presentation His Imperial Majesty inspected the Guard of Honour of the 1st Batt. Connaught Rangers, 1st King George's Own Sappers and Miners.

Before the presentation of the above officers took place the King-Emperor presented Albert Medals to the following officers, warrant and non-commissioned officers of the Indian Ordnance Department, which were conferred on them for their gallantry in saving life on the occasion of the explosion of cordite at Hyderabad (Sind) and Ferozepur in 1906.

Albert Medal of the First Class.—Captain G. C. Donovan and Sub-Conductor A. E. Purkis.

Albert Medal of the Second Class.—Major-General C. A. Anderson, Major M. S. Clarke Campbell, Captain H. Clarke, Assistant Commissionary and Hon. Lieutenant F. Hensely, Conductor H. Pargiter, Sergeant A. J. Robinson, Sergeant G. Smith, and Sergeant D. Daw.

Their Imperial Majesties gave a dinner-party this evening, to which the following had the honour of being invited :—The Governor-General of India and Lady Hardinge of Penshurst, the Roman Catholic Archbishop of Agra, the Roman Catholic Archbishop of Madras, the Raja of Jhind, the

APPENDIX A

Raja of Kapurthala, the Raja of Pudukottai, the Maharaja Rana of Jhalawar, the Nawab Bahadur of Murshidabad.

Additional Members of the Council of the Governor-General.—The Hon. Mr. C. W. N. Graham (President Bengal Chamber of Commerce), the Maharaja Adhiraja Bahadur of Burdwan, the Hon. Raja of Dighapatia, the Hon. Maulvi Syed Shamsul Huda, the Hon. the Raja of Kurupam, the Hon. Nawab Saiyid Muhammad Sahib Bahadur, the Hon. Babu Bhupendra Nath Basu, the Hon. Mr. Sachchidananda Sinha.

The Commissioner (Fyzabad Division) and Mrs. Holmes, the Hon. Khan Zulfikar Ali Khan of Maier Kotla, the Hon. Malik Umar Hayat Khan, Tiwana, the Hon. Mr. J. M. Macpherson, the Director-General of the Indian Medical Service and Mrs. Lukis, the Director-General of Telegraphs in India and Mrs. Dempster, the Inspector-General of Excise and Salt and Mrs. Todhunter, the Hon. Mr. G. H. B. Kenrick (Advocate-General, Bengal), the Hon. Mr. C. H. Kesteven, the Hon. Kour Sir Ranbir Singh of Patiala, the Hon. Sir Ghulam Muhammad Ali Khan Bahadur, K.C.I.E., Prince of Arcot.

The Secretary to the Government of India in the Home Department, the Hon. Mr. E. D. MacLagan (Secretary to the Government of India in the Department of Revenue and Agriculture), the Hon. Mr. H. Sharp (Secretary to the Government of India in the Department of Education), the Hon. Mr. W. B. Gordon (Secretary to the Government of India in the Public Works Department), the Financial Commissioner of Panjab and Mrs. Meredith, the Hon. Mr. P. C. Lyon (Member of the Board of Revenue, Eastern Bengal and Assam) and Mrs. Lyon, the Hon. Mr. R. C. C. Carr, I.C.S. (Member of the Board of Revenue, Madras), the Commissioner of Northern India Salt and Revenue and Mrs. Arthur.

The Hon. Mr. Justice F. A. Robertson (a Judge of the Chief Court, Panjab) and Mrs. Robertson, the Hon. Mr. Justice A. Kensington (a Judge of the Chief Court, Panjab) and Mrs. Kensington, the Hon. Mr. Justice D. C. Johnstone (a Judge of the Chief Court, Panjab) and Mrs. Johnstone, the Chief Secretary to the Government of Madras and Member of the Madras Legislative Council and Lady Stuart, the Director of Supplies and Transport and Mrs. Mansfield.

Major-General W. Du G. Gray (Inspector-General of Volunteers in India), the General Officer Commanding the 5th (Mhow) Division and Mrs. Blomfield, Major-General T. D. Pilcher (commanding the Sirhind Brigade), Major-General G. C. Kitson (Quartermaster-General in India).

The Hon. Mr. A. K. L. Stuart (Senior Member of Board of Revenue, Madras, and a Member of the Madras Legislative Council), the Hon. Mr. J. McC. Douie (First Financial Commissioner, Panjab, and a Member of the Panjab Legislative Council) and Mrs. Douie.

The Hon. Mr. P. G. Melitus (Member of Board of Revenue, Eastern Bengal and Assam, and a Member of the Eastern Bengal and Assam Legislative Council) and Mrs. Melitus, the Hon. Mr. A. H. Diack (Second Financial Commissioner, Panjab, and a Member of the Panjab Legislative Council) and Mrs. Diack, Surgeon-General W. B. Bannerman and Miss Bannerman, the Hon. Mr. D. J. Macpherson (Member of Board of Revenue, Bengal, and Member of the Bengal Legislative Council) and Mrs. Macpherson.

APPENDIX A

The Rev. J. C. R. Ewing (Vice-Chancellor of the Panjab University), the Commissioner of Delhi Division and Mrs. Dallas, the Political Agent of the Phulkian States and Bhawalpur and Mrs. Atkins, Colonel Viscount Hardinge (C.B., A.D.C. to the King-Emperor) and Viscountess Hardinge, Colonel Nawab Sir Muhammad Aslam Khan, Sardar Bahadur (A.D.C. to the King-Emperor), Raja Sir Harnam Singh of Kapurthala and Rani Lady Harnam Singh.

The Inspector-General of Police of the Panjab and Mrs. Lee-French, the Raja Dhiraj of Shahpura, the Maharaja of Moharbhanj, the Nawab of Bhanganapalle, the Raja of Sarangarh, the Surgeon to the Governor-General of India and Mrs. O'Kinealy, the Comptroller of the Governor-General's Household and Mrs. Mackenzie, Captains Burn and Todd (Aides-de-Camp-in-Waiting to His Excellency the Governor-General).

Ladies and Gentlemen of the Household.—Duke of Teck (Silver Stick and personal Aide-de-Camp), the Right Hon. the Marquis of Crewe (Minister in Attendance), the Right Hon. the Earl of Durham (Lord High Steward), the Duchess of Devonshire (Mistress of the Robes), the Earl of Shaftesbury (Lord Chamberlain to Her Imperial Majesty), the Countess of Shaftesbury (Lady-in-Waiting), the Lord Annaly (Lord-in-Waiting), the Lord Stamfordham (Private Secretary to His Imperial Majesty), the Hon. Venetia Baring (Maid of Honour), Major-General Sir S. S. Beatson (Private Secretary to Her Imperial Majesty), Lieut.-Colonel Sir J. R. Dunlop-Smith (Political A.D.C. to the Secretary of State), Lieut.-Colonel the Hon. Sir D. W. G. Keppel (Master of the Household), Lieut.-Colonel Sir R. Havelock Charles (Sergeant-Surgeon to His Imperial Majesty), Captain B. Godfrey-Faussett, Rear-Admiral Sir C. Keppel.

December 14.

DELHI.

Mounted Procession to the Review Ground.

The Governor-General's Personal Staff.

Capt. R. Raban.	Capt. R. E. T. Hogg.	Major Hon. W. Cadogan.
Major H. R. Stockley.	Hon. Col. Nawab Sir Hafiz Muhammad Abdulla Khan.	Major E. D. Money.
Hon. Col. Sir Muhammad Aslam Khan.	Col. Viscount Hardinge.	Col. Stanton.
Col. Goodwin.	Br.-Gen. H. D'U. Keary.	Br.-Gen. C. J. Melliss.
Br.-Gen. Birdwood.	Sir E. Henry.	Br.-Gen. Mercer.
Lt.-Gen. Sir H. L. Smith-Dorrien.		Gen. Sir E. Barrow.
Lord Stamfordham.		The Lord-in-Waiting.

Bodyguard.

Household Cavalry Orderlies with Standard.

APPENDIX A

THE KING-EMPEROR.

Adjutant, Bodyguard.		Commandant, Bodyguard.
The Duke of Teck.		The Governor-General.
Major Lord C. Fitzmaurice.	Br.-Gen. Grimston.	Col. Maxwell.
The Maharaja of Bikaner.		The Maharaja of Gwalior.
Royal Groom.		Royal Groom.

THE QUEEN-EMPRESS
(in a carriage with the Mistress of the Robes and the Lord High Steward).

Commandant, Imperial Cadet Corps.	Major-Gen. Sir Pratap Singh.
Lt.-Col. H. D. Watson.	Major-Gen. Sir Stuart Beatson.
Capt. H. Hill.	Capt. L. F. Ashburner.

Second Carriage.—Lady Hardinge, Marquis of Crewe, Lord Chamberlain to the Queen-Empress, Aide-de-Camp.

Imperial Cadet Corps.

ORDER OF MARCH, ROYAL REVIEW.

HIS IMPERIAL MAJESTY THE KING-EMPEROR'S PROCESSION.

Army Headquarters Staff.
Foreign General Officers and Military Attachés.
The Commander-in-Chief's Personal Staff.
The Governor-General's Personal Staff.

Capt. Raban.	Capt. Hogg.	Major Cadogan.
Major Stockley.	Hon. Col. Hafiz Muhammad Abdulla Khan.	Major Money.
Hon. Col. Muhammad Aslam Khan.	Col. Viscount Hardinge.	Col. Stanton.
Col. Goodwin.	Br.-Gen. Keary.	Br.-Gen. Melliss.
Br.-Gen. Birdwood.	Sir E. Henry.	Br.-Gen. Mercer.
Lt.-Gen. Sir H. L. Smith-Dorrien.		Gen. Sir E. Barrow.
Lord Stamfordham.		The Lord-in-Waiting.

First Division Bodyguard.

Household Cavalry Orderlies with Standard.

THE KING-EMPEROR.

Adjutant, Bodyguard.		Commandant, Bodyguard.
The Duke of Teck.		The Governor-General.
Major Lord C. Fitzmaurice.	Br.-Gen. Grimston.	Col. Maxwell.
The Maharaja of Bikaner.		The Maharaja of Gwalior.
Royal Groom.		Royal Groom.

Second Division Bodyguard.

APPENDIX A

HER IMPERIAL MAJESTY THE QUEEN-EMPRESS'S PROCESSION.

First Division, Imperial Cadet Corps.

THE QUEEN-EMPRESS

(in a carriage with the Mistress of the Robes and the Lord High Steward).

Commandant, Imperial Cadet Corps.	Hon. Major-Gen. Sir Pratap Singh.
Lt.-Col. H. D. Watson.	Major-Gen. Sir Stuart Beatson.
Capt. H. Hill.	Capt. Ashburner.

Second Carriage.—Lady Hardinge, Marquis of Crewe, Lord Chamberlain to the Queen-Empress, Aide-de-Camp.

Second Division, Imperial Cadet Corps.

Guards of Honour were furnished :—

At the Saluting Point by Royal Navy and Royal Marine Artillery.

At the Imperial Camp by the 1st Batt. Seaforth Highlanders and 45th Sikhs.

THE INVESTITURE.

PROCESSION TO THE DAIS.

Delhi Herald, Major Stockley, Captain Hogg, Major Money, Lieut.-Colonel Bird, Lieut.-Colonel Sir H. Charles, Prince George of Battenberg, Major C. Wigram, Lieut.-Colonel Sir D. Keppel, Major Lord C. Fitz-maurice, Captain Godfrey-Faussett, Commander Sir C. Cust, Sir James Dunlop-Smith, Major-General Sir Stuart Beatson, Sir Colin Keppel, Sir Edward Henry, Lieut.-General Sir H. Smith-Dorrien, Sir J. Hewett, the Lord-in-Waiting, the Lord Stamfordham, the Lord Chamberlain to the Queen-Empress, the Lord High Steward.

THE QUEEN-EMPRESS. THE KING-EMPEROR.

Pages.—Maharaja Kishen Singh of Bharatpur, Maharaja Sumer Singh of Jodhpur, Maharaja Kunwar Sadul Singh of Bikaner, Vir Singh (grandson of the Maharaja of Orchha), Maharaja Kumar Kimmatsinghji of Idar, Sahibzada Muhammad Wahidaz Zafar Khan of Bhopal, the Thakur Saheb of Palitana, Raja Kumar Chandra Singh of Sailana, Maharaja Kumar Gulab Singh of Rewa, Maharaja Mandhata Singh of Sailana.

The Duke of Teck, the Hon. Venetia Baring, the Mistress of the Robes, the Marquis of Crewe, Sir H. McMahon, the Assistant Herald.

The Guard of Honour mounted outside the Investiture Tent was furnished by the 1st Batt. Seaforth Highlanders and the 5th Sikhs.

December 15.

DELHI.

PROCESSION TO LAY FOUNDATION-STONE OF NEW DELHI.

First Carriage.

THE KING-EMPEROR. THE QUEEN-EMPRESS.

Second Carriage.—The Mistress of the Robes, the Marquis of Crewe, the Lord High Steward, and the Duke of Teck.

Third Carriage.—The Countess of Shaftesbury, the Hon. Venetia Baring, the Lord Chamberlain to the Queen-Empress, and the Lord Stamfordham.

Brigadier-General Sir R. Grimston and Major Lord C. Fitzmaurice were in attendance on horseback.

PROCESSION TO THE REVIEW OF POLICE.

First Division of Escort.

Orderly. Orderly.

Orderly with Royal Standard.

THE KING-EMPEROR.

The Duke of Teck. The Governor-General.

Major Lord Charles Fitzmaurice. General Sir R. Grimston.

The Maharaja of Bikaner. The Nawab of Rampur. Major-Gen. Sir Pratap Singh. The Maharaja of Gwalior.

Gen. Sir E. Barrow. Lord Annaly. The Commander-in-Chief.

Major-Gen. Sir S. Beatson. Lt.-Gen. Sir E. Smith-Dorrien. Lord Stamfordham.

Colonel Maxwell. A.D.C. to Governor-General.

Royal Groom. Royal Groom.

THE QUEEN-EMPRESS

(in a carriage with the Mistress of the Robes and the Lord High Steward).

Captain Hill. Lt.-Col. Watson.

Lady Hardinge

(in a carriage with the Marquis of Crewe and the Lord Chamberlain to the Queen-Empress).

Second Division of Escort.

The Escort was furnished by the 13th Hussars and the 17th Cavalry.

PROCESSION TO THE MILITARY TOURNAMENT.

First Carriage.

THE KING-EMPEROR. THE QUEEN-EMPRESS.

Second Carriage.—The Mistress of the Robes, the Marquis of Crewe, the Duke of Teck, and the Lord High Steward.

Third Carriage.—The Countess of Shaftesbury, the Hon. Venetia Baring, and the Lord Chamberlain to the Queen-Empress.

Major Lord C. Fitzmaurice and Major Wigram were in attendance on horseback.

The route was by the Kingsway, Princess Road, and the Parade Road.

The Escort was furnished by the Volunteer Light Horse, detachments of the 1st Lancers, the 6th Cavalry, and the 39th Central India Horse.

APPENDIX A

December 16.

AGRA.

QUEEN-EMPRESS'S CAMP.

Guards of Honour were mounted at the station by the 13th Rajputs, and at the Circuit House by the 18th Royal Irish Regiment.

December 17.

KING-EMPEROR'S CAMP.

The King-Emperor's train stopped at Arrah this morning and His Imperial Majesty, attended by his Suite, was present at Divine Service in Arrah Church. After the Service the King-Emperor inspected the Behar Light Horse and visited Arrah House and returned to the train, which left for Bikna Thori.

AGRA.

QUEEN-EMPRESS'S CAMP.

In the evening Her Imperial Majesty gave a dinner-party, to which the following ladies and gentlemen had the honour of being invited :—The Bishop of Lucknow, Mr. and Mrs. Reynolds, Mr. and Mrs. Lyle, Mr. and Mrs. Mardan, Colonel and Mrs. Downing, Colonel and Mrs. Camilleri, Major and Mrs. Austin Smith, and Major and Mrs. Buchanan.

December 19.

JAIPUR.

QUEEN-EMPRESS'S CAMP.

Guard of Honour at Agra : Royal Irish Regiment.
Escort at Agra : 13th Hussars.
Guard of Honour at Jaipur Station : 30th Rajputs.
Guard of Honour at Jaipur Residency : 42nd Deoli Regiment.

Her Imperial Majesty gave a dinner-party this evening. The following ladies and gentlemen had the honour to be invited :—Colonel and Mrs. Showers, the Hon. Nawab Sir Faiyaz Ali Khan, Major Fisher, Sir Swinton and Lady Jacob, Major Shelley, Mr. Lanson, Mr. Berkeley, the Rev. Dr. Jameson, and Mrs. Stothard.

December 21.

AJMER.

QUEEN-EMPRESS'S CAMP.

Guards of Honour were furnished at Ajmer station by the 44th

Merwara Infantry, and the Bombay, Baroda and Central India Railway Rifle Volunteers.

Her Imperial Majesty proceeded direct from the station to the Mayo College, the Escort being supplied by the 27th Light Cavalry.

In the evening Her Imperial Majesty gave a dinner-party, to which the following ladies and gentlemen had the honour to be invited :—Sir Elliot and Lady Colvin and Miss Colvin, Colonel Stratton, Lieut.-Colonel Poingdestre, Lieut.-Colonel Deane, Mr. and Mrs. Waddington, and Mrs. Saunders.

December 24.

KASRA, NIPAL.

King-Emperor's Camp.

The King-Emperor arrived at Kasra Camp last night.

His Imperial Majesty attended Divine Service in camp this morning. The sermon was preached by the Rev. John Godber.

Sir Henry and Lady McMahon, Miss McMahon, and Lieut.-Colonel and Mrs. Manners-Smith had the honour of being invited to luncheon with His Imperial Majesty.

Christmas Day.

The King-Emperor attended Divine Service in camp this morning. His Imperial Majesty was attended by the whole of his Suite.

December 26.

KOTAH.

Queen-Empress's Camp.

In the evening Her Imperial Majesty gave a dinner-party, to which the following ladies and gentlemen had the honour to be invited :—Colonel and Mrs. Mathews, Lieut.-Colonel and Mrs. Carr White, Mr. and Mrs. Robinson, Mr. and Mrs. Devon, and Mr. Sutton.

December 28.

NARKATIAGANJ.

King-Emperor's Camp.

The King-Emperor, attended by the whole of his Suite, left Kasra Camp this morning.

His Imperial Majesty was accompanied to Bikna Thori Station by His Excellency the Prime Minister of Nipal. After His Excellency with his sons (General Mohan Shum Shere Jung Rana Bahadur, Lieut.-General Baber Shum Shere Jung Rana Bahadur, and Lieut.-General Kishen Shum

Shere Jung Rana Bahadur) had taken leave of His Imperial Majesty, the Royal special train left Bikna Thori Station at 6 P.M. Lieut.-Colonel Manners-Smith and Mr. H. C. Streatfield were in attendance on the platform.

December 30.

CALCUTTA.

Arrival at Howrah.

Walking Procession from Howrah Station to the Pontoon and from the Landing-Stage at Prinsep's Ghat to the Pandal.

H.E. the Governor-General's Staff.

Captain Maclachlan.	Major the Hon. W. Cadogan.	Captain Holmes.
Captain Hogg.		Lt.-Col. Bird.
Hon. J. Fortescue.	Br.-Gen. Mercer.	Mr. F. H. Lucas.
Colonel Stanton.	Br.-Gen. Birdwood.	Br.-Gen. Keary.
Lt.-Col. Sir R. Havelock Charles.	Major Lord Charles Fitzmaurice.	Major C. Wigram.
Captain B. G. Godfrey-Faussett.	Commander Sir C. Cust.	The Hon. Sir D. Keppel.
Sir James Dunlop-Smith.	Major-Gen. Sir Stuart Beatson.	Rear-Admiral Sir C. Keppel.
Sir E. Henry.	Gen. Sir E. Barrow.	Lt.-Gen. Sir H. L. Smith-Dorrien.

Lord Stamfordham.	The Lord-in-Waiting.
The Lord Chamberlain to the Queen-Empress.	The Lord High Steward.
THE QUEEN-EMPRESS.	THE KING-EMPEROR.
Attendants.	Attendants.
H.E. Lady Hardinge.	H.E. the Governor-General.

H.H. the Duke of Teck.	The Mistress of the Robes.	The Marquis of Crewe.

The Hon. Venetia Baring.	The Countess of Shaftesbury.

H.H. the Maharaja of Bikaner.	H.H. the Maharaja of Gwalior.	Hon. Major-Gen. Sir Pratap Singh.

Br.-Gen. Sir R. Grimston.	Sir Henry McMahon.

Mounted Procession from Prinsep's Ghat to Government House, Calcutta.

G.O.C. 8th Lucknow Division and Staff.

Captain Maclachlan.	Major the Hon. W. Cadogan.	Captain Holmes.
Captain Hogg.		Br.-Gen. Mercer.
Colonel Stanton.	Br.-Gen. Birdwood.	Br.-Gen. Keary.
Captain B. G. Godfrey-Faussett.	Commander Sir C. Cust.	The Hon. Sir D. Keppel.

APPENDIX A

Br.-Gen. Sir R. Grimston. Sir E. Henry. Major-Gen. Sir Stuart Beatson.

Lt.-Gen. Sir H. Smith-Dorrien. General Sir E. Barrow.

The Master of Ceremonies. The Lord-in-Waiting. The Lord Stamfordham.

The Maharaja of Bikaner. The Maharaja of Gwalior. Sir Pratap Singh.

Composite Squadron of Light Horse.

Calcutta Light Horse.

O.C. Calcutta Light Horse. THEIR IMPERIAL MAJESTIES (in a carriage). O.C. Bodyguard. O.C. Escort.

The Duke of Teck.

Major C. Wigram. Royal Groom. Major the Lord Charles Fitzmaurice. Royal Groom.

Carriage Escort of 2 N.C.O.'s and 4 Sowars of the Bodyguard.

Second Carriage.—The Mistress of the Robes, the Marquis of Crewe, Rear-Admiral Sir C. Keppel.

Third Carriage.—The Countess of Shaftesbury, the Lord High Steward, Lt.-Col. Sir J. Dunlop-Smith, Lt.-Col. Sir R. Havelock Charles.

Fourth Carriage.—The Hon. Venetia Baring, the Lord Chamberlain to the Queen-Empress, Mr. F. H. Lucas.

Fifth Carriage.—Lieutenant-Colonel Bird, the Hon. J. Fortescue.

The Bodyguard.

Indian Cavalry Regiment.

The route, which was lined by troops, was by the Ellenborough course south of Havildar's Tank, Red Road, Government Place East, and Old Court House Street, entering Government House by the north gate.

The Escort was furnished by U Battery Royal Horse Artillery, the 8th Hussars, Calcutta Light Horse, Light Horse Composite Squadron, the Governor-General's Bodyguard, 4th Cavalry (one squadron), 16th Cavalry.

On arrival at Government House the King-Emperor and Queen-Empress were received by the Governor-General and Lady Hardinge.

The following were also assembled at Government House to receive Their Imperial Majesties :—The Commander-in-Chief with his Staff, the heads of Local Governments and Administrations, the Most Rev. the Bishop of Calcutta, the Metropolitan of India and Ceylon, the Members of the Governor-General's Executive Council, the Naval Commander-in-Chief of the East Indies with his Staff, the Chief of the General Staff, the President and Members of the Railway Board, the Additional Members of the Governor-General's Legislative Council, the Secretaries and Deputy Secretaries of the Government of India, the Headquarters Staff of the Army, the heads of Civil and Military Departments, the Hon. the Chief Justice of Bengal, the Puisne Judges of the High Court.

The King-Emperor inspected the Guard of Honour of the East Yorkshire Regiment and the 66th Panjabis. After the inspection the following had the honour of being presented to Their Imperial Majesties by the Governor-General :—The Chief Justice, the Bishop of Calcutta, the Members of the Executive Council, the Naval Commander-in-Chief, the Chief of the General Staff, the President and Members of the Railway Board, the

APPENDIX A

Additional Members of the Legislative Council, the Secretaries to the Government of India, after which the senior officers of the Army Headquarters Staff had the honour of being presented by the Commander-in-Chief, and the Puisne Judges by the Chief Justice.

December 31.

GOVERNMENT HOUSE, CALCUTTA.

The King-Emperor and Queen-Empress attended Divine Service at the Cathedral this morning.

The procession from Government House to the Cathedral was as follows :—

First Carriage.

THE KING-EMPEROR. THE QUEEN-EMPRESS.

Second Carriage.—The Mistress of the Robes, the Duke of Teck, and Captain Godfrey-Faussett, R.N. (Equerry-in-Waiting).

Third Carriage.—The Marquis of Crewe, the Lord High Steward, and Major Lord Charles Fitzmaurice (Equerry-in-Waiting).

The route to the Cathedral was by the Red Road, Mayo Road, and Chowringhee.

The Escort was furnished by the 8th Hussars.

January 2.

CALCUTTA.

MOUNTED PROCESSION FROM THE DUFFERIN STATUE TO THE REVIEW GROUND.

Army Headquarters Staff.

H.E. the Governor-General's Staff.

Captain Maclachlan.		Captain Holmes.
Major the Hon. W. G. S. Cadogan.	Captain Hogg.	Major Graeme.
Major Money.	Colonel Stanton.	Br.-Gen. Mercer.
Br.-Gen. Keary.	The Hon. Sir Derek Keppel.	Br.-Gen. Birdwood.
Lieut.-Gen. Sir H. Smith-Dorrien.		Gen. Sir E. Barrow.
Lord Stamfordham.		The Lord-in-Waiting.

First Division Bodyguard.

N.C.O., 8th Hussars with Standard.

THE KING-EMPEROR.

		Commandant, Bodyguard.
H.E. the Commander-in-Chief.	H.E. the Governor-General.	H.H. the Duke of Teck.
Major Lord Charles Fitzmaurice.	Br.-Gen. Grimston.	Colonel Maxwell.

APPENDIX A

H.H. the Maharaja of Bikaner. | H.H. the Maharaja of Gwalior. | Sir Pratap Singh.

Royal Groom. | Royal Groom.

THE QUEEN-EMPRESS

(in a carriage with the Mistress of the Robes and the Lord High Steward).

Adjutant of the Bodyguard.

Major H. R. Stockley. | Major Gen. Sir Stuart Beatson.

H.E. Lady Hardinge

(in a carriage with the Marquis of Crewe and the Lord Chamberlain to the Queen-Empress).

Second Division Bodyguard.

January 3.

CALCUTTA.

This afternoon the King-Emperor and Queen-Empress honoured the Calcutta Races with their presence.

Their Imperial Majesties left Government House at 2.30 P.M., and a procession of carriages was formed as follows :—

First Carriage.

THE KING-EMPEROR. THE QUEEN-EMPRESS.

Second Carriage.—The Mistress of the Robes, the Marquis of Crewe, the Duke of Teck.

Third Carriage.—The Countess of Shaftesbury, the Lord Chamberlain to the Queen-Empress, General Sir E. Barrow.

Fourth Carriage.—The Hon. Venetia Baring, Lord Stamfordham, Sir Henry McMahon.

Fifth Carriage.—Commander Sir C. Cust, Rear-Admiral Sir C. Keppel (Equerries-in-Waiting).

Major Lord Charles Fitzmaurice and Major Wigram were in attendance on horseback.

The Escort, under the command of Major Keighley, was furnished by the Governor-General's Bodyguard.

The route of the procession was by the Red Road, the Jail Road, and the east side of the Racecourse to the Grand Stand.

January 4.

CALCUTTA.

Last night the King-Emperor and Queen-Empress honoured with their presence a military tattoo, and also witnessed the illuminations and a display of fireworks, which took place on the Maidan between Government House and the fort.

Their Imperial Majesties arrived at the Lawrence Statue at 9.30, and were conducted to their seats on the dais by the Governor-General and Lady Hardinge. The following gentlemen—members of the Illuminations Committee—then had the honour of being presented to the King-Emperor and the Queen-Empress by His Excellency :—

Mr. J. G. Apcar, Raja Kristo Das Law, Mr. Emerson, Babu Charu Chandar Malik. Colonel Ward, Captain Brancker, and Risaldar Chapal Singh, organisers of the torchlight tattoo, also had the honour of being presented.

Their Imperial Majesties' Suite in attendance were assembled below to the right and left of the dais.

At the conclusion of the display the King-Emperor and Queen-Empress returned to Government House.

The King-Emperor this night held an Investiture.

His Imperial Majesty entered the Throne-room at 9 P.M., attended by the Governor-General, the Duke of Teck, the Marquis of Crewe, the Lord High Steward, and the Equerries-in-Waiting.

The following gentlemen were then severally introduced into His Imperial Majesty's presence, when the King-Emperor conferred upon them the honour of knighthood, and invested them with the insignia of the division of the Order into which they had been admitted :—

To be Knights Commander of the Royal Victorian Order.—The Nawab Bahadur of Murshidabad, Major-General B. T. Mahon, Major-General Sir A. A. Barrett, Major-General G. C. Kitson.

To be Knights Bachelor.—Mr. D. Yule, the Hon. Mr. F. L. Halliday.

To be Commanders of the Royal Victorian Order.—The Hon. Mr. C. J. Stevenson-Moore, Mr. C. B. Bayley.

To be Companions of the Order of the Indian Empire.—The Hon. Mr. W. C. Madge, Colonel B. W. Marlow, Major L. Rogers, Mahamahopadhyaya Hara Prasad Shastri, Mr. J. H. Kerr.

To be Members of the Fourth Class of the Royal Victorian Order.—Captain G. H. Wills, Lieut.-Colonel R. Bird, Major the Hon. H. J. Fraser, Captain the Hon. A. O. W. Weld-Forester, Captain V. A. S. Keighley.

To be Members of the Fifth Class of the Royal Victorian Order.—Mr. C. Stead, Mr. F. C. T. Halliday, Mr. C. A. Tegart, Mr. H. S. H. Pilkington, Mr. Amir Ahmad.

To be Companions of the Imperial Service Order.—Mr. H. L. French, Shaikh Shadi, Babu Upendra Nath Chatterji, Rai Bahadur Rala Ram, Mr. T. W. Payne, Babu Narayan Kishen Sen, Mr. T. O. Drake, Mr C. W. Caston, Mr. J. E. Lacey, Mr. Ahsan-ud-Din Ahmad, Mr. G. W. Marshall.

The Kaisar-i-Hind Medal of the First Class.—Mr. J. T. Stark, Rai Hari Mohan Chandra Bahadur, Mr. E. G. Barton.

After the Investiture the King-Emperor and Queen-Empress held a Court.

January 5.

CALCUTTA.

Procession to the Pageant.

First Carriage.

THE KING-EMPEROR. THE QUEEN-EMPRESS.

Second Carriage.—The Mistress of the Robes, the Marquis of Crewe, the Duke of Teck, the Lord High Steward.

Third Carriage.—The Countess of Shaftesbury, the Lord Chamberlain to the Queen-Empress, Lord Stamfordham, Commander Sir C. Cust.

Fourth Carriage.—The Hon. Venetia Baring, the Commander-in-Chief, Rear-Admiral Sir Colin Keppel.

Major Lord Charles Fitzmaurice and Major Wigram were in attendance on horseback.

The remainder of the suite were in attendance in the *pandal*, in front of which a Guard of Honour of the Middlesex Regiment and the 27th Panjabis was mounted. On arrival the King-Emperor and Queen-Empress were received by the Lieutenant-Governor of Bengal, the Nawab of Murshidabad, the Maharajadhiraja of Burdwan (President of the Imperial Reception Executive Committee), Hon. Sir Cecil Graham and Dr. Rash Behari Ghose (Vice-President), the Maharaja of Darbhanga (President of the Pageant Sub-Committee), and the Hon. Mr. Norman MacLeod, and were conducted to the front of the pavilion, where Their Imperial Majesties were received by the Governor-General and Lady Hardinge and conducted to their seats on the dais.

The Maharaja of Gidhour then handed a *Pesh Kash* of 101 gold mohurs on a *tahli* to the Nawab of Murshidabad, who on behalf of the people of Bengal, Behar, and Orissa and Eastern Bengal and Assam, handed it to the King-Emperor.

The following then had the honour of being presented to Their Imperial Majesties by the Nawab of Murshidabad :—

The Maharajadhiraja of Burdwan, Prince Amir Adr Mirja Abid Ali, the Maharaja of Gidhour, the Maharaja of Darbhanga, the Hon. Maharaja of Dinajpur, Maharaja Sir Prodyot Coomar Tagore, the Maharaja of Chota Nagpur, the Maharaja of Surang, the Maharaja of Nattore, the Hon. Maharaja of Cassimbazar, Maharaja of Narsingpur, the Maharaja of Krishnagar, Raja Bahadur Benod Krishna Deb, Raja Peary Mohun Mookerjee, the Hon. Raja of Dighapatiya, Nawab Shamsh-ul-ulama, Saiyed Imdad Imam, the Maharaja Kumar of Hathwa, Sir Alexander Apcar, Sir Rajendra Nath Mookerjee, the Hon. Sir Cecil Graham, Major-General Drummond, Dr. Rash Behary Ghose, the Hon. Mr. F. H. Stewart, the Hon. Babu Bhupendra Nath Basu, Mr. R. H. A. Gresson, the Hon. Mr. Norman MacLeod, the Hon. Mr. J. G. Apcar, the Hon. Babu Deva Prasad Sarvadicary, Mr. E. O. Emerson, Sir Jyoti Singh, Sir Jyoti Singh of Pachote.

The Maharajadhiraja of Burdwan presented the programmes to Their Imperial Majesties, and the Pageant, which consisted of the Nawroz Procession and the Dasehara Procession and the dance of the Orissa Paiks, then commenced.

At the conclusion of the Pageant the following had the honour of being presented to their Imperial Majesties :—

Dr. Dennison Ross, Mr. Lascelles, Captain Meadows, Mr. Thornton.

After taking tea the King-Emperor and Queen-Empress left the dais and were conducted to their carriage, attended by the Maharaja Sir Prodyot Coomar Tagore and the Maharaja of Nattore, who held the State umbrellas, and also by the Maharaja Kumar of Mourbhang and the Mirza of Murshidabad, pages to the Queen-Empress. Their Imperial Majesties then drove in procession, making a circuit of the grounds on which the Pageant took place, and returned to the Government House by the Red Road.

The Escort, under the command of Major McClellan, was furnished by the 8th Hussars and 4th Cavalry.

January 6.

CALCUTTA.

This morning at 8.30 the King-Emperor mounted his charger and left Government House, attended by the Commander-in-Chief, the Duke of Teck, General Sir E. Barrow, Major-General Sir G. C. Kitson, Major-General Sir B. T. Mahon, Brigadier-General Sir R. Grimston, Major Lord Charles Fitzmaurice, and Major Wigram (Equerries-in-Waiting).

The King-Emperor inspected the following military camps on the Maidan :—U Battery Royal Horse Artillery, 74th Battery Royal Field Artillery, 8th Hussars, No. 70 Company Royal Garrison Artillery, 2nd Batt. East Yorkshire Regiment, 2nd Batt. the Black Watch, 3rd Batt. Middlesex Regiment, a wing of the 1st Batt. Middlesex Regiment, the 66th Panjabis, the 2nd Batt. 10th Gurkha Rifles.

His Imperial Majesty then rode to Kidderpur and Alipur, and inspected the camps of the detachment of the 2nd Lancers, the 4th Cavalry, the 16th Cavalry, and the 27th Panjabis.

The King-Emperor returned from Alipur to Fort William, where the 2nd Rifle Brigade and the 88th Carnatic Infantry were drawn up in line on their parade grounds.

His Imperial Majesty returned from the Fort to Government House by motor.

In the forenoon the King-Emperor received a deputation from the University of Calcutta. His Imperial Majesty entered the Throne-room at 10.30, attended by the Governor-General, the Lord Steward, the Duke of Teck, Lord Stamfordham, Lieut.-General Sir H. L. Smith-Dorrien, Brigadier-General W. R. Birdwood, Brigadier-General H. D'U. Keary, Colonel Stanton, Brigadier-General Mercer, the Maharaja of Gwalior, the Hon. Major-General Sir Pratap Singh, the Maharaja of Bikaner, Captain Godfrey-Faussett, R.N., Major Lord Charles Fitzmaurice (Equerries-in-Waiting).

Dr. Ashutosh Mukerjee (Vice-Chancellor) then, on behalf of the University, presented an Address to the King-Emperor, to which His Imperial Majesty was graciously pleased to read a reply.

Before entering the Throne-room the King-Emperor was graciously pleased to present to Dr. Ashutosh Mukerjee portraits of Their Imperial Majesties to be preserved by the University as mementoes of the King-Emperor's visit to Calcutta.

This morning the Queen-Empress visited the Young Women's Christian Association, the Presidency General Hospital, the Dufferin Hospital, and the Medical College Hospital.

APPENDIX A

Her Imperial Majesty left Government House by motor, attended by Lady Hardinge, the Duchess of Devonshire, Sir Havelock Charles, and Colonel O'Kinealy.

On arrival at the Young Women's Christian Association the Queen-Empress was received by Mrs. Noel Paton, the President.

After making an inspection of the institute, Her Imperial Majesty proceeded to the Presidency General Hospital, where the Queen-Empress was received by Surgeon-General Sir Charles Lukis, Colonel Harris, Colonel Pilgrim, and the staff of the hospital. Her Imperial Majesty visited the various wards in the main building and in the Woodburn block, and then proceeded to the Dufferin Hospital. The Queen-Empress was received by the Lieutenant-Governor of Bengal and Miss Platts (the surgeon-in-charge).

After inspecting the hospital Her Imperial Majesty visited the Medical College Hospital, on arrival at which the Queen-Empress was received by Colonel Drury and the staff of the hospital. Her Imperial Majesty inspected the Prince of Wales's block and the Eden Hospital, and then returned to Government House.

January 7.

CALCUTTA.

The King-Emperor and Queen-Empress attended Divine Service at the Cathedral this morning.

The procession from Government House to the Cathedral was as follows :—

First Carriage.

THE KING-EMPEROR. THE QUEEN-EMPRESS.

Second Carriage.—The Mistress of the Robes, the Duke of Teck, Captain Godfrey-Faussett, R.N. (Equerry-in-Waiting).

Third Carriage.—The Lord High Steward, Commander Sir Charles Cust (Equerry-in-Waiting).

Captain Holmes and Captain Maclachlan (extra Aides-de-Camp) were in attendance on horseback.

The route to the Cathedral was by the Mayo Road and Chowringee. The Escort was furnished by the 8th Hussars and 16th Cavalry.

January 8.

CALCUTTA.

The King-Emperor and Queen-Empress proceeded from Government House to Prinsep's Ghat at 11 A.M. this morning.

The following gentlemen had the honour of taking leave of Their Imperial Majesties at Government House :—

The Commander-in-Chief with his Staff.

The heads of Local Governments and Administrations.

The Most Rev. the Bishop of Calcutta, Metropolitan of India and Ceylon.

APPENDIX A

The Members of the Governor-General's Executive Council.
The Naval Commander-in-Chief with his staff.
The President and Members of the Railway Board.
Additional Members of the Governor-General's Legislative Council.
The Secretaries and Deputy Secretaries to the Government of India.
The Headquarters Staff of the Army.
The heads of Civil and Military Departments.
The Chief Justice of Bengal.
The Puisne Judges of the High Court.
Ruling Chiefs.

The King-Emperor and Queen-Empress then entered their carriage and drove from Government House to Prinsep's Ghat.

The procession was in the following order :—

Captain Holmes.		Major the Hon. W. Cadogan.
Major Graeme.		Brigadier-General Mercer.
Colonel H. R. Stanton.	Brigadier-General Birdwood.	Brigadier-General Keary.
General Sir E. Barrow.		Sir Henry McMahon.
The Maharaja of Bikaner.	The Maharaja of Gwalior.	Hon. Major-General Sir Pratap Singh.

First Carriage.

THE KING-EMPEROR.	THE QUEEN-EMPRESS.
(On Horseback)	(On Horseback)
Colonel Apostolides.	Major Keighley.
	Brigadier-General Cookson.
Major Wigram.	Brigadier-General Sir R. Grimston.

Second Carriage.—The Mistress of the Robes, The Marquis of Crewe, Rear-Admiral Sir Colin Keppel.

Third Carriage.—The Duke of Teck, the Countess of Shaftesbury, Commander Sir C. Cust, Sir Derek Keppel.

Fourth Carriage.—Hon. Venetia Baring, the Lord High Steward, Sir R. Havelock Charles.

Fifth Carriage.—The Lord Chamberlain to the Queen-Empress, Lord Stamfordham, Mr. F. H. Lucas.

As Their Imperial Majesties entered their carriage the National Anthem was played, and a salute of 101 guns was fired from the ramparts of Fort William.

The Escort, under the command of Brigadier-General Cookson, was furnished by—

U Battery Royal Horse Artillery.
8th Hussars.
The Calcutta Light Horse.
Composite Squadron Light Horse.

APPENDIX A

The Governor-General's Bodyguard.
16th Cavalry.

On arrival at the Ghat the King-Emperor and Queen-Empress were received by the Governor-General and Lady Hardinge. The following were also present :—

The Lieutenant-Governor of Bengal with his Staff.
Members of the Bengal Executive Council.
The Ruling and feudatory Chiefs of Bengal.
The principal nobles of Bengal.
Members of the Bengal Legislative Council.

Representatives of—

The Bengal Chamber of Commerce.
The Commissioners of the Port of Calcutta.
The British Indian Association.
The Trades Association.
The Bengal National Chamber of Commerce.
The Bihar Landholders' Association.
The University of Calcutta.
The Commissioners of the Calcutta Corporation.

The Hon. Mr. Slacke (Vice-President) then, on behalf of the Legislative Council of Bengal, presented an Address to Their Imperial Majesties, to which the King-Emperor was graciously pleased to read a reply.

The King-Emperor and Queen-Empress then proceeded on board the steamer *Howrah*, where Their Imperial Majesties were received by the Vice-Chairman of the Port Commissioners, the Port Officer of Calcutta, and the Deputy Conservator of the Port of Calcutta.

The procession from the Ghat to the steamer was in the following order :—

The Governor-General's Staff.

Captain Holmes.	Major Graeme.	Major the Hon. W. Cadogan.
Mr. F. H. Lucas.	Colonel Stanton.	Brigadier-General Mercer.
Brigadier-General Keary.	Sir R. Havelock Charles.	Brigadier-General Birdwood.

Major Wigram.	Sir Derek Keppel.
Commander Sir C. Cust.	Rear-Admiral Sir Colin Keppel.
General Sir A. Barrow.	Lord Stamfordham.
The Lord Chamberlain to the Queen-Empress.	The Lord High Steward.
THE QUEEN-EMPRESS.	THE KING-EMPEROR.
Lady Hardinge.	The Governor-General.

The Duke of Teck.	The Mistress of the Robes.	The Marquis of Crewe.

The Hon. Venetia Baring.	The Countess of Shaftesbury.

The Maharaja of Bikaner.	The Maharaja of Gwalior.	Hon. Major-General Sir Pratap Singh.

Brigadier-General Sir R. Grimston.	Sir Henry McMahon.

APPENDIX A

As the steamer left Prinsep's Ghat a salute of 101 guns was fired by H.M.S. *Highflyer*.

The steamer, escorted by six ferry boats manned by the Calcutta Port Volunteers, proceeded up the Hugli River to Howrah landing-stage, where Their Imperial Majesties disembarked and were received by the Commissioner of the Burdwan Division, the Magistrate of Howrah, and the Agent of the Bengal-Nagpur Railway.

The procession was then re-formed, and the King-Emperor and Queen-Empress proceeded to Howrah Station.

The Governor-General and Lady Hardinge then had the honour of taking leave, and Their Imperial Majesties entered the Royal train, which left for Bombay at 12.15 P.M.

The National Anthem was played, and a salute of 101 guns was fired from the ramparts of Fort William as the train left Howrah Station.

Guards of Honour of the 3rd Batt. Middlesex Regiment and the 2nd Batt. 10th Gurkhas, the 2nd Rifle Brigade and the Eastern Bengal State Railway Volunteers, and the Bengal-Nagpur Railway Volunteer Rifles, were mounted at Government House, the Prinsep's Ghat, and Howrah Station respectively.

January 9.

KING-EMPEROR'S CAMP, NAGPUR.

The King-Emperor and Queen-Empress, with their Suite in attendance, arrived at Nagpur at 2.15 P.M. to-day, and on alighting from the train were received by the Chief Commissioner, the Lord Bishop of Nagpur, and the General Officer Commanding the Jubbulpur Brigade.

Their Imperial Majesties paid a visit to the Fort, and proceeded again at 3.15 P.M. by special train for Bombay.

January 10.

H.M.S. *MEDINA*, BOMBAY.

The King-Emperor and Queen-Empress arrived at Bombay at 12 noon.

Their Imperial Majesties were received at the Victoria terminus by the Governor-General, the Governor of Bombay and Lady Clarke.

A Guard of Honour of the Great Indian Peninsula Railway Volunteers was mounted at the station.

The King-Emperor having inspected the Guard of Honour, Their Imperial Majesties were escorted to their carriage and a procession was formed as follows :—

First Carriage.

THE KING-EMPEROR. THE QUEEN-EMPRESS.

Second Carriage.—His Excellency the Governor-General, the Marquis of Crewe.

APPENDIX A

Third Carriage.—The Mistress of the Robes, His Highness the Duke of Teck, Commander Sir C. Cust, Rear-Admiral Sir Colin Keppel.

Fourth Carriage.—His Excellency the Governor of Bombay, Lady Clarke, Lord Stamfordham.

Fifth Carriage.—The Countess of Shaftesbury, the Lord High Steward, the Hon. Sir Derek Keppel.

Sixth Carriage.—The Hon. Venetia Baring, the Lord Chamberlain to the Queen-Empress, Sir R. Havelock Charles.

Major-General Sir R. Grimston and Major Clive Wigram were in attendance on horseback.

The route was by Hornby Road, Esplanade Road, and Apollo Bandar Road.

The Escort was furnished by Y Battery Royal Horse Artillery, 7th Dragoon Guards, Bombay Light Horse, 26th Cavalry, and the Governor's Bodyguard.

On arrival at the amphitheatre Their Imperial Majesties alighted from their carriage, and the King-Emperor having inspected the Guard of Honour of the Norfolk Regiment, a procession was formed to the pavilion in the following order :—

Procession at the Bandar, Bombay.

H.E. The Governor of Bombay's Staff.

H.E. The Governor-General's Staff.

Captain Grissell.	Captain Hogg.	Major Humphreys.
Mr. Jacomb Hood.	Mr. F. H. Lucas.	The Hon. J. Fortescue.
Sir R. Havelock Charles.	Captain Godfrey-Faussett.	Major Lord C. Fitzmaurice.
The Hon. Sir Derek Keppel.	Sir James Dunlop-Smith.	Commander Sir C. Cust.
Rear-Admiral Sir Colin Keppel.	Sir Edward Henry.	Major-Gen. Sir Stuart Beatson.
Gen. Sir H. Smith-Dorrien.	The Lord-in-Waiting.	Lord Stamfordham.

The Lord Chamberlain to the Queen-Empress.	The Lord High Steward.
THE QUEEN-EMPRESS.	THE KING-EMPEROR.

H.H. the Duke of Teck.	H.E. the Gov.-Gen.	The Marquis of Crewe.
Lady Clarke.	H.E. the Gov. of Bombay.	The Mistress of the Robes.

The Hon. Venetia Baring.	The Countess of Shaftesbury.
Major C. Wigram.	Brig.-Gen. Sir R. Grimston.

Their Imperial Majesties having taken their seats in the pavilion, Sir R. Lamb, Vice-President of the Bombay Legislative Council, on behalf of the Council, read an Address of Farewell, to which the King-Emperor was graciously pleased to reply.

The following gentlemen then had the honour of being presented to Their Imperial Majesties by the Governor of Bombay :—The Chief Justice of Bombay, the Bishop of Bombay, the Judges of the High Court, the Additional Members of the Legislative Council of His Excellency the Governor-General, the Commissioner of Customs, the General Officer Commanding the 6th (Poona) Division, the General Officer Commanding the Bombay Brigade, the Commissioner (Northern Division), the Foreign Consular Officers, the Native Chiefs present, and the Sheriff of Bombay.

The King-Emperor and Queen-Empress, attended by the Governor-General, the Governor of Bombay, and Lady Clarke, and the ladies and gentlemen of the Suite in attendance, then embarked and left the Apollo Bandar for H.M.S. *Medina*.

The King-Emperor and Queen-Empress gave a luncheon-party on board H.M.S. *Medina*, to which the following had the honour of being invited :—The Governor-General, the Governor of Bombay and Lady Clarke, His Highness the Aga Khan, Captain Lumsden, Sir Charles Cleveland, Lieut.-Colonel Maxwell, Major Greig, Captain Tod, Captain Muir, Major-General Sir R. Grimston, Major Money, Captain Maclachlan, Captain Hogg, Captain Raben.

After luncheon the King-Emperor invested the Maharao Raja of Bundi with the insignia of a Knight Grand Cross of the Victorian Order.

His Imperial Majesty's Indian Suite took leave of the King-Emperor and Queen-Empress.

At 6 P.M., the Governor-General having taken leave of their Imperial Majesties, H.M.S. *Medina* left for Port Sudan.

January 17.

H.M.S. *MEDINA*, PORT SUDAN.

The King and Queen arrived at Port Sudan at 7.15 A.M.

This morning a salute of 21 guns was fired from the saluting battery as H.M.S. *Medina* entered the harbour.

At 7.30 A.M. His Majesty received Field-Marshal the Viscount Kitchener, and afterwards the King received the Governor-General, who was the bearer of a letter of greeting to Their Majesties from His Highness the Khedive.

The Governor-General was accompanied by Lewa Ramzi Taher Pasha, chief A.D.C. to the Khedive.

At 8 A.M. the King and Queen disembarked, attended by their Suite, and were received on the quay by Field-Marshal the Viscount Kitchener, the Governor-General and Lady Wingate, and Major-General Sir R. Baron von Slatin, with their respective Staffs, and Mr. Graham Kerr (Governor Red Sea Province).

Guards of Honour of the 1st Batt. Alexandra Princess of Wales's Own Yorkshire Regiment and the 8th Batt. Egyptian Army were mounted opposite the pavilion on the quay.

Having inspected the Guards of Honour, His Majesty returned to the dais.

The Governor-General then read an Address of Welcome to the King and Queen, to which His Majesty was graciously pleased to reply.

APPENDIX A

Certain Sheikhs and notables then had the honour of receiving presents from His Majesty.

January 20.

H.M.S. *MEDINA*, PORT SAID.

The King and Queen arrived at Port Said this morning.

At 1.15 P.M. the King received a visit from the Khedive. His Highness remained to luncheon with Their Majesties on board H.M.S. *Medina*, and the following had the honour of being invited :—

His Highness Kiamel Pasha (ex-Grand Vizier), Muzuffer Bey Kiamel, Major-General Sir John Maxwell, His Excellency Said Zoulificar Pasha (Grand Master of the Ceremonies), El Leja Watson Pasha, Prince D'Arenberg (President Suez Canal), Mr. H. T. Anstruther, Mr. R. S. Donkin, Count de Serionne, Mahomed Mahmund Bey (Governor of Port Said), Councillor M. Cheetham, Mr. E. C. Blech (British Consul-General, Port Said), Captain O. A. G. FitzGerald, and Captain Darell (A.D.C. to the General Officer Commanding the troops in Egypt).

After luncheon the Khedive having taken leave of the King, His Majesty disembarked and inspected the Guards of Honour of the 1st Batt. Scots Guards under the command of Major Carpenter-Garnier, and the 3rd Batt. Egyptian Army, under the command of El Yusbashi Mahommed Effendi Bahgat.

In the afternoon the Queen received a deputation of ladies from Port Said, and Her Majesty was graciously pleased to accept a bouquet, presented by Mrs. Blech.

The following, with the Suite in attendance, had the honour of being included in Their Majesties' dinner-party on board H.M.S. *Medina* this evening :—

Field-Marshal the Viscount Kitchener of Khartoum, Major-General Sir John Maxwell, El Lewa Watson Pasha, Colonel Macauley, Councillor M. Cheetham, Captain William Goodenough, R.N., Captain Michael Culme-Seymour, R.N., Captain Henry Bruce, R.N., Captain Clement Greatorex, R.N., Flag-Captain Alfred Chatfield, R.N., and Commander George Tomlin.

January 24.

H.M.S. *MEDINA*, MALTA.

The King and Queen arrived at Malta at 10 A.M. this morning.

As H.M.S. *Medina* entered the Grand Harbour, salutes of 21 guns were fired from Forts Ricasoli and St. Elmo, from His Majesty's ships, and the ships of the French Fleet in harbour, and from the saluting battery.

On arrival the King received the Governor on board H.M.S. *Medina*.

His Majesty then received the Naval Commander-in-Chief, by whom the Admirals and Captains of the Mediterranean Fleet had the honour of being presented to His Majesty. Admiral A. E. H. Boué de Lapeyrère,

Rear-Admiral F. P. Moreau, and the Captains of the ships of the French Fleet also had the honour of being presented to Their Majesties by the Commander-in-Chief.

Later the King honoured Admiral A. E. H. Boué de Lapeyrère with a visit on board the French flagship *Danton*.

This evening the King and Queen honoured the Naval Commander-in-Chief and Lady Poë with their presence at a dinner-party at Admiralty House, and afterwards attended a gala performance at the Opera. The Duchess of Devonshire, the Countess of Shaftesbury, the Hon. Venetia Baring, the Duke of Teck, the Marquis of Crewe, the Earl of Shaftesbury, the Lord Annaly, the Lord Stamfordham, Lieut.-General Sir Horace Smith-Dorrien, Rear-Admiral Sir Colin Keppel, Commander Sir Charles Cust, and Captain B. Godfrey-Faussett, R.N., were in attendance.

Guards of Honour of the Royal Marine Light Infantry and the 2nd Batt. King's Own Malta Militia were mounted at Admiralty House and the Opera House respectively.

January 30.

H.M.S. *MEDINA*, GIBRALTAR.

The King and Queen arrived at Gibraltar at 10 o'clock this morning.

As H.M.S. *Medina* entered the harbour salutes of 21 guns were fired from the Portuguese men-of-war, His Majesty's ships in harbour, and from the saluting battery.

On arrival His Majesty received the Governor, the Colonial Secretary, the Captain of the Portuguese man-of-war, Rear-Admiral Pelham, and the Captains of His Majesty's ships in harbour.

The King then received in audience Sir Maurice de Bunsen, British Ambassador, Madrid.

His Majesty also received Sir Reginald Lister, British Minister, Tangier.

Deputations from the Exchange Committee and Chamber of Commerce, the Roman Catholic Community, and the Hebrew Community, were afterwards received in turn by Their Majesties, followed by a Special Mission sent by the Sultan of Morocco.

Si Mohammed el Guebbas (Commissioner for Foreign Affairs), the Pasha of Tangier, and the Members of the Mission were introduced to Their Majesties by Sir Reginald Lister.

Si Mohammed el Guebbas then read an Address of Welcome from the Sultan, to which His Majesty was graciously pleased to reply.

In the afternoon the King and Queen drove to the Colonial Hospital, where they were received by Dr. W. Turner (Colonial Surgeon), Sir Frederick Evans (Chairman), and the Members of the Board of Hospital Commissioners.

After visiting the various wards Their Majesties drove to the Waterworks, where they were received by Mr. W. W. Copeland (Engineer), Colonel A. Grant (Chairman), and the Members of the Board of Sanitary Commissioners.

The Queen then opened the new reservoir works by firing the first mine.

APPENDIX A

The King and Queen honoured the Governor and Lady Hunter with a visit at Government House, where they remained to tea and then returned on board H.M.S. *Medina.*

January 31.

H.M.S. *MEDINA*, GIBRALTAR.

This morning at 9 A.M. the Infante Don Carlos, escorted by a Spanish naval squadron, arrived at Gibraltar.

Salutes of 21 guns were fired from His Majesty's ships in harbour and the saluting battery as the squadron entered the harbour.

At 9.30 A.M. the Infante visited the King and Queen on board H.M.S. *Medina*, where he was received by the Duke of Teck and the Lord High Steward.

His Royal Highness was accompanied by the Governor of Algeçiras, and attended by his personal Suite and the Admiral and Captains of the ships of the Spanish squadron, who had the honour of being presented to Their Majesties.

The King afterwards visited the Infante on board the Spanish flagship.

This afternoon Their Majesties drove to the Military Hospital.

First Carriage.

THE KING, THE QUEEN, AND THE GOVERNOR.

Second Carriage.—Lady Hunter, the Duke of Teck, Lieut.-General Sir H. Smith-Dorrien, and Commander Sir Charles Cust.

Third Carriage.—The Countess of Shaftesbury, The Marquis of Crewe, the Earl of Shaftesbury, and Sir Richard Havelock Charles.

After visiting the hospital Their Majesties proceeded to the Mount, where they honoured the Admiral-Superintendent and Mrs. Pelham with a visit and remained to tea.

After tea Their Majesties returned on board H.M.S. *Medina.*

February 4.

H.M.S. *MEDINA*, SPITHEAD.

H.M.S. *Medina* arrived at Spithead at 10 A.M. this morning.

The King and Queen attended Divine Service on board at 10.30 A.M., and afterwards Their Majesties received the Captains of the cruisers of the Escort :—

Captain Goodenough, H.M.S. *Cochrane* ; Captain Michael Culme-Seymour, H.M.S. *Argyll* ; Captain H. H. Bruce, H.M.S. *Defence* ; and Captain Greatorex, H.M.S. *Natal.*

APPENDIX A

February 5.

ARRIVAL AT PORTSMOUTH.

Previous to disembarking this morning the King received on board H.M.S. *Medina* the Rt. Hon. Winston Spencer-Churchill, M.P. (First Lord of the Admiralty), and Lords Commissioners of the Admiralty, Admiral Sir Arthur Moore (Commander-in-Chief at Portsmouth), Rear-Admiral A. G. Tate (Superintendent, Portsmouth Dockyard), and the Flag Officers with their personal Staffs, and the Captains of His Majesty's ships in harbour and at Spithead.

Their Majesties disembarked shortly after 10 o'clock, and were received on the jetty by the Duke of Wellington (Acting Lord-Lieutenant of the County of Hampshire), General Sir C. W. H. Douglas (General Officer Commanding-in-Chief, Southern Command), and Major-General W. E. Blewitt (General Officer Commanding Southern Coast Defences).

Royal salutes were fired from His Majesty's ships and the land forts at Portsmouth at 9 o'clock, and Guards of Honour of the Royal Marine Light Infantry (under the command of Captain Norman O. Burge) and of the Royal Marine Artillery (under the command of Captain Lancelot D. Briscoe) were mounted at the South Railway Jetty.

An Address was presented to Their Majesties by the Mayor of Portsmouth (Sir Scott Foster) on board H.M.S. *Medina* on behalf of the Corporation of Portsmouth, to which the King handed a reply.

ARRIVAL AT VICTORIA.

The King and Queen were met on arrival at Victoria Station by Prince and Princess Christian of Schleswig-Holstein with Princess Victoria and Princess Marie Louise of Schleswig-Holstein, Princess Louise (Duchess of Argyll) and the Duke of Argyll, the Duchess of Albany, Princess Louis of Battenberg and Princess Louise of Battenberg, the Countess Feodore Gleichen and the Countess Helena Gleichen.

The Members of the Corps Diplomatique as follows were present :—

Their Excellencies the French Ambassador, the German Ambassador, the Countess Benckendorff, the Austro-Hungarian Ambassador, the Spanish Ambassador, the Turkish Ambassador, the Italian Ambassador and the Marchesa Imperiali, the Netherlands Minister, the Countess de Lalaing, the Brazilian Minister, the Swedish Minister and the Countess Wrangel, the Danish Minister, the Uruguayan Minister, the Colombian Minister, the Norwegian Minister and Madame Vogt, the Liberian Minister and Madame Cromelin, Madame Gennadius, the Bulgarian Minister and Madame Tzokow, the Argentine Minister and Madame de Dominguez, the Chilian Minister and Madame de Edwards, the Siamese Minister, the Persian Minister, and the Mexican Minister and Madame de Beistigui.

The Haytian Minister-Resident, the Guatemalan Chargé d'Affaires, the Peruvian Chargé d'Affaires, the Cuban Chargé d'Affaires, the Bolivian Chargé d'Affaires and Madame Suarez, the Japanese Chargé d'Affaires, the Portuguese Chargé d'Affaires, the United States Chargé d'Affaires, the Swiss

Chargé d'Affaires, the Servian Chargé d'Affaires and Madame Grouitch, and Monsieur Vouros (Greek Legation).

Their Excellencies the Russian Ambassador, the Belgian Minister, the Greek Minister, the Chinese Minister, the Chargés d'Affaires for Costa Rica and for Roumania, Madame de Villa Urrutia, Madame Regis de Oliveira, Madame Perez Triana, and Mrs. Yamaza were unavoidably prevented from attending.

The following members of the Government in the Cabinet were present at Victoria Station upon the arrival of the King and Queen :—

The Rt. Hon. H. H. Asquith, M.P. (Prime Minister and First Lord of the Treasury), the Earl Carrington (Lord Privy Seal) and the Countess Carrington, the Viscount Haldane (Secretary of State for War), the Rt. Hon. R. McKenna, M.P. (Secretary of State for the Home Department) and Mrs. McKenna, the Rt. Hon. Sir Edward Grey, Bt., M.P. (Secretary of State for Foreign Affairs), the Rt. Hon. L. Harcourt, M.P. (Secretary of State for the Colonies) and Mrs. Harcourt, and the Rt. Hon. H. Samuel, M.P. (Postmaster-General).

There were also present :—

The Archbishop of Canterbury, the Duke of Norfolk, the Duke of Devonshire, the Marquis and Marchioness of Lansdowne, the Marchioness of Crewe, the Marquis de Soveral, Earl of Aberdeen, the Earl and Countess of Bessborough, the Earl and Countess Grey, Field-Marshal the Earl Roberts, the Viscount Esher, General the Lord William Seymour, the Lord and Lady Sandhurst, the Lord Revelstoke, the Lord Strathcona and Mount Royal (High Commissioner for the Dominion of Canada), the Rt. Hon. Sir George Reid (High Commissioner for the Commonwealth of Australia), the Rt. Hon. Ameer Ali (member of the Judicial Committee of the Privy Council) and Mrs. Ali, Admiral the Hon. Sir Edmund Fremantle (Rear-Admiral of the United Kingdom), Field-Marshal Sir W. G. Nicholson (Chief of the Imperial General Staff), the Hon. Sir Richard Solomon (High Commissioner for the Union of South Africa), Lieut.-General Sir Arthur Paget (General Officer Commanding-in-Chief, Eastern Command), Sir Richmond Ritchie (Permanent Under-Secretary of State for India), the Hon. Sir W. Hall Jones (High Commissioner for the Dominion of New Zealand), Sir Theodore Morison and the Members of the Council of the Secretary of State for India, Rear-Admiral Sir Adolphus FitzGeorge, Colonel Sir Augustus FitzGeorge, Major-General Sir A. E. Codrington (General Officer Commanding the London District), Colonel R. Scott-Kerr (Commanding Grenadier Guards), Colonel the Hon. W. Lambton (Commanding Coldstream Guards), Colonel G. J. Cuthbert (Commanding Scots Guards), and Mr. Edward White (Chairman of the London County Council).

The Lady Gweneth Ponsonby had the honour of presenting a bouquet to the Queen.

The Rt. Hon. Sir Thomas Crosby (Lord Mayor of London) and the Lady Mayoress, the Sheriffs of London, and the Lord Mayors of Birmingham, Bristol, Cardiff, Dublin, Liverpool, Leeds, Manchester, Norwich, Sheffield, and York, and the Lord Provosts of Aberdeen, Dundee, Edinburgh, Glasgow, and Perth were present.

A Guard of Honour of the 3rd Batt. Grenadier Guards, with the Colour and Band of the regiment, under the command of Captain B. N. Brooke, was mounted at the station.

PROCESSION TO THE PALACE.

The King having inspected the Guard of Honour, a Royal carriage procession was formed in the following order :—

First Carriage.

(Plain Road Landau and Four Bay Horses.)

HIS MAJESTY THE KING.

HER MAJESTY THE QUEEN.

HIS ROYAL HIGHNESS THE PRINCE OF WALES.

Second Carriage.

(Plain Road Landau and Four Bay Horses.)

The Duchess of Devonshire (Mistress of the Robes), the Duke of Teck (Personal Aide-de-Camp to the King), the Earl of Durham (Lord High Steward), Commander Sir Charles Cust, Bt., R.N. (Equerry-in-Waiting).

Third Carriage.

(Plain Road Landau and Four Bay Horses.)

The Countess of Shaftesbury (Lady-in-Waiting), the Marquis of Crewe (Secretary of State for India), the Earl of Shaftesbury (Lord Chamberlain to the Queen), the Lord Annaly (Lord-in-Waiting).

Fourth Carriage.

(Plain Road Landau and Four Bay Horses.)

The Hon. Venetia Baring (Maid of Honour), the Rt. Hon. Sir William Carington (Keeper of the Privy Purse), the Lord Stamfordham (Private Secretary), the Hon. Sir Derek Keppel (Equerry-in-Waiting).

Fifth Carriage.

(Plain Road Landau and Four Bay Horses.)

Lieut.-General Sir H. Smith-Dorrien (A.D.C. General-in-Waiting), Sir Edward Henry (Commissioner of Metropolitan Police), Major-General Sir Stuart Beatson (extra Equerry), Captain Bryan Godfrey-Faussett, R.N. (Equerry-in-Waiting).

Sixth Carriage.

(Plain Road Landau and Four Bay Horses.)

Colonel Sir James Dunlop-Smith (Political A.D.C. to the Secretary of State for India), Sir Richard Havelock Charles (Sergeant-Surgeon), Mr. F. H. Lucas (Private Secretary to the Secretary of State for India), the Hon. John Fortescue (Librarian).

Major Lord Charles Fitzmaurice and Major Clive Wigram (Equerries-in-Waiting) were in attendance upon horseback.

Their Majesties were escorted from Victoria Station to the Palace by a Captain's Escort of the Royal Horse Guards, under the command of Major the Viscount Crichton.

The route of the Royal procession was by Buckingham Palace Road, Victoria Street, Parliament Square, Parliament Street, Whitehall, the Admiralty Arch, and the Mall.

Princess Mary, Prince George, and Prince John met Their Majesties at the Grand Entrance to the Palace.

The Earl Spencer (Lord Chamberlain), the Master of the Household, the Hon. Sidney Greville (Paymaster of the Household), Sir Walter Campbell, Mr. Harry L. Verney, and Captain Philip Hunloke (Grooms-in-Waiting), Sir Francis Laking, Bt., the Countess of Minto, the Lady Ampthill, and the Lady Desborough (Ladies in Waiting), the Lady Eva Dugdale (Woman of the Bedchamber in Waiting), the Hon. Katharine Villiers and the Hon. Mabel Gye (Maids of Honour in Waiting), the Hon. A. Nelson Hood, Mr. E. W. Wallington, and Lieut.-Colonel F. Dugdale (Treasurer, Private Secretary, and Equerry to the Queen), Mlle. Dussau and Mr. H. P. Hansell, were in attendance at the Palace upon the arrival of the King and Queen ; and the Earl of Granard (Master of the Horse), Colonel Sir Douglas Dawson (Comptroller in the Lord Chamberlain's Department), the Hon. Arthur Walsh (His Majesty's Master of the Ceremonies), the Hon. Richard Moreton (Deputy-Master of the Ceremonies), Captain the Hon. Sir Charles Wentworth FitzWilliam (Crown Equerry), Lieut.-Colonel Sir F. Ponsonby (Equerry to the King), and Colonel G. C. Nugent (Field Officer in Brigade Waiting) were in attendance at the railway station.

February 6.

BUCKINGHAM PALACE.

The King and Queen were present this morning in St. Paul's Cathedral at a Service of Thanksgiving for Their Majesties' safe return to this country.

Their Majesties, accompanied by the Prince of Wales, Princess Mary and Prince George, left the Palace at 11.40 o'clock, escorted by a Captain's Escort of 1st Life Guards, under the command of Captain the Lord Hugh Grosvenor, a State Procession having been formed in the following order :—

First Carriage.

THE KING. THE QUEEN.

THE PRINCE OF WALES AND PRINCESS MARY.

The following were in attendance on horseback :—

Major-General Sir A. E. Codrington (General Officer Commanding the London District).	Lt.-Gen. Sir H. L. Smith-Dorrien (Aide-de-Camp General-in-Waiting).

APPENDIX A

Major the Lord Charles Fitzmaurice (Equerry-in-Waiting). Major Clive Wigram (Equerry-in-Waiting). Capt. the Hon. Sir Charles Wentworth Fitzwilliam (Crown Equerry).

Colonel G. C. Nugent (Field Officer in Brigade Waiting). Lieut.-Colonel the Duke of Teck (Silver-Stick-in-Waiting).

Capt. the Hon. J. F. Forbes Trefusis (Adjutant in Brigade Waiting). Captain G. E. M. Mundy (Silver Stick Adjutant).

Second Carriage.—Prince George, the Duchess of Devonshire (Mistress of the Robes), the Countess of Shaftesbury (Lady-in-Waiting), the Earl of Granard (Master of the Horse).

Third Carriage.—The Hon. Venetia Baring (Maid of Honour in Waiting), the Earl of Durham (Lord High Steward), the Earl of Shaftesbury (Lord Chamberlain to the Queen).

Fourth Carriage.—The Lord Annaly (Lord-in-Waiting), Lieut.-Colonel the Rt. Hon. Sir W. Carington (Keeper of the Privy Purse), Lieut.-Colonel the Lord Stamfordham (Private Secretary), Captain Philip Hunloke (Groom-in-Waiting).

Fifth Carriage.—Commander Sir Charles Cust, Bt., R.N., Equerry-in-Waiting), the Hon. Sir Derek Keppel (Equerry-in-Waiting), Lieut.-Colonel Sir Frederick Ponsonby (Equerry-in-Waiting), Captain B. Godfrey-Faussett, R.N. (Equerry-in-Waiting).

The King's Guard of the 1st Batt. Grenadier Guards, with the Colour and Band of the regiment, under the command of Captain L. V. Colby, was mounted in the Quadrangle of the Palace.

The route of the Royal Procession was by the Mall, Marlborough Gate, Pall Mall, Trafalgar Square, the Strand, Fleet Street, and Ludgate Hill to St. Paul's Cathedral.

The Procession halted at Trafalgar Square, and the King received a deputation from the Westminster City Council, headed by the Mayor, who presented an Address of Welcome to the King and Queen, to which His Majesty handed a reply.

The King and Queen were received at Temple Bar by the Lord Mayor, the Sheriffs, and members of the Court of Aldermen and Common Council.

The Lord Mayor, in accordance with ancient custom, surrendered the City Sword to the King, which His Majesty returned.

The King and Queen afterwards proceeded to the Cathedral, where a Guard of Honour of the 1st Batt. Coldstream Guards, under the command of Captain W. A. Fuller-Maitland, was mounted.

A Detachment of the London Diocesan Church Lads' Brigade lined the steps leading to the West Door of the Cathedral.

Queen Alexandra, accompanied by the Princess Victoria, attended by Her Majesty's Suite, and escorted by a Captain's Escort of 1st Life Guards under the command of Lieutenant L. H. Hardy, had proceeded beforehand to St. Paul's Cathedral.

APPENDIX A

Prince and Princess Christian of Schleswig-Holstein, Princesses Victoria and Marie Louise of Schleswig-Holstein, Princess Louise (Duchess of Argyll) and the Duke of Argyll, the Duchess of Albany, Prince Arthur of Connaught, Princess Louis of Battenberg, with Prince George and Princess Louise of Battenberg, the Duchess of Teck and Prince George of Teck, and the Countesses Feodore and Helena Gleichen had previously arrived and taken their appointed places.

Their Majesties were received at the Cathedral by the Dean and Chapter, together with the Lord Mayor and Sheriffs.

The Archbishop of Canterbury, the Archbishop of York, and Bishop Boyd Carpenter (Clerk of the Closet) were present.

The King, the Queen, and Queen Alexandra were conducted to their seats, a procession being formed in the following order :—

Minor Canons.
Prebendaries.
Bishops.
Clerk of the Closet.
Archbishop of York.
Archbishop of Canterbury.
Canons Residentiary.
Sheriffs.
The Lord Mayor (bearing the Pearl Sword).

Senior Canon.	THE QUEEN.	THE KING.	Dean of St. Paul's.

Prince of Wales.	Queen Alexandra.

The Princess Victoria.	Prince George.	Princess Mary.

The Earl of Durham (Lord High Steward).	The Earl of Granard (Master of the Horse).
The Countess of Shaftesbury (Lady of the Bedchamber to the Queen).	The Duchess of Devonshire (Mistress of the Robes to the Queen).
Admiral Sir M. Culme-Seymour, Bt. (Vice-Admiral of the United Kingdom).	Field-Marshal the Lord Grenfell (Gold-Stick-in-Waiting).

The Earl Howe (Lord Chamberlain to Queen Alexandra).	The Lord Annaly (Lord-in-Waiting to the King).	The Earl of Shaftesbury (Lord Chamberlain to the Queen).
The Hon. Venetia Baring (Maid of Honour to the Queen).	The Countess of Gosford (Lady of the Bedchamber to Queen Alexandra).	The Hon. Charlotte Knollys (Woman of the Bedchamber to Queen Alexandra).
The Earl of Gosford (Vice-Chamberlain to Queen Alexandra).	Lieut.-Colonel the Rt. Hon. Sir William Carington (Keeper of the Privy Purse).	The Lord Stamfordham (Private Secretary to the King).
Capt. B. Godfrey-Faussett (Equerry to the King).	Commander Sir Charles Cust, Bt., R.N. (Equerry to the King).	The Hon. Sir Derek Keppel (Equerry to the King).

Lt.-Col. Sir Frederick Ponsonby (Equerry to the King).

Capt. the Hon. Sir Charles Fitzwilliam (Crown Equerry).

Lt.-Gen. Sir H. L. Smith-Dorrien (Aide-de-Camp General-in-Waiting).

Major-Gen. Sir A. E. Codrington (General Officer Commanding the London District).

Major the Lord Charles Fitzmaurice (Equerry-in-Waiting to the King).

Captain Philip Hunloke (Groom-in-Waiting to the King).

Major Clive Wigram (Equerry-in-Waiting to the King).

Colonel Henry Streatfeild (Equerry-in-Waiting to Queen Alexandra).

Colonel Sir Arthur Davidson (Equerry-in-Waiting to Queen Alexandra).

Colonel G. C. Nugent (Field Officer in Brigade Waiting).

Lieut.-Colonel the Duke of Teck (Silver-Stick-in-Waiting).

The National Anthem was then sung, being followed by the special form of service appointed for the occasion.

At the conclusion of the service the Recessional Hymn was sung, during which Their Majesties were conducted by the Lord Mayor, the Clerk of the Closet, and the Dean and Chapter to the West Door of the Cathedral, where the Royal Procession was re-formed and proceeded by way of Ludgate Hill, New Bridge Street, the Embankment, Northumberland Avenue, Admiralty Arch, and the Mall to Buckingham Palace.

In addition to Their Majesties' Suites, the following were on duty in the Cathedral :—

Colonel Sir Douglas Dawson (Comptroller of the Lord Chamberlain's Department), the Hon. Arthur Walsh (Master of the Ceremonies), the Hon. Richard Moreton (Marshal of the Ceremonies), the Rt. Hon. Sir S. Ponsonby-Fane, Mr. Lionel Cust, Sir David Erskine, Mr. Arnold Royle, Major-General Sir John Slade, Mr. Horace West, Mr. Percy Armytage, Vice-Admiral Charles Windham, Mr. Thomas Kingscote, Captain Gerald Ellis, Colonel H. Fludyer, Mr. Montague Eliot, and Colonel Lord William Cecil (Gentlemen Ushers), and Mr. R. F. Synge (Deputy-Marshal of the Ceremonies).

Major J. C. Brinton (late 2nd Life Guards), Captain Phillips and Lieutenant A. Leigh Bennet (Coldstream Guards), Major McCalmont and Lieutenant Lord Arthur Hay (Irish Guards), and the gentlemen of the Lord Chamberlain's Department were also on duty in the Cathedral.

Amongst those present at the Service were :—

Their Excellencies the Ambassadors, Foreign Ministers and Chefs de Mission, the Cabinet Ministers and other Members of the Government, ex-Cabinet Ministers, the Speaker, Members of the Houses of Parliament, the Lord Mayors and Lord Provosts of the United Kingdom, the Mayors of the Metropolitan boroughs, the Chairman and Members of the London County Council, the Permanent Officials of the various departments of the State, the Council of the Secretary of State for India, officers of the Army and Navy, a detachment of officers and men from H.M.S. *Medina*, His Majesty's Judges, the Aldermen and Common Councilmen of the City of London, representatives of the City Companies, the Households of the King and Queen, Queen Alexandra and the Royal Family, officials and visitors from India and the Colonies.

The route to and from Buckingham Palace and St. Paul's Cathedral was lined with troops.

APPENDIX B

THE KING-EMPEROR'S STAFF IN INDIA.

Permanent Staff.

Brigadier-General R. E. Grimston, Military Secretary.
Major E. D. Money (1st Gurkha Rifles), Assistant Military Secretary.
Major A. R. Stockley (1st Sappers and Miners), Assistant Military Secretary.
Captain R. E. T. Hogg (38th Central India Horse), Assistant Military Secretary.
Lieut.-Colonel R. Bird (Indian Medical Service), Surgeon.

EXTRA STAFF AT DELHI.

Attached.

Sir John Hewett, President Durbar Committee.
Colonel Sir Henry McMahon, Master of the Ceremonies.

The King's Honorary Aides-de-Camp.

Hon. Major-General the Maharaja of Gwalior.
Hon. Major-General Sir Pratap Singh.
Hon. Colonel Nawab Sir Aslam Khan.
Hon. Colonel the Maharaja of Bikaner.
Hon. Colonel the Nawab of Rampur.
Hon. Colonel Nawab Sir Hafiz Khan.

Extra Equerry.

Lieut.-Colonel H. D. Watson (9th Gurkha Rifles).

The King's Aides-de-Camp.

Brigadier-General W. R. Birdwood.
Brigadier-General H. D'U. Keary.
Brigadier-General C. J. Melliss.

Colonel H. E. Stanton.
Colonel Viscount Hardinge.
Colonel F. Goodwin.

Extra Aides-de-Camp.

Major the Hon. W. G. S. Cadogan (10th Hussars).
Captain L. F. Ashburner (Royal Fusiliers).
Captain H. Hill (Royal Welsh Fusiliers).
Captain R. Raban (1st Skinner's Horse).

British Officers from Indian Regiments.

Captain G. Craster (6th Cavalry).
Captain J. K. Gatacre (11th Lancers).
Major E. C. Corbyn (18th Lancers).
Captain E. L. Popham (26th Cavalry).
Captain A. B. Eckford (39th Central India Horse).
Captain F. E. G. Talbot (14th Sikhs).
Captain B. E. A. Manson (61st Pioneers).
Captain T. Oakes (102nd Grenadiers).
Captain N. R. Anderson (130th Baluchis).
Major F. G. C. Ross (2nd Battalion 2nd Gurkha Rifles).
Lieut.-Colonel H. L. Roberts (16th Cavalry).

Indian Officers from Indian Regiments.

Cavalry.

Risaldar Ismail Khan (1st Lancers, Skinner's Horse).
Risaldar Ramjas (6th Cavalry).
Ressaidar Anup Singh (11th Lancers).
Risaldar Gul Nawaz Khan (18th Lancers).
Risaldar Saiyid Abdullah (26th Cavalry).
Risaldar Lall Khan (38th Central India Horse).
Risaldar Mumtaz Ali Khan (39th Central India Horse).

Infantry.

Subadar Gulab Singh (14th Sikhs).
Subadar Ram Das (61st Pioneers).
Subadar Sahib Din (102nd Grenadiers).
Subadar Sultan Mir (130th Baluchis).
Subadar Jangbir Thapa (1st Batt. 1st Gurkha Rifles).
Subadar Rudrnarain Nagarkoti (2nd Batt. 1st Gurkha Rifles).
Subadar Jangbir Thapa (1st Batt. 2nd Gurkha Rifles).
Subadar Sital Singh Lama (2nd Batt. 2nd Gurkha Rifles).
Subadar Mihr Din (1st Sappers and Miners).

STAFF IN NIPAL.

Brigadier-General R. E. Grimston.
Captain R. E. T. Hogg (38th Central India Horse).
Lieut.-Colonel H. D. Watson (9th Gurkha Rifles).

APPENDIX B

STAFF FOR THE QUEEN-EMPRESS'S RAJPUTANA TOUR.

Lieut.-Colonel A. D. G. Bannerman.
Major E. D. Money (1st Gurkha Rifles).
Captain H. Hill (Royal Welsh Fusiliers).
Lieut.-Colonel R. Bird, Surgeon.

EXTRA STAFF AT CALCUTTA.

The King's Honorary Aides-de-Camp.

Extra Aides-de-Camp.

Major Hon. W. G. S. Cadogan (10th Hussars).
Captain A. F. C. Maclachlan (King's Royal Rifles).
Major L. O. Graeme (Cameron Highlanders).
Captain H. Holmes (Royal Irish Fusiliers).

EXTRA STAFF AT BOMBAY.

Extra Aides-de-Camp on Arrival.

Captain B. S. Grissell (Norfolk Regiment).
Major L. O. Graeme (Cameron Highlanders).
Captain L. F. Ashburner (Royal Fusiliers).
Major G. G. P. Humphreys (127th Baluch Infantry).

Extra Aides-de-Camp on Departure.

Major G. G. P. Humphreys (127th Baluch Infantry).
Captain R. Raban (1st Lancers).
Captain A. F. C. Maclachlan (King's Royal Rifles).
Captain B. S. Grissell (Norfolk Regiment).

APPENDIX C

REGIMENTS IN INDIA WITH WHICH THE KING IS ASSOCIATED AS COLONEL-IN-CHIEF.

British Service.

10th Prince of Wales's Own Royal Hussars.
Royal Artillery.
Royal Engineers.
The Royal Fusiliers.
The Norfolk Regiment.
The Royal Welsh Fusiliers.
The King's Royal Rifle Corps.
The Queen's Own Cameron Highlanders.
Princess Victoria's (Royal Irish Fusiliers).

Indian Service.

1st Duke of York's Own Lancers (Skinner's Horse).
6th King Edward's Own Cavalry.
11th King Edward's Own Lancers (Probyn's Horse).
102nd King Edward's Own Grenadiers.
2nd King Edward's Own Gurkha Rifles (the Sirmoor Rifles).
18th King George's Own Lancers.
26th King George's Own Light Cavalry.
38th King George's Own Central India Horse.
39th King George's Own Central India Horse.
1st King George's Own Sappers and Miners.
14th King George's Own Ferozepur Sikhs.
61st King George's Own Pioneers.
130th King George's Own Baluchis (Jacob's Rifles).
1st King George's Own Gurkha Rifles (The Malaun Regiment).

REGIMENT WITH WHICH THE QUEEN IS ASSOCIATED.

127th Queen Mary's Own Baluch Light Infantry.

APPENDIX D

THE PRAYER OF THE SIKHS ON THE 13TH OF DECEMBER.

SRI WAHGURU JI KI FATAH!

Having first remembered the Sword meditate on Guru Nanak;
Then on Guru Angad, Amar Das, and Ram Das; may they assist us!
Remember Arjan, Har Gobind, and the holy Hari Rai;
Meditate on the holy Hari Krishan, a sight of whom dispelled all sorrow.
Remember Teg Bahadar, and the nine treasures shall come hastening to your homes.
Ye holy Gurus, everywhere assist us!
May the tenth King, the holy GURU GOVIND SINGH, everywhere assist us.
God Himself knoweth, He Himself acteth; it is He who adjusteth.
Standing in His presence, NANAK, make supplication.

Sikhs of the true Immortal God, turn your thoughts to the teachings of the Granth Sahib and the deeds of the Khalsa; utter Wahguru!

Meditating on the Deathless One, endowed with all power, compassionate, and just, utter Wahguru!

Meditating on the deeds of those who worshipped the Name, plied the sword, ate and distributed their food in companionship and overlooked others' faults, O Khalsa, utter Wahguru!

O Deathless Creator, illimitable, this creature forgetting Thy name is so attached to worldly goods, that he hath forgotten the Real Thing. Without Thy Supreme mercy how shall we cross the ocean of the world? O great King, lust, wrath, greed, worldly love, jealousy, and other evil passions greatly trouble our minds, but on coming towards Thee worldly maladies and afflictions are healed and dispelled. Show us such favour that we may by word and deed be Thine, and that in all things we may obtain Thine assistance and support.

Grant to thy Sikhs the gift of Sikhism, the gift of the Guru's instruction, the gift of faith, the gift of confidence in Thee, and the gift of reading and understanding the holy Granth Sahib.

May the Sikh choirs, mansions, and banners ever abide! Victory to the faith ; May the minds of the Sikhs be humble but their intellects exalted ! Utter Wahguru ! Wahguru !! Wahaguru !!!

O Primal Father, Everlasting Creator, we Thy humble worshippers are to-day assembled at the spot where our Messenger of salvation, the true Guru Teg Bahadar, seeing the people of India the victims of an oppressive and unjust Government, made the following prophecy in 1675 A.D.

"I behold coming from across the ocean a race of men who will spread peace and dispense justice and root out tyranny and oppression." By Thy mercy, O God, his words have proved true, for the British Government, which confers happiness on its subjects, has been firmly established in India. We Sikhs of the Gurus in the midst of our happiness and rejoicing to-day specially render Thee our humble gratitude and thanks that our beloved Emperor has come to the City where our holy Guru the Bestower of salvation uttered the above fateful prophecy, in order to place the Crown of the realm of many lands on his head.

O Eternal God, may this peaceful and just sovereignty ever endure and may the Emperor George and his gracious consort Queen Mary with their family abide in happiness, and may their Empire extend and prosper !

Beloved Sikh brethren, let us of one mind thank the Cherisher of the world through Whose favour we have beheld this magnificent coronation ceremony, and let us conclude the great event with three cheers of *Sat Siri Akal* for the safekeeping and prosperity of Their Majesties and the Royal Family.

THE END